Performance-Based
ACQUISITION
Pathways to Excellence

Gregory A. Garrett

National Contract Management Association
8260 Greensboro Drive, Suite 200
McLean, VA 22102
800-344-8096
www.ncmahq.org

©2005 by National Contract Management Association
All rights reserved. Published 2005
Printed in the United States of America
ISBN 0-9700897-1-6

Contents

Foreword

Performance-Based Acquisition: Pathways to Excellence is another outstanding book by the best-selling author, highly acclaimed speaker, and successful practicing industry leader Gregory A. Garrett. The book takes a thought-provoking and holistic view of the world of performance-based buying and selling and focuses on the acquisition of complex products, services, and integrated solutions in both the public and the private business sectors.

Garrett has a tremendous talent for taking a highly complex subject like performance-based acquisition and breaking it down into simple, logical actions and proven-effective best practices. This book examines the world of performance-based buying and selling from the viewpoints of both government and industry. In his classic style, Garrett artfully weaves into each chapter numerous best practices and two or more case studies from world-class companies, including CH2M Hill, CISCO Systems, Dell, Home Depot, Honda, The Limited, Toyota, and many others. Plus, he has included numerous excellent case studies from a variety of U.S. federal government agencies, including the Department of Defense (DOD), Defense Contract Management Agency (DCMA), Defense Advanced Research Projects Agency (DARPA), Defense Acquisition University (DAU), Office of Personnel Management (OPM), Department of Homeland Security (DHS), Department of Agriculture (DoA), Department of Veteran Affairs (VA), and Department of Health and Human Services (HHS).

The book begins with the introduction of a simple model, titled

"Performance-Based Acquisition: The Essential Elements," which is composed of several building blocks supporting the 4Ps: people, processes, performance, and price. The rest of the book drills down into each of the 4 Ps, demonstrating and illustrating how each is essential to the art and science of performance-based acquisition.

Chapters 2 and 3 discuss the essential element of people—principally what buying and selling leaders should know and do and the importance of building teamwork in integrated project teams, composed of a buyer, a seller, and subcontractors. Chapters 4, 5, and 6 address the essential element of processes, discussing how key trends are affecting e-business buying and selling processes, the process for managing opportunity and risk in complex acquisitions, and the process for creating a supplier value chain. Chapters 7 and 8 discuss the essential element of performance, including a compelling discussion of the five critical components of performance-based contracts and the need for organizations to create performance-balanced scorecards to achieve higher levels of success. Chapter 9 addresses the essential element of price, thereby providing a comprehensive discussion of pricing strategies, methods, arrangements, and analysis techniques.

Chapter 10 looks into the future of business and goes beyond performance-based acquisition into a world of high-performance organizations (HPOs). Here, the author provides interesting insight into the three key drivers of potential future business success: (1) performance-based culture, (2) extended enterprise value chain, and (3) high-performance project discipline. The logic and insights in Chapter 10 alone are worth the price of the book. Clearly, this book is a must-read for anyone who is in the public or private business sectors and is involved in performance-based buying or selling of products, services, and integrated solutions.

William C. Pursch, Ph.D., CPCM
President, Pursch Associates
Past National President,
National Contract Management Association (NCMA)

Preface

This is a one-of-a-kind book that provides a comprehensive and compelling discussion of the four essential elements to improve the buying and selling of products, services, and integrated solutions (people, processes, performance, and price). In both the public and the private business sectors, organizations are seeking proven, effective, and performance-oriented best practices to buy and sell more quickly, conveniently, and cost-efficiently.

What makes this text unique is how the author skillfully blends such a diversity of integrated performance-focused topics, ranging from what senior executives and chief acquisition and purchasing officers should know and do, to the process for managing opportunity and risk in complex acquisitions, to the understanding of key e-business trends, to the creation of a supplier value chain for critical components of performance-based contracts.

Gregory A. Garrett, international educator, highly acclaimed speaker, and practicing industry leader has taken his tremendous knowledge and vast business experience from both the U.S. government and industry to simplify the complex world of performance-based acquisition.

Garrett is also the best-selling author of *World-Class Contracting* (third edition, CCH, 2003), *Managing Complex Outsourced Projects* (CCH, 2004), *Contract Negotiations* (CCH, 2005), and is the co-author of *Contract Management Organizational Assessment Tools* (NCMA, 2005). He has used his 25 years of successful experience in both the public and the private business sectors, where he managed more than $30 billion of complex contracts and programs worldwide, to share numerous proven-effective case studies, tools, and best practices to improve performance-based buying and selling.

We at the National Contract Management Association are delighted to publish this outstanding new text, *Performance-Based Acquisition: Pathways to Excellence*. This book is a follow-on to a successful series of articles we have published in our monthly *Contract Management* magazine. Realizing the importance of performance-based acquisition to both buying and selling communities, we plan to provide a nationwide series of one-day seminars based on this book.

We are confident you will find this book a valuable reference tool for many years to come.

Sincerely,
Steve Boshears, Colonel, U.S. Army (Retired)
Chief Knowledge Officer
National Contract Management Association (NCMA)

Dedication

To the men and women of our U.S. Armed Forces, who have sacrificed so much for the freedom we all enjoy. I dedicate this book and this poem, "Old Glory," written by my son Christopher J. Garrett.

By: Christopher J. Garrett

"Old Glory"

There she is waving high above me.
Each and every day of my life, I look up at her for inspiration and courage.
She was born, like a phoenix,
Out of the fires of war.
Neither through the rain nor the snow,
Nor through the fall of bombs will she ever waiver.
No armies of any foreign land will ever step foot on her sacred land.
Deep in my heart, I know that after I and my children's children are dead and gone,
That she will continue to gleam with pride.
She stands for so much good,
Yet ill will is all that some can muster.
Freedom and liberty are her friends;
Intolerance and ignorance are her foes.
She has waved gallantly in every major war for over two hundred years.
From Yorktown, to the Halls of Montezuma, to the Shores of Tripoli,
To Gettysburg, to the coast of Normandy,
To the islands Okinawa and Iwo Jima,
And finally today to Baghdad, she has battled courageously.
In acts of liberation not conquest she has marched
On the streets of cities of fallen despots,
Securing freedom for all.
She has been beaten,
Betrayed, burned and
Raped in the streets of nations
That she has freed from totalitarian rule.
Even though she has wept and bled
Upon the field of combat to liberate persecuted people,
Her foes speak of nothing but her supposed evil.
Dignifiedly, she waves each and every day,
From her outpost on the moon,
Looking down upon our world with pride.
She is proud.
She is brave.
She has fought for the freedoms of many
And defeated all.
She is humble,
Never arrogant.
That is why each and every morning,
I wake up and thank God
That I was born in the U.S.A.
God Bless Old Glory.
Long may she wave.

Acknowledgments

I would like to thank the following individuals for their guidance, support, contributions, friendship, and inspiration:

- William C. Pursch, Ph.D., CPCM,

- W. Gregor MacFarlan, CPCM,

- Rene G. Rendon, DBA, CPCM, CFCM,

- Neal J. Couture, CPCM,

- Steve Boshears, CPCM,

- Gail A. Parrott.

Special thanks to Barbara Hanson for her continued outstanding administrative support and to the NCMA editorial and design staff for their excellent work.

NCMA editorial and design staff:
Amy Miedema, *Director of Communications*
Kathryn Mullan, M.A., *Assistant Editor*
David Danner, M.A., *Senior Graphic Designer*
Ioana Condrut, *Junior Graphic Designer*

Introduction

Today, performance-based acquisition is a hot topic because every organization in both the public and the private business sectors wants to buy or sell products, services, and integrated solutions more cost-efficiently and rapidly. The world we live in is composed of a diverse and continually evolving mixture of people, processes, technologies, laws, and regulations that collectively drive business transactions. Thus, creating a more collaborative, cost-effective, and performance-based approach to buying and selling products, services, and integrated solutions is a broad and multifaceted challenge.

This book provides a big-picture view of the nature of performance-based acquisition (buying and selling) by focusing on the following essential elements: people, processes, performance, and price. This book is not intended to restate government regulations on performance-based contracts (PBCs) or to examine performance-based business solely from a buyer's perspective or services-based perspective.

In Chapter 1, the high-level concept of performance-based acquisition and the four essential elements are each briefly discussed. Chapter 1 also includes two compelling case studies featuring Dell and Home Depot, describing their respective success in performance-based buying and selling by focusing on the four essential elements that drive consistently high performance results. Chapters 2–9 provide more detailed discussion, with case studies, tools, and best practices about one of the four essential elements.

Chapters 2 and 3 are focused on the essential element of people.

Chapter 2 discusses what senior executives and chief acquisition and purchasing officers should know and do to improve buying and selling, including a case study from the Defense Contract Management Agency (DCMA). Chapter 3 examines the need for teamwork when buying and selling, often involving multiple parties with multifunctional areas working together on integrated project teams to provide customer solutions. Chapter 3 also provides an excellent discussion of the value of leadership and the actions required to build leaders at every level of an organization to ensure success. Clearly, effective leadership is fundamental to any performance-based organization.

Chapters 4, 5, and 6 are focused on the essential element of processes. Chapter 4 provides a high-level, insightful examination of e-business: how to improve buying and selling, especially how e-business is changing the way we do business. Chapter 5 provides a broad process focus to the art and science of managing opportunity and risk in complex acquisition programs and related projects. Chapter 5 contains numerous best practices and proven-effective tools for identifying, analyzing, and mitigating risks in order to maximize opportunities. Chapter 6 discusses the world of outsourcing and the process to create a higher level of performance through a supplier value chain. The text artfully integrates the aspects of customer relationship management (CRM), supply chain management (SCM), and supplier relationship management (SRM) into the vision or concept of a supplier value chain. The discussion is complemented with numerous case studies (Cisco, Ford, IBM, The Limited, and others) and best practices aimed at improving the buying and selling processes.

Chapters 7 and 8 are focused on the essential element of performance. Chapter 7 discusses the critical components of a performance-based contract, with a brief examination of each component. Chapter 8 provides an interesting discussion of the pros and cons of performance-based scorecards, often referred to as balanced scorecards or supplier report cards. Chapter 8 also provides several successful case studies from various organizations and companies, including Honda, Raytheon, Toyota, and others—organizations all focused on improving performance results.

Chapter 9 is focused on the essential element of price. It provides a comprehensive discussion of pricing strategies, methods, and arrangements and of how price is a key element of perceived value by many buyers. The discussion of pricing provides numerous tools, techniques, and best practices useful for everyone involved in buying or selling products, services, or integrated solutions.

Chapter 10 looks beyond the current view of performance-based

acquisition into the future—the evolution of high-performance organizations (HPOs). The discussion provides a fast-forward insight into
the conceptual world of a future business state, where HPOs domi-
nate and operate in an integrated performance-based culture, that
transcends all of their business actions. HPOs operate in a realm of
well-educated and highly trained people who use integrated, multifunctional business processes that are connected through globally
accessible, extended enterprise-wide converged (voice, data, and
video) information networks. Those networks consistently meet or
exceed their well-communicated individual, team, and organizational
performance targets. These targets are tied to each individual's pay
treatment while simultaneously leveraging pricing strategies, methods, and arrangements to achieve acquisition excellence, profitability, and long-term customer loyalty.

Clearly, this is not your typical book on government or commercial
buying or selling. This book goes well beyond "the box" by taking a
simple, holistic, and practical view of what it takes to consistently
achieve business success in both the public and the private business
sectors. The 100+ best practices and 25+ case studies are intended to
provide simple yet proven-effective pathways to excellence.

Furthermore, the book provides three value-added appendices:

■ Appendix A—The Seven Steps to Performance-Based Services
Acquisition;

■ Appendix B—The Acquisition Bid/No-Bid Assessment Tool; and

■ Appendix C—Glossary of Key Terms.

Plus, the book contains an extensive bibliography listing reference materials and a user-friendly index for quick book references.
My hope is you will find this book a thought-provoking and valuable
reference and guide.

Sincerely,
Gregory A. Garrett

CHAPTER 01

Performance-Based Acquisition: The Essential Elements

Performance-based acquisition (PBA) is no longer an option; it is a business necessity in both the public and the private business sectors. The U.S. federal government has mandated that agencies and departments comply with certain performance-based guidelines and requirements, pursuant to the *Federal Acquisition Regulation* (*FAR*) and specific agency policies. In both the public and the private sectors, PBA is viewed as a strategic method to manage business by promoting flexibility and innovation and by creating win–win solutions through effective communication, organizational goal alignment, and clear accountability between buyer(s), seller(s), and subcontractors.

In the words of the great artist, scientist, and inventor Leonardo da Vinci, "Simplicity is the ultimate sophistication." With this concept in mind, some people have asked this simple question: "What are the essential elements of performance-based acquisition?" Experts in U.S. federal government contract and acquisition management have stated that the essential elements of PBA are the following: performance requirements, performance standards, performance measures and metrics, contractual incentives, and appropriately tailored terms and conditions that are specific to the unique acquisition environment—all clearly documented in a mutually agreed-to performance-based contract.

Clearly, these items are all critical components for planning, awarding, and executing a performance-based acquisition; however, they are not the true essential elements of success. The real essential elements of success in performance-based acquisition are much broader and far simpler, yet challenging: the four Ps—people, processes, performance, and price, in that order. Too often organizational leaders become overly focused on reducing the price or driving down costs, thereby causing leaders to make penny-wise but pound-foolish decisions (i.e., eliminating key people, reducing training and professional development, hiring the cheapest supplier rather than the best supplier, and focusing more on the use of overly complex performance scorecards rather than on truly important actions, such as retaining the most talented people and creating succession plans to build leaders).

Although some experts will disagree with the premise of the four Ps because they think it is too simplistic, I think they miss the point. Many senior executives in both the public and the private sectors spend too little real time building strong business relationships with their people (especially mentoring and coaching their team members to build leadership skills).

To be perfectly clear, I believe all aspects of business should be performance-based or performance-oriented. This book is not intended to merely cite U.S. federal government regulations of what should be in a performance-based contract or to restate the government's perspective on performance-based services acquisition. I believe all buying and selling should be performance focused; thus, all buying and selling organizations should develop a performance-based culture.

Because most people learn and retain more of what they see than of what they read or hear, **Figure 1.1** (p. 21) is provided to visually reinforce the four Ps as the essential elements of PBA. Furthermore, the figure depicts how most acquisition portfolios are composed of several major programs and numerous related contracts and projects.

Likewise, Figure 1.1 illustrates how typically performance-based acquisitions involve a buyer, seller (prime contractor), and numerous subcontractors—all working together on integrated project teams to achieve customer-focused needs and goals within an established budget.

Case Studies

To further demonstrate the power of the four Ps, the following case studies from two world-class organizations document the organizations' actions to achieve consistently high performance.

Case Study—Dell

Dell's business model has made many other business models in the industry obsolete. Dell's speed to the market (or cycle time) and its revenue-per-dollar of capital investment are the highest of any personal computer manufacturer. Dell's inventory turn or velocity

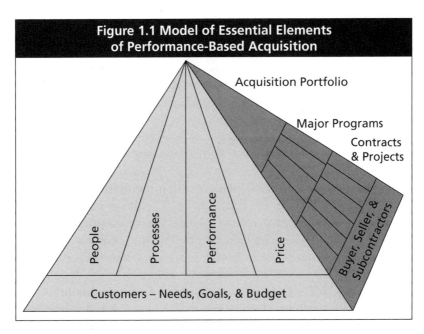

Figure 1.1 Model of Essential Elements of Performance-Based Acquisition

(revenue per dollar of inventory) is an outstanding score of 100 or world-class performance. So, how does Dell do it? Dell focuses on the four Ps—people, processes, performance, and price.[1] At Dell, the four Ps are demonstrated by the following actions:

- **People**—Dell hires only the best and brightest and continually recruits top-notch people. Dell has excellent training and employee development programs. Dell has very high management retention.

- **Processes**—Dell is highly process oriented and customer focused. The key operating process is the supply chain, through a sophisticated extended-enterprise manufacturing system. Dell's processes allow it to operate at very low inventory levels. Dell's process for payment before shipment ensures high asset efficiency.

- **Performance**—Dell's organizational processes are highly customer focused and performance based. Dell extensively uses performance metrics, which are well documented, communicated, and understood, so people in the organization know where they are at any given time and can consistently execute their jobs.

- **Price**—At Dell, as a result of its people, processes, and performance, the company is able to sell computers at lower prices and still grow profitable revenue.

Case Study—Home Depot

During the past few years, Home Depot's annual revenues have grown 42 percent, net earnings have grown 65 percent, and cash has increased from $200 million to $2.9 billion. As a result, Home Depot was listed as number 22 in the "Business Week 50" in 2004.[2] So, how did Home Depot do it?

Home Depot now focuses on the four Ps—people, processes, performance, and price—as explained by the following actions:

- **People**—Home Depot raised the education standards for store managers, thereby encouraged the hiring of military veterans, especially officers, who had received leadership training during their military tours of duty; expanded companywide training programs; and focused on employee accountability and customer service.

- **Processes**—Home Depot developed integrated business processes and instilled disciplined, customer-focused approaches to business activities. Home Depot dramatically accelerated investment in information technology using enterprise resource planning tools, with SAP software for finance and PeopleSoft software for human resources. Furthermore, Home Depot consolidated purchasing and marketing processes.

- **Performance**—Home Depot improved its performance by returning to the basics: focusing on building leaders, providing more education, holding people accountable, developing organizational processes, executing in a highly disciplined manner, and using specific performance metrics extensively. Home Depot focused on key performance areas, including productivity, customer satisfaction, inventory reduction, and cost efficiency.

- **Price**—Home Depot's new strategies to improve people, processes, and performance have allowed it to lower prices and to grow more profitable revenues.

Important Look at the Essential Elements—The Four Ps

The following explanation of the four Ps will be of valuable assistance to readers.

People

The first essential element of performance-based acquisition is people. The most important ingredient to achieving success in buying or selling products, services, or solutions is selecting the right people. Some may argue that the number of people is most important. However, although the correct number of people is always vital for success, the quality of those people in an organization is most important, including their having the following characteristics:

■ Integrity,

■ Communication skills,

■ Dedication,

■ Education,

■ Energy,

■ Experience,

■ Interpersonal skills,

■ Leadership,

■ Persistence,

■ Professional continuing education and training,

■ Professional certification,

■ Teamwork, and

■ Work ethic.

In addition to selecting the right people for an acquisition project, an organization must strive to retain the right people. The following 10 strategies are proven best practices for retaining the right people:

1. Create a culture of respect, trust, and business integrity.

2. Clearly communicate vision, mission, and performance goals to everyone in the organization.

3. Tie organizational strategies to individual and team goals.

4. Tie pay to performance on both an individual and a team basis.

5. Provide quality, timely, and cost-effective individual and team-based training for everyone.

6. Create and implement succession planning for key positions and key people.

7. Build leadership skills for all team members.

8. Create and implement recognition and reward programs.

9. Hold people accountable and provide timely feedback to help improve individual and team performance.

10. Provide coaching, mentoring, and knowledge-transfer programs for all team members.

Case Study—E-mentoring, U.S. Office of Personnel Management

Office of Personnel Management (OPM) officials have added electronic monitoring, or e-mentoring, to OPM's multiagency Web portal, GoLearn.gov. Portal users can find experts in their fields in minutes. About 20,000 visitors have used this feature since its introduction in January 2004, according to OPM officials, who have recently upgraded the service.

A survey conducted last year shows that senior-level executives recognize the value of mentors. More than half said a mentor helped them succeed. But 60 percent of the women and 72 percent of the men surveyed did not have a mentor.

OPM officials also provide the service to other agencies, including the Bureau of Alcohol, Tobacco, Firearms and Explosives; the Department of Housing and Urban Development; the Department of Energy; and the General Services Administration.[3]

Companies such as General Electric, NCR, Proctor & Gamble, IBM, and others have long and distinguished records of retaining talent and of developing leaders while using a combination of in-house training, coaching, and mentoring, which are complemented by outside professional trainers, consultants, and academicians. Unfortunately, many organizations in both the public and the private business sectors do not focus enough time and effort on retaining talent—the right people. Thus, organizations that suffer from high turnover usually have increased costs, lower productivity, and fewer future leaders.

Although people and their salaries and benefits are often the largest expense in many organizations, the right people are, indeed, the organization's greatest asset. Remember, truly talented people often overcome numerous acquisition obstacles and find a way to achieve success.

Processes

The second essential element of performance-based acquisition is processes. It is imperative for every organization involved in an acquisition to clearly define, document, and implement well-developed, integrated (multifunctional) acquisition processes. Today, more and more organizations are involved in complex acquisitions and are developing organizational methodologies that are designed to integrate all key business processes in a consistent manner and that are based on proven best practices. Well-defined, documented, communicated, and effectively implemented processes are required for leveraging the power of e-business, managing opportunity and risk, creating supplier value chains, and integrating various functional areas.

A process that clearly defines roles, responsibilities, key actions, information systems, related tools, and hand-offs among people can prove to be very valuable if people follow the process. After one realizes that all work is completed through processes and that process inconsistency increases costs and yields inconsistent performance results, the steps of improving and integrating business processes are indeed essential to success. Of course, all processes must be regularly evaluated to identify and implement potential process improvement actions.

Numerous organizations use the power of enterprise software applications to help facilitate a more disciplined and integrated use of business processes that will drive higher levels of acquisition performance and more consistent results. Companies such as Boeing, General Electric, Lockheed Martin, Northrop Grumman, and many others have implemented enterprise resource planning software applications, which were developed by Baan, Deltek, Oracle, SAP, and others, with varying degrees of success.

Enterprise software applications have also been developed in numerous functional areas to improve the acquisition process, including enterprise contract management software developed by CACI (formerly AMS), I-Many, Nextance, and others; enterprise capture management software developed by Map ROI formerly Privia, Inc. and others; and enterprise project management software developed by Microsoft, Primavera, Scitor, and others. Enterprise software applications and related information systems can be powerful tools to facilitate more disciplined and consistent processes. It is important to remember that the underlying processes and the people's understanding of the use of the software are what really drive performance.

Worldwide organizations are focusing on benchmarking, and their processes are based on proven, research-based, capability maturity models. Those models were created by or for professional associations, including the following:

- *Business Development Capability Maturity Model (BD-CMM)*— Created by Shipley & Associates in partnership with the Association for Proposal Management Professionals for improving business development processes and results;

- *Capability Maturity Model Integration (CMMI)*— Created by the Software Engineering Institute for improving software development processes and results;

- *Contract Management Maturity Model (CMMM) and the Contract Management Maturity Assessment Tool (CMMAT)*—Created by Garrett and Rendon in partnership with the National Contract Management Association for improving contract management processes for both buyers and sellers;[4] and

- *Organizational Project Management Maturity Model (OPM3)*— Created by the Project Management Institute for improving project management processes and results.

Clearly, the tasks of developing and implementing efficient and effective acquisition-related processes are critical for buyers and sellers, in both the public and the private business sectors.

Performance

The third essential element of performance-based acquisition is performance. Typically, performance is evaluated in terms of the following factors:

- Cost/expense (within budget percentage or dollar amount);

- Customer (satisfaction or loyalty index rating);

- Cycle time (period of time from order to delivery);

- Employee (satisfaction or engagement rating);

- Profitability (percentage or dollar amount);

- Quality (product or service reliability, ease of use, maintainability, etc.);

- Revenue (dollar amount);

- Schedule (percentage of on-time delivery); and

- Technical (meet product or service requirements).

Increasingly organizations are using performance-based contracts and various performance report cards—sometimes referred to as balanced scorecards—to evaluate or assess the ability of their organization, their suppliers, or both so they can meet or exceed their diverse acquisition-related goals. Measuring performance requires that each organization involved develops an appropriate performance plan for its organization and for each major acquisition program that it participates in as buyer, seller, or subcontractor. **Table 1.1** (p. 28) provides a summary of some key performance areas and most commonly used performance metrics.

Performance-related acquisition best practices include the following:

- Create and document a balanced performance plan.

- Know what is (are) the most important performance area(s).

- Place the greatest reward on the most important performance area(s).

- Select fewer performance areas (three to five).

- Select fewer performance measures and metrics for each performance measure and area (one to three).

- Use a blend of objective and subjective performance measures and metrics.

- Keep the performance plan as simple as possible.

- Communicate the performance plan to everyone involved in the acquisition.

Table 1.1 Key Performance Areas and Metrics

Customer and Supplier Key Performance Areas	Checklist of Customer and Supplier Key Performance Metrics

Financial	❏ Return on investment
	❏ Within budget (planned expenses compared to actual expenses)
	❏ Cost reduction (current costs compared to future costs)
	    ❏ Implementation costs
	    ❏ Operations costs
	    ❏ Maintenance costs
	    ❏ Support costs
	❏ Return on assets
	❏ Net present value
	❏ Cost performance index
	❏ Revenue generated (annual and quarterly)
	❏ Days of sales outstanding
	❏ Revenue or expense to headcount
	❏ Inventory turns

Schedule	❏ No. of milestones on time ❏ Percentage of on-time delivery (mutually agreed-to date) ❏ No. of days cycle time (order to delivery) ❏ Earned value method ❏ Schedule performance index
Technical	❏ Capacity volume ❏ Operating time and usage ❏ Capabilities and features ❏ Speed ❏ No. of product failures or outages
Quality	❏ Mean time between failure ❏ Mean time to repair ❏ No. of complaints ❏ No. of defects

After one realizes that performance is always a matter of perspective and timing, it is best to develop a mutually agreed-to, well-documented, well-communicated, and simple acquisition performance plan before the contract award. The acquisition performance plan should then become a basis for considering, for instance, a quality assurance surveillance plan and all acquisition progress reporting.

Price

The fourth and final essential element of performance-based acquisition is price. Fundamentally, the right people will develop the right processes and together, those elements will drive the right performance, after which performance should drive the right pricing strategy, methods, and arrangements. Pricing strategy is usually determined according to performance and numerous market-related factors. There are two primary categories of pricing strategies:

- **Lowest price technically acceptable**—Price is the principal attribute for determining an award.

- **Best value**—Other factors (schedule, quality, technical, extent of subcontracting to small businesses, past performance) may be considered as important as or more important than price for determining an award.

Clearly, buyers generally look for the lowest reasonable price on products and services that they believe will meet or exceed their needs. In a competitive pricing environment, most buyers are willing to pay more than the lowest price for products and services they perceive to be of a higher quality or better overall value. Buyers must determine what is most important to them—price or other related factors. Sellers must determine if they can provide sufficient perceived value to their customers and can differentiate their products and services from those of their competitors. If so, then sellers can price their products and services at higher levels because their customers will be willing to pay more.

In addition, an organization must select the appropriate pricing method(s)—cost-based, value-based, or activity-based. Each method is discussed in more detail in chapter 9.

In addition to the right pricing strategy, it is critical to select the right pricing arrangement, commonly referred to as the type of contract. The right pricing arrangement depends on numerous factors such as these:

- Adequacy of the seller's cost-estimating and cost-accounting systems,

- Administrative costs to both parties,

- Commercial availability of the products or services,

- Extent of research and development required,

- Other unique acquisition-related factors, and

- Urgency of the requirements.

The most common type of contract or pricing arrangement, which is extensively used in both public and private business sectors, is the firm-fixed-price (FFP). The FFP pricing arrangement places the greatest financial risk on the seller of the products, services, or both. **Figure 1.2** (this page) depicts the range of contract types or pricing arrangements available and the sharing of financial risk between the parties.

Firm-Fixed Price (FFP)	Fixed-Price Incentive (FPI)	Fixed-Price Redeterminable (FPR)	Cost Sharing (CS)	Time & Material (T&M)	Cost-Plus Incentive Fee (CPIF)	Cost-Plus-Award Fee (CPAF)	Cost-Plus-Fixed Fee (CPFF)
				(BUYER)			
Low Risk							High Risk
				(SELLER)			
High Risk							Low Risk

Figure 1.2 The Range of Types of Contracts or Pricing Arrangements

Summary

To summarize, the true essential elements of performance-based acquisition are the four Ps—people, processes, performance, and price. Although all of the four Ps are important, people are always the most important factor in achieving success. Together, the right people using the right processes will achieve the right performance, which should drive the right price (strategy, method, and arrangement) for the specific acquisition situation. In the next chapter, we will focus on the importance of leadership, especially what senior executives and chief acquisition officers should know and do to improve acquisition management.

Questions to Consider

1. How well does your organization hire, train, and retain the best people?

2. Does your organization develop, document, and consistently execute its integrated business processes?

3. How effectively does your organization develop, implement, and track performance results?

4. What pricing strategy and pricing arrangements does your organization typically select? How well is the approach working?

Endnotes

1. Larry Bossidy and Ram Charan, *Confronting Reality* (Boston: Harvard Business School Press, 2004).

2. Ibid.

3. Megan Lisagor, "E-Mentoring: A Tool for Federal Workers," *Federal Computer Week*, January 24, 2005, 50.

4. Gregory A. Garrett and Rene G. Rendon, *Contract Management Organizational Assessment Tools* (McLean, VA: NCMA, 2005).

What Senior Executives and Chief Acquisition Officers Should Know and Do to Improve Performance Results

Introduction

Senior executives in both government and industry face many challenges, some common to both and others unique to their marketplace, industry, and perspective as buyer or seller. Common challenges faced by senior executives in both the public and the private business sectors include the following:

- Responding to increased customer demands and higher expectations,

- Meeting the challenge of competition for resources,

- Finding solutions for the loss of key talent,

- Reducing costs,

- Reducing cycle times,

- Reducing inventories,

- Improving quality,

- Improving customer satisfaction,

- Improving information technology infrastructure,

- Building high-performance teams,

- Developing future leaders,

- Improving knowledge transfer,

- Managing change, and

- Improving buying and selling processes and results.

Performance-based acquisition (PBA) is all about improving results from a customer's or user's perspective and from an organizational perspective. PBA is about motivating people to improve business processes to achieve higher levels of performance while reducing prices through innovative problem-solving approaches to overcome challenges.

Industry—Senior Executives' Challenges

According to PricewaterhouseCoopers' eighth annual survey of 1,300 chief executive officers (CEOs) worldwide (January 2005), industry leaders say overregulation remains the most serious threat to business growth. However, most CEOs are upbeat about revenue prospects. Key findings from the survey include the following:

- 60 percent stated government overregulation is their major concern;

- 46 percent cited the rising cost of social welfare as a major business concern;

- 41 percent said they were very confident of increasing revenue;

- 36 percent stated they considered terrorism a major concern to their business;

- 25 percent stated loss of key talent to competitors as a major concern; and

- 25 percent believe they are managing governance, risk management, and compliance effectively.[1]

U.S. Government—Senior Executives' Challenges

According to recent surveys, interviews, and public presentations by numerous senior executives and chief acquisition officers (CAOs) in the U.S. government, the following are some of their major concerns:

■ Aging workforce with serious potential skill gaps (2007 and beyond);

■ Lengthy procurement acquisition lead time;

■ Privatization or competitive sourcing that causes a loss of jobs and a loss of control;

■ Expense of upgrading facilities such as for information technology and security;

■ Overly restrictive personnel policies, rules, and regulations;

■ Closure of necessary facilities;

■ Political influence in critical decision-making;

■ Budget planning, authorization, and appropriation processes, plus details, delays, and funding shortages;

■ Asset identification and valuation; and

■ Analysis of outsourcing and spending.

Clearly, senior executives in both the public and the private business sectors face significant challenges regarding people, processes, performance, and price. As the saying goes, "With great power comes great responsibility." Unfortunately, far too many senior executives are viewed by their customers, team members, and suppliers as people who talk the talk but do not walk the talk. Talk is necessary but cheap. Strategic planning is good but not sufficient. In today's business acquisition environment, consistent high performance or excellent execution is what is most highly valued. So, let us examine an organization that is facing and addressing those important business challenges.

Case Study—Defense Contract Management Agency

The Defense Contract Management Agency (DCMA) is a U.S. Department of Defense (DOD) organization composed of thousands of people. DCMA includes active duty military personnel and civilians, all dedicated to providing quality contract management support for the DOD and various civilian agencies, including the National Aeronautics and Space Administration (NASA). DCMA's people perform a wide range of professional services, including preaward surveys, quality assurance, change management, contract administration, in-plant inspections, engineering, technical support, and much more. DCMA's personnel are deployed throughout the world in support of the DOD. DCMA's military personnel are represented by every branch of the U.S. Armed Forces.

DCMA is well led by Major General Darryl Scott, USAF. In May 2004, General Scott spoke at the Washington, D.C., chapter meeting of National Contract Management Association (NCMA) about the opportunities and challenges facing DCMA. General Scott described the primary challenges he faced in providing contract management support to his customers. Like many senior executives, General Scott stated that his principal challenges involved his organization's people, processes, and culture.

Specifically, General Scott stated the following challenges were most critical to DCMA's ongoing success:

- **People**—DCMA's workforce is aging rapidly. The average employee is 50 years old. Numerous critical skill areas, including various advanced engineering and technical support positions, are at critically low staffing levels, with few or no replacements who are fully trained, experienced, or available. DCMA has significantly increased its hiring program for those specialized skills and has created a robust intern program to develop a skills pipeline.

- **Processes**—DCMA's environment is evolving from rigid rules, regulations, manuals, and highly detailed specifications to a more flexible set of business guidelines for each functional area. DCMA has developed its new business guidelines on the basis of proven best practices, which have been adapted from both internal and external benchmarking.

- **Performance**—DCMA's performance has historically been viewed by most of its customers to be good to excellent. Yet, there are clearly numerous areas for further improvement that have been identified by internal and external audits, surveys, and assessments. DCMA is creating an environment and culture of high performance, which is based on continuous process improvements. Furthermore, DCMA is reorganizing from a geographic focus to a customer focus in an effort to better understand and fulfill customers' requirements.

■ **Price**—DCMA is essentially funded by its DOD and civilian agency customers as a professional services organization. Thus, DCMA, like any commercial organization, is continually evaluating how to get better, faster, and cheaper while achieving its vital mission.

Ways to Improve Performance

Essentially, too many business leaders in both the public and the private sectors have either lost sight of the big picture, or the critical execution of details, or both. Business leaders must perform a difficult balancing act and must always focus on creating a positive, ethical, performance-based culture. At the same time, they must understand and keep an eye on the critical execution details, while empowering team members, not micromanaging. Some executives understand the big picture of where they are and where they want to be, but they have little clue as how to get from point A to point B. Other executives are astute about cost, price, or technical issues but lack the skill to grasp the big picture of what is truly important for the organization to consistently achieve high performance for years and decades.

Therefore, what should senior executives in both the public and the private sectors, including U.S. federal government agency CAOs, know and do to improve buying and selling? Well, because we are dealing with senior executives, the answer must be kept simple, clear, and concise as shown in **Table 2.1**.

Responsibilities for Improving Performance Results

Here's a discussion of the seven items listed in the table.

Table 2.1 Seven Great Responsibilities of Senior Executives to Improve Performance Results
1. Create and communicate a vision of high performance.
2. Develop great talent.
3. Build a performance-based culture.
4. Creat customer-focused, integrated project teams.
5. Ensure excellence in execution.
6. Hold individuals and teams accountable for high performance results.
7. Empower, recognize, and reward individual and team performance results.

1. **Create and communicate a vision of high performance.** Finding someone who views the organization from multiple perspectives—customer, supplier, employee, cost, schedule, technical, and quality perspectives—in both the short term (three years or less) and the long term (beyond three years) is a real challenge. So the first great responsibility of any executive is to create and effectively communicate a vision of the big picture. As Stephen Covey, author of the best-selling book *The Seven Habits of Highly Effective People* (1989), says one should "begin with the end in mind." The end state for every organization should be the creation of a successful organization that meets or exceeds all performance goals on a consistent basis. The senior executives must create and drive the goals to achieve the vision. Chapters 3–10 will discuss key aspects of a vision and goals that senior executives should address and communicate.

2. **Develop great talent.** The second great responsibility of any executive is to develop great talent. Building leadership skills at every level of an organization—through empowering, providing education, coaching, mentoring, and cross-training—is essential to the organization's evolving and it achieving higher levels of performance. Unfortunately, most organizations give this important responsibility only lip service and a small budget for training. Jack Welch, former CEO of General Electric, was an exception. Welch always seemed to find the time in his busy schedule—during more than 25 years as CEO—to coach, mentor, and provide periodic live classroom training to business leaders with the highest potential. Chapter 3 will provide a more detailed discussion of developing great talent.

3. **Build a performance-based culture.** Executives must think outside the box. Senior executives should strive to build a true performance-based culture. That culture exists when everything is done with high-performance results in mind, including the following:

   ■ Performance-based vision,

   ■ Performance-based opportunity and risk management,

   ■ Performance-based organizational goals,

   ■ Performance-based individual and team goals,

- Performance-based measures and metrics,

- Performance-based payment (to individuals and suppliers),

- Performance-based contracts,

- Performance-based promotions,

- Performance-based teams, and

- Performance-based buying and selling.

Chapter 10 will provide a more detailed discussion of building a performance-based culture.

4. **Create customer-focused, integrated project teams**. Nearly all work is accomplished through teamwork. Thus, creating high-performance integrated project teams is essential to business success. An integrated project team is a fully combined team (buyer, seller [prime contractor], and subcontractors). Everyone works together with clearly defined roles and responsibilities, and everyone focuses on a meeting a customer's or user's needs. An integrated project team can achieve tremendous performance results by getting everyone to sing and dance to the same tune at the same time, which is easy to say but often very hard to accomplish. Chapters 3 and 10 provide more details about the importance of creating customer-focused integrated project teams.

5. **Ensure excellence in execution**. Senior executives must stay laser-focused on critical execution details: As the old saying goes, "The devil is in the details." Executives must ensure that the organization does not lose sight of the essential details that are vital for achieving success, from both customer and organizational perspectives. Ensuring excellence in execution is a central theme of this book. Chapters 3–9 provide best practices and case studies, which focus on improving buying and selling processes, performance, and price.

6. **Hold individuals and teams accountable for high-performance results**. If a senior executive does everything else right, but does not hold individuals and teams accountable for high-performance results, the executive's organization will fail to consistently achieve success. Senior executives must create an environment where

individuals and teams are held accountable for both successes and failures. While intelligent risk-taking must be encouraged and occasional failures must be understood, individuals and teams must be aware that there are real consequences for failure, especially failure to comply with laws, government regulations, company policies and procedures, and contractual terms and conditions. Compliance, accountability, and discipline are vital aspects of an organization that continually achieves excellent results. Chapters 3, 7, 8, and 10 provide the greater insights, tools, and best practices that will hold individuals and teams accountable for improving their buying and selling.

7. **Empower, recognize, and reward individual and team performance results.** All senior executives in both the public and the private sectors must embrace and practice pay for performance. Multiple factors affect whether or not any employee is satisfied with his or her job, including these:

- Job security,

- Professional development,

- Complexity of job,

- Opportunities for travel,

- Opportunities for advancement,

- Organizational culture,

- Flexibility of hours, and

- Fringe benefits.

Salary is clearly a vital factor, especially if an employee feels s/he is underpaid in comparison to low-performing peers, employees, or supervisors. A pay-for-performance compensation package is one that is tied to the organization's, team's, and individual's goals and objectives. Pay-for-performance compensation systems have proven to be effective tools to stimulate higher levels of performance in thousands of organizations worldwide. But, money is not enough. Many simple and less-expensive actions go a long way to helping the organization motivate and retain talent, including the following:

- Saying "thank you";

- Sending letters of appreciation;

- Presenting small, appropriate gifts;

- Finding opportunities for professional development (training programs, professional seminars, paid-for education, degree-based programs);

- Treating people with respect;

- Offering expanded responsibilities;

- Giving people real empowerment;

- Expanding their fringe benefits;

- Offering flexible work hours; and

- Allowing people to work in a virtual office.

Chapters 3, 8, and 10 will provide an expanded discussion of the need to recognize and reward individual and team performance so employees can improve buying and selling.

Summary
In the first chapter, "Performance-Based Acquisition: The Essential Elements," we introduced a simple model to provide a holistic view of what it takes to achieve higher levels of performance when buying and selling products, services, and solutions in today's complex business world. The essential elements of the performance-based acquisition model include the 4 Ps—people, processes, performance, and price. In this chapter, we have discussed the essential element of people, specifically what challenges both private industry and government senior executives face and what they should know and do to improve performance results. We introduced and briefly discussed the "Seven Great Responsibilities of Senior Executives to Improve Performance Results." Chapters 3–10 provide greater detail about what should or could be accomplished to improve performance results by taking

both a broad and deep view of people, processes, performance, and price. Chapter 10 will help tie it all together with a compelling view of the future.

Chapter 3 will continue the discussion about the essential element of people by closely examining the topic of teamwork. At the completion of each of the following chapters, there will be a summary of key best practices that are intended to help you retain the most important points so you can improve performance results. Knowledge is good, but the application of knowledge to obtain excellence is best!

Questions to Consider

1. Which of the senior executive challenges discussed are the most important for your organization to overcome? (Pick three or more.)

2. Of the "Seven Great Responsibilities of Senior Executives to Improve Performance Results," which one or two are the most important for improving your organization's performance?

3. Which one or two of the "Seven Great Responsibilities of Senior Executives to Improve Performance Results" are the most difficult to implement in your organization?

4. On a scale of 1 to 10 (from lowest to highest), how would you rate your senior executives' ability to consistently achieve high-performance results?

Endnote

1. PricewaterhouseCoopers, "Eighth Annual Survey of Chief Executive Officers," January 2005.

CHAPTER 03

Acquisition Teamwork: Roles, Responsibilities, and More

Introduction

The intent of this book is to make the subject of performance-based acquisition (PBA) accessible and logical for all and to shift the paradigm from traditional acquisition-thinking to collaborative, performance-oriented teamwork that focuses on program performance, improvement, and innovation, not simply on contract compliance. PBA offers the potential to dramatically transform the nature of service delivery and to permit both the government and industry to tap the enormous creative energy and innovative nature of their team members.

A team is a group of people working together for a common goal. An acquisition team includes members of various functional organizations—buyer, seller (prime contractor), and supply-chain partners (subcontractors)—working together to achieve common customer goals. Today, acquisition teams are typically called integrated solution teams, or integrated project teams (IPTs). The IPTs share responsibility, authority, and resources to achieve their collective missions. Teamwork is demonstrated by effective, open, and honest communication daily. All teams members must possess a positive, can-do attitude. Truly effective IPTs realize that diversity, individuality, and creativity are vital to success. Everyone must be totally committed to cost, schedule, and quality standards of excellence and must have achieving customer goals as the primary focus of all team activities.[1]

Time to Build a High-Performance Team

Why is it that everyone understands that a high-performance sports team takes months, if not years, to become consistently successful, yet many senior business executives in both government and industry often expect their acquisition teams, or IPTs (which have frequently been put together with available talent), to become instantly successful? Too many senior executives talk about the need to provide flawless execution, but they allow their IPTs to be set up for failure.

The following are a number of common business challenges that set up acquisition programs and related projects for poor or failing results:

- Failure to select the right team members;

- Failure to give the IPT (multiparty and multifunctional team) sufficient time to plan and build a team;

- Failure to understand and document customers' performance-based requirements;

- Failure to develop joint (buyer and seller) performance measures and metrics;

- Failure to develop and document agreed-to acceptance criteria;

- Unrealistic delivery dates promised by the seller's sales teams or executives; and

- Premature sales team commitment to prototype products, services, or solutions that do not yet meet buyer needs.

There is no set period of time for a group of individuals working together—either in person, virtually, or in some combination—to evolve through the typical steps or phases of team building—forming, storming, norming, and performing—so the team can achieve peak performance (see **Figure 3.1**, p. 45). Each IPT is unique, and some teams require more time than others. However, top IPT leaders know how to help accelerate the team-building process by using their knowledge of the people on the team and of what it takes to be successful.

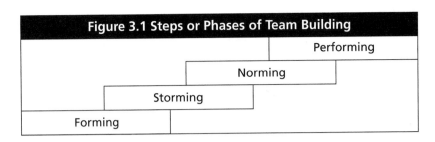

Figure 3.1 Steps or Phases of Team Building

Complex Program Phases and Control Gates

Every large and complex acquisition program goes through various phases during its life cycle. Different organizations have given the distinct phases a wide variety of names or numerical designations, as illustrated in **Figure 3.2** (p. 46). Typically, before a program transitions from one phase to another in the acquisition life cycle, there is a control gate. A control gate is often an executive approval process for evaluating program-related opportunities and risks and for deciding whether or not to continue with the program.

Unfortunately, in both the public and the private sectors, programs are often delayed for extended periods because of overly bureaucratic executive reviews and approval processes, which all too often merely rubber-stamp continuing the acquisition. If a control gate does not add value to a program and the related projects, then it should be eliminated. The use of phases and control gates can serve as an effective tool for leveraging the acquisition team's expertise to evaluate opportunities and mitigate risks throughout the acquisition life cycle. Every phase and control gate should be well understood by all parties involved in the acquisition, add value to the process, and help maximize program success. The key aspects of using acquisition lifecycle phases and control gates are to have the right people managing the program and related projects at the right time. Plus, it is vital to have the right people with the appropriate expertise conducting control gate reviews.

Acquisition Teamwork Process

Figure 3.3 (p. 47) lists the key inputs, tools, techniques, and outputs that are essential to ensure success of large and complex acquisition programs and related projects.

Inputs and Dealing with People

This section deals with the major inputs to acquisition teamwork, especially the people and their involvement. Those people who are involved with a complex acquisition program, including team mem-

Figure 3.2 Program Phases and Control Gates

	Study Period		Implementation Period		Operations Period	
	Formulation		Implementation		Operations	

NASA Phases

| Pre-Phase A: Preliminary Requirements Analysis | Phase A: Mission Needs and Conceptual Trade Studies | Phase B: Concept Definition | Phase C: Design and Development | Phase D: Fabrication, Integration, Test, and Certification | Phase E: Pre-Operations | Phase F: Operations/Disposal |

DOD Phases

| Pre-Phase 0: Determination of Mission Need | Phase 0: Concept Exploration and Definition | Phase I: Demonstration and Validation | Phase II: Engineering and Manufacturing Development | | Phase III: Production and Deployment | Phase IV: Operations and Support |

Typical High-Tech Commerical Business Phases

| Product Requirements Phase | Product Definition Phase | Product Proposal Phase | Product Devel. Phase | Engineer. Model Phase | Int. Test Phase | External Test Phase | Production Phase | Manufacturing Sales, and Support Phase |

Control gates: New Initiative Approval — System Concept Approval — Development Approval — Production Approval — Operational Approval

Adapted from Kevin Forsberg, Hal Mooz, and Howard Cotterman, *Visualizing Project Management* (New York: John Wiley & Sons, 2001).

Figure 3.3 Acquisition Teamwork Process

Inputs	Tools and Techniques	Outputs

■ People
  • Buyer (Needs and Goals)
  • Seller (Value-Chain)
■ Leadership Development
■ Roles and Responsibilities
■ Training
	Business Conduct
	■ Project Charter Outline
	■ Code of Conduct
	Accountability and Responsibility
	■ Responsibility Assignment Matrix
	■ Multiparty Participation Matrix
	■ Project Team Member Objectives and Assessment Tool
	Leadership Development
	■ Talk the Talk
	■ Walk the Talk
	■ Build Leaders at Every Level
	■ Make a Difference
		■ Highly Effective Integrated Project Team
		  • Exceeds Customer Needs
		  • Obtains Positive Customer Feedback
		  • Ensures On-Time Delivery
		  • Provides Quality Products and Services
		  • Exhibits Excellent Teamwork
		  • Delivers Within Budget

bers from the buyer, seller, and subcontractors, will determine the success or failure of any program by their actions and inaction. There are many barriers to successful teamwork, including the following:

■ Personality conflicts,

■ Egos,

■ Management style,

■ Language,

■ Lack of attention,

■ Lack of Motivation,

■ Lack of technical knowledge,

■ Lack of respect towards others,

■ Closed mind, and

■ Lack of focus.[2]

Note also that all IPT members must be engaged in and committed to the following actions:

■ Interdependence rather than independence;

■ Desire to do whatever is necessary, within appropriate ethical and legal guidelines, to make the project succeed;

■ Focus on doing what is right for the customer or user; and

■ Placement of team needs above individual needs.

Building teamwork is not easy; sustaining teamwork, especially at a high level of performance, is a significant challenge. Therefore, selecting the right people for a team is very important. Likewise, if conflicts among team members cannot be resolved quickly and effectively, removing poor performers and teamwork disrupters is equally important. Finally, while all team members are important, the team leader is most important, because the team leader motivates and drives the whole team to achieve customer goals. **Figure 3.4** (p. 49) provides a sample IPT structure, adapted from the book *Managing Complex Outsourced Projects* by Gregory A. Garrett, to illustrate how important the project leader is for pulling together a multiparty and multifunctional team to achieve success.[3]

Leadership Development

Although some people seem to be natural-born leaders, most people develop leadership skills over time through formal education, professional training, work experience, and personal coaching and mentoring. A project leader's challenge is to tap into the available discretionary effort of team members. In other words, a successful project leader motivates or stimulates people to achieve a higher level of performance. Helping individuals develop their leadership skills takes time and the commitment of senior leaders of an organization. Thus senior leadership must create a culture or environment that supports leadership development by encouraging innovation, appropriate risk

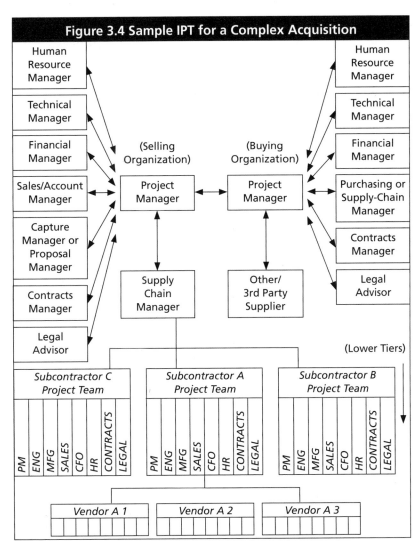

Figure 3.4 Sample IPT for a Complex Acquisition

Adapted from Gregory A. Garrett, *Managing Complex Outsourced Projects* (*Chicago: CHH Incorporated*, 2004).

taking, and professional and ethical business practices.

Most organizations need highly skilled and experienced leaders who are able to adapt their leadership style, including the application of tools and techniques, to various project situations. An individual who possesses only one leadership style, with limited tools and techniques, will fail in most situations because of that person's inflexibility or inability to successfully adapt to changing environments. One of the greatest challenges of leadership development is helping individuals understand when, where, and how to adapt their leadership style to a specific situation, and which of the various leadership tools and techniques should be applied or tailored to the situation. Every organization should strive to develop leaders at every level. Leadership development should be a part of the personal plan of every member of an organization and of the IPT.

Roles and Responsibilities

Roles and responsibilities are the specific contributions expected from each team member to accomplish the project or customer goals. Team member contributions can include formal and informal offerings. Formal team member contributions typically include the expected roles and responsibilities of a specific functional discipline. Informal contributions by team members often vary according to personal strengths such as computer skills, negotiating skills, writing skills, planning skills, analytical or technical skills, and communication skills.

Every project team must create its own unique roles and responsibilities on the basis of the project's requirements and the talents of the team members. IPT members' roles and responsibilities must evolve with the changing environment. Likewise, team members must be comfortable in an environment where change is frequent and expected. Many organizations spend a great deal of time and money developing standard documents defining the roles and responsibilities of employees. While having such standard documents is good, being able to tailor them quickly and cost-effectively is better—and critical in today's ever-changing business environment.[4]

Team members' roles and responsibilities should include the following:

- A clear and concise statement of each member's objectives and expected results;

- An understanding of the individual's scope of work and level of accountability; and

- An understanding of the individual's span of control over resources, including people, funds, facilities, and equipment.

Personnel Training

Both team-building training and leadership-development training can take many forms, offered through multimedia, range in cost dramatically, and vary in effectiveness. However, every organization needs to take appropriate action to build teams and develop leaders. The important questions are the following:

- Whom do we spend our time and money on?

- How much time and money should we invest in team building and leadership development?

- Do we conduct the team-building training and leadership-development training with internal organization resources, or do we outsource?

- If we outsource team-building training and leadership-development training, then whom do we hire to do the job?

- How do we evaluate the results versus expenditures on team-building training and leadership-development training?

- What should project leaders and team members be taught?

- What competency-based model is appropriate for our organization?

- How important are the following key programs and related project actions?

  - Create a code of conduct.

  - Create a vision.

  - Develop a mission statement.

  - Develop a project charter.

  - Define performance-based requirements.

  - Create customer-focused project goals.

  - Create clear team member roles and responsibilities.

  - Provide team members feedback and coaching.

  - Manage project budget and schedule.

  - Motivate team members to a higher level of performance.

- Ensure appropriate team communications.

- Mitigate team risks.

- Resolve team conflicts.

- Remove teamwork obstacles.

- Recognize and reward teamwork and excellent results.

■ What media should our team-building and leadership training use (CD-ROMs, Web-based courses, Web broadcasts, classroom [on site or off site], audiotapes, videotapes, satellite broadcasts)?

Clearly, developing strong teams and individual leadership skills is important to every organization, especially for IPT leaders who are responsible for managing large, complex, programs and related projects. While nearly every organization recognizes the need for team building, leadership development, and succession planning at all levels of the organization, few organizations do it well.

Tools and Techniques

The following tools and techniques have been proven effective for building, sustaining, and improving teamwork in complex acquisitions. The key to successfully implementing those tools and techniques is knowing when to use them and how to tailor them to the specific situation.

Business Conduct: Tools and Techniques. First, a leader should examine the project charter. *A key action in gaining recognition and support for a new IPT is to formally charter the project, program, or program management office (PMO).* The project or program charter should perform several functions, including the following:

■ Identify the project or program and its importance to the organization.

■ Appoint an IPT leader.

■ Acknowledge the members of the multifunctional IPT (buyer, seller, and subcontractors).

■ Establish top-level responsibilities and authority.

■ Establish the resource commitment (people, funds, and facilities).

■ Confirm the project or program's executive sponsor or champion.

■ State the overall customer-focused project goals.

Table 3.1 (this page) provides a program or project charter outline to help teams develop effective formal charters for their major programs or projects.

Table 3.1 Program or Project Charter Outline
Project Name or Title: _____
Date: _____
Importance of the Project: _____
Overall Scope of Project: _____
Project Leader: _____
Project Team Members and Roles: _____
Project Leader's Authority and Responsibilities: _____
Customer-Focused Project Goals: _____
Resource Commitment: _____
Project Executive Sponsor or Champion: _____

Code of Conduct. Table 3.2 (this page) provides a sample code of conduct. The sample code of conduct has been successfully used by senior program management directors and vice presidents at Lucent Technologies to simply and concisely convey the importance of mutual respect that will build teamwork and achieve project success.

Most organizations and companies have detailed guidelines for professional and ethical business practices to ensure their employees are good corporate citizens who obey all appropriate federal, state, and local laws, regulations, and business guidelines. Today more than ever, professional business conduct is imperative to achieve success in both the short term and the long term. When developing IPTs, with buyers, sellers, and subcontractors working closely together, professional and ethical behavior by all team members is mandatory. **Figure 3.5** (p. 55) illustrates some of the common legal conduct issues that must be addressed to ensure proper employee business conduct.

Case Study—CH2M HILL Strategic Project Management

CH2M HILL strategic project management system emphasizes the consistent use of a standard project delivery process, including developing teams, chartering projects, planning work, endorsing, executing, managing change, closing, and learning.

Those overarching processes are totally integrated with the Project Management Institute's *A Guide to the Project Management Body of Knowledge* and are aligned with the ISO 10006 global standards for project management. The core processes are scalable and matched with Web-based technologies and tools that enable project managers to deliver projects efficiently and to provide accurate project status reporting to all levels of management and clients.

The project manager development framework, along with this Web-

Table 3.2 Sample IPT Code of Conduct
R = Be Respectful of others time, opinions, ideas, and contributions.
E = Empower people to make decisions and do their job.
S = Support both the team and each individual team member.
P = Practice professional behavior at all times.
E = Escalate and handle problems early before they become crises.
C = Have a Can-do attitude.
T = Trust others to listen and do the right thing.

Figure 3.5. Legal Conduct Issues

Conflict of Interest	Defective Pricing	Product Substitution	Cost Mischarging	False Claims
├Bribes	├Principal	├Principal	├Labor	├Original Contract
├Kickbacks	└Supplier Vendors and Subcontractors	└Supplier Vendors and Subcontractors	├Materials	└Contract Changes
└Insider Information			├Research	
			└Indirect	

Adapted from Kevin Forsberg, Hal Mooz, and Howard Cotterman, *Visualizing Project Management* (New York: John Wiley & Sons, 2001).

based performance enhancement process, has been invaluable in the recognition and growth of project managers and project delivery teams. Clear roles, responsibilities, and pathways for greater achievement have created a very attractive workplace environment.[5]

Accountability and Responsibility: Tools and Techniques

Accountability and responsibility are the backbone or foundation for teamwork and essential to achieve high performance.

Responsibility Assignment Matrix. One of the easiest yet most effective ways to communicate who does what on a project is through the use of a responsibility assignment matrix. **Table 3.3** (this page) provides a basic outline of a responsibility assignment matrix that can be tailored for any project.

Table 3.4 (p. 56) provides another example of how a responsibility assignment matrix can be developed to ensure that all team members

Table 3.3 Responsibility Assignment Matrix Outline

Team Member Role, Name, Phone, and E-mail	Phase											
	Concept			Design			Implementation			Operations and Maintenance		
	Task	Task	Task	Task	Task	Task	Task	Task	Task	Task	Task	Task

Table 3.4 Completed Responsibility Assignment Matrix

Role	Responsibilitie
Project Leader	• Creates project plan, working with team members; includes identification of deliverables, work tasks, resources, and timeline • Ensures information is communicated throughout team and among team members • Monitors work tasks to ensure overall timeline is met • Ensures company approvals are secured • Oversees Alert-Jeopardy-Escalation Plan and ensures timely resolution of issues • Oversees contract management plan and ensures approved changes are communicated to team • Develops risk mitigation plan while working with team members
Proposal Manager	• Acts as single point of contact regarding development of customer deliverables • Collects inputs; then edits, formats, and produces finished deliverables • Runs bid and proposal reviews • Oversees production, packaging, and shipment of customer deliverables
Sales Manager	• Acts as the single point of contact to address all customer matters • Develops win themes and strategies • Leads completion of competitive assessment • Translates customer business needs into technical and delivery requirements • Serves as a surrogate for the customer to answer questions and to provide assumptions or direction regarding missing or unclear information • Writes executive summary
Technical Manager	• Acts as the single point of contact to address all technical matters • Identifies, organizes, and directs technical personnel to complete technical response • Identifies, organizes, and directs technical support to design the solution • Translates customer business needs into technical requirements for the solution • Certifies that all components of the solution are properly reflected in the pricing • Identifies and recommends strategies to mitigate technical risks
Project (Delivery) Manager	• Acts as the single point of contact to address all delivery matters • Identifies, organizes, and directs program management, ordering and billing, engineering, installation, documentation, and training • Identifies, organizes, and directs support resources to create a delivery plan • Translates customer business needs into delivery requirements for the solution • Certifies that all components of the delivery plan are properly reflected in the pricing • Identifies and recommends strategies to mitigate delivery risks
Pricing Manager	• Acts as single point of contact to address all pricing matters • Identifies, organizes, and directs pricing personnel to complete pricing response • Supports business manager in development of business case • Ensures appropriate approvals have been secured for pricing included in response • Certifies pricing is complete and accurate • Identifies and recommends strategies to mitigate pricing risks
Contract Manager	• Acts as single point of contact to address all contractual matters • Identifies, organizes, and directs contracts, legal, and purchasing personnel to complete contractual response • Certifies that all terms and conditions are consistent with company polices and that all contractual language has been properly approved • Identifies and recommends strategies to mitigate contractual risk.

Adapted from Gregory A. Garrett and Reginald J. Kipke, *The Capture Management Life-Cycle* (Chicago: CCH Incorporated, 2003).

clearly understand their roles and responsibilities. The form summarizes the roles and responsibilities of the core members of a capture team.

Multiparty Participation Matrix. When one deals with a buyer, a seller, and subcontractors, it is vital that everyone understands who does what—including which party has the lead role in specific project activities throughout the project's life cycle. **Table 3.5** (See pp. 58-61) is a multiparty participation matrix that is designed to help clarify each party's respective role throughout the typical process of integrated project management.

Team Member Assessment: Tools and Techniques. As an example of team member objectives and an assessment tool, **Table 3.6** (See p. 62) provides a proven-effective means for project leaders to work with team members. Using the table, they can mutually establish IPT member objectives and expected results, which will contribute to project success. In addition, Table 3.6 allows the project leader and team members to use the same form throughout the year to assess results and project effects.

Project Leadership Development: Tools and Techniques. How many times have you heard people in a project leadership position say the right words—"talk the talk"—but fail to deliver on their promises? Unfortunately, too many public and private sector organizations and companies suffer from a leadership gap: there are too many managers and too few leaders. Time and time again, companies have stagnated or declined because of failures of leadership. Many believe that leadership is an elusive quality, that a person is either born with it or not, and that it cannot be developed or taught. Others view leadership as a skill that blends art and science and can be developed or taught successfully.

Regardless of an individual's position, however, leadership skills are important to professional development and success. Real leaders, after all, know how to talk the talk, walk the walk, build leaders at every level, and make a difference.

Step 1: Talk the Talk. There are three key aspects to being able to successfully deliver a message as a leader. Those aspects include knowing how to deliver the message, paying attention to appearance, and knowing what to say.

A. **Knowing it is in the delivery**. To improve communications skills,

Table 3.5 Multiparty Participation Matrix					
Integrated Project Management	**Buyer**	**Seller**	**Subcontractors or Supply-Chain Partners**		
Process Element			**A**	**B**	**C**
1.0 CONCEPT					
1.1 Describe Project and Determine Project Management Need					
1.1.1 Create Opportunity Overview					
1.1.2 Determine Need for Project Management Services					
1.1.3 Assign Project Manager and Provide Funding					
1.1.4 Determine Project and Project Management Level					
1.2 Conduct Project Risk Assessment					
1.2.1 Conduct Business Case and Technical Design Reviews					
1.2.2 Write Project Qualification Report					
1.2.3 Review Project Qualification Report					
1.3 Obtain Decision to Proceed					
2.0 PRE-AWARD PLANNING					
2.1 Identify Planning Resources					
2.2 Assess Levels of Participation					
2.3 Convene Planning Team					
2.4 Develop Preliminary Project Plan					
2.4.1 Review and Understand Customer Requirements					
2.4.2 Revise Preliminary Scope Statement					
2.4.3 Develop Preliminary Work Breakdown Structure					
2.4.4 Develop Preliminary Project Schedule					
2.4.5 Develop Preliminary Staffing Plan					
2.4.6 Develop Preliminary Project Budget					
2.4.7 Develop Preliminary Test and Acceptance Plan					
2.4.8 Develop Preliminary Risk Management Plan					
2.4.9 Develop Proposal Baseline Configuration					
2.5 Support Proposal and Contract Negotiation Process					
2.5.1 Develop Preferred and Mandatory Terms and Conditions					
2.5.2 Finalize Bid/No-Bid Decision					
2.5.3 Submit Proposal					
2.5.4 Assist in Contract Negotiations					
2.5.5 Revise Risk Management Plan					
2.5.6 Document Lessons Learned					
3.0 POST-AWARD PLANNING					

Table 3.5 Multiparty Participation Matrix					
Process Element			**A**	**B**	**C**
3.1 Review and Summarize Contract					
3.1.1 Validate Customer Requirements Through Internal Requirements Analysis					
3.1.2 Review Contract Requirements and Prepare Contract Tracking Summary					
3.1.3 Prepare Functional Baseline					
3.1.4 Attend Post-Award Orientation with Customer					
3.2 Reissue Project Charter and Build Project Team					
3.2.1 Determine Project Team Structure					
3.2.2 Reissue Project Charter					
3.2.3 Develop Resource Responsibility Matrix					
3.2.4 Finalize Staffing Plan					
3.2.5 Obtain Resource Commitment					
3.2.6 Obtain Logistical Support					
3.3 Conduct Internal Project Kickoff Meeting					
3.4 Conduct Project Plan Workshop					
3.4.1 Plan Workshop and Notify Team Members					
3.4.2 Develop Project Plan					
3.4.2.1 Create Baseline WBS at Work Package Level					
3.4.2.2 Create Baseline Project Budget					
3.4.2.3 Create Baseline Project Schedule					
3.4.2.4 Develop Supporting Project Plan Elements					
3.4.3 Prepare Supporting Plans					
3.4.3.1 Revise Risk Management Plan					
3.4.3.2 Prepare Finance Plan					
3.4.3.3 Prepare Baseline Implementation Plan					
3.4.3.4 Prepare Customer Relations Plan					
3.4.3.5 Prepare Baseline Subcontracting Plan					
3.4.3.6 Prepare Quality Assurance Plan					
3.4.3.7 Prepare Training Plan					
3.4.3.8 Prepare Safety Plan					
3.4.3.9 Prepare Product Baseline and Test and Acceptance Plan					
3.4.3.10 Prepare Transition Plan					
3.4.3.11 Prepare Life Cycle Management Plan					
3.4.3.12 Prepare Baseline Configuration Management and Change Control Plan					
3.4.3.13 Prepare Project Management Plan					
3.4.4 Develop Allocated Baseline and Detailed System Design					

Table 3.5 Multiparty Participation Matrix					
Process Element			A	B	C
3.4.5 Document and Distribute Kickoff and Workshop Minutes					
3.5 Develop Integrated Project Plan					
3.5.1 Coordinate Supporting Plans					
3.5.2 Prepare Baseline Project Plan for Customer Review					
3.6 Hold Customer Kickoff Meeting					
3.6.1 Develop and Distribute the Agenda					
3.6.2 Establish Roles and Responsibilities					
3.6.3 Review Baseline Project Plan					
3.6.4 Review Change Control Process					
3.7 Finalize Baseline Project Plan					
4.0 IMPLEMENTATION					
4.1 Establish and Maintain Project Management Information System					
4.1.1 Organize and Coordinate Project Information Flow					
4.1.2 Receive and Review Project Status Reports					
4.2 Monitor and Control Project					
4.2.1 Audit Project Performance					
4.2.2 Issue Regular Project Status Reports					
4.2.3 Hold Regular Project Status Meetings					
4.3 Manage Cost, Schedule, and Resource Variance					
4.3.1 Manage Cost Variance					
4.3.2 Manage Schedule Variance					
4.3.3 Manage Resource Use					
4.4 Control Changes to Project					
4.4.1 Identify and Communicate Change					
4.4.2 Evaluate Effect on Budget, Schedule, and Architectural Baseline					
4.4.3 Execute Contract Change					
4.4.4 Implement Change					
4.5 Manage Technical Progress					
4.5.1 Review Technical Progress					
4.5.2 Conduct Quality Reviews					
4.6 Manage Contract with Customer					
4.6.1 Review Customer Contract Compliance					
4.6.2 Document and Control Contract Changes					
4.6.3 Monitor Customer Billing and Payment					
4.7 Manage Suppliers					

Table 3.5 Multiparty Participation Matrix					
Process Element			A	B	C
4.7.1 Review Supplier Performance					
4.7.2 Manage Subcontract Changes					
4.7.3 Review Supplier Billing and Monitor Payments					
4.8 Manage Risk					
4.8.1 Review Status of High-Risk Events					
4.8.2 Reassess Risk Based on Environmental and Project Changes					
4.9 Manage Test and Acceptance					
4.9.1 Perform Predelivery/Milestone Test and Acceptance					
4.9.2 Perform Final System Test and Acceptance					
4.10 Obtain Customer Sign-Off					
5.0 CLOSE-OUT					
5.1 Transition to Operations and Support					
5.1.1 Hold Customer Satisfaction Review					
5.1.2 Hold Transition Meeting					
5.1.3 Establish Customer Follow-Up and Monitoring Process					
5.2 Close Out Project Internally					
5.2.1 Prepare and Review Final Schedule and Cost Reports					
5.2.3 Verify Final Project Billing					
5.2.4 Finalize Historical Project Documentation					
5.3 Hold Final Project Team Critique and Review					
5.3.1 Review all Plans to Ensure Project Completion					
5.3.2 Provide Team and Individual Recognition					
5.3.3 Disperse Project Team					

Legend: I = Information only, P = Participate in process, L = Lead process

leaders need to do the following:

- *Learn to be a proactive listener.* Think before talking.

- *Deliver messages in person or by telephone.* Do this delivery with passion, commitment, and a positive can-do attitude; people usually can spot a fake.

- *Use tone, pauses, loudness, pitch, and inflection.* These approaches communicate what is important.

- *Use body language to reinforce verbal communication.* This

Table 3.6 IPT Member Objectives and Assessment Tools and Techniques

Employee Name:_____

Location:_____

Date:_____

Fiscal Year: From:_____

To:_____

Integrated Project Team Name:_____

Organization:_____

Individual Business Objectives	Actual Results and Project Effect	Supervisor Assessment
Desired Teamwork Behaviors	Demonstrated Behaviors and Project Effect	Supervisor Assessment
Project Leadership Characteristics	Actual Results and Project Effect	Supervisor Assessment
Professional Development Objectives	Actual Results and Project Effect	Supervisor Assessment

Employee Comments:_____

❑ Objectives

❑ Quarterly Assessment

❑ End-of-Year Assessment

Employee Signature:_____

Employee Name Printed:_____

Date:_____

Employee Supervisor Signature:_____

Supervisor Name Printed:_____

Date:_____

physical approach includes eye contact, hand motions and gestures, and facial expressions.

■ *Practice, develop, and refine your communication skills daily.*

B. **Looking like a leader.** Some people foolishly believe that saying the right things makes appearance unimportant. Wrong! Appearance always matters because it communicates volumes about you. While being physically attractive does help in some instances, how you choose to dress, stand, sit, and use other nonverbal physical communication methods and techniques will have a dramatic effect on how effectively you deliver your message. (See **Table 3.7** below for tips on how to look the part of an effective leader.)

Table 3.7 Checklist to Look the Part of a Leader
❑ Dress the part. Select appropriate attire for business meetings, presentations, conferences, and so forth.
❑ Err on the side of overdressing. Unfortunately, today's "business casual" is getting too casual!
❑ Use proper posture. People are less likely to respect slouchers or take them seriously.
❑ Maintain neat personal grooming. Make sure that hair (including facial hair) and nails are kept neatly trimmed.
❑ Use appropriate professional audio or visual aids. These aids can help support your physical presence at important meetings and presentations.
❑ Maintain physical fitness (as appropriate). A healthy physique can demonstrate your personal commitment and discipline.

C. **Knowing what to say.** To talk the talk effectively, a person must know what to say. If you are serious about improving your leadership skills, then communicate the customers' needs rather than their desires to your team members, and share with the team the status of the marketplace. It also is vitally important to communicate your company's goals and vision precisely and repeatedly, thus ensuring that everyone knows their role and responsibilities, as well as the performance metrics to achieve those goals. In addition, regularly explain your organization's business challenges regarding budget, expenses, schedule, and quality to everyone involved. Finally, communicate the importance of creating a performance-based culture. And, be sure to reward results.

Step 2: Walk the Talk. Learning to practice real project leadership is challenging. Leadership is not about micromanagement; it is about becoming a force multiplier. Novice project leaders often make the mistake of doing the work that their team members are responsible for doing instead of holding team members accountable, providing appropriate coaching and support or changing personnel when needed. Novice project leaders frequently fail to quickly recognize team members' strengths and weaknesses, which will result in additional problems and potential project failure. Finally, novice project leaders are hesitant to remove poor performers or divisive individuals from their teams; instead, they allow poor performers to negatively affect team and project performance for an extended period of time. The following proven best practices can help motivate others to accomplish your desired results.

■ Listen to your customers and team members, and understand their needs and desires.

■ Take proactive, appropriate actions to help customers and team members achieve their needs and desires.

■ Teach your employees and customers about leadership by honoring commitments.

■ Hold people accountable for their actions or inactions and results.

■ Conduct frequent meetings with all team members either in person, through teleconferencing, or through the Internet.

■ Display a positive, can-do attitude with a blend of realism and practicality.

■ Conduct frequent buyer and seller meetings with key decision makers to discuss relationship and project performance goals compared to results, using agreed-on performance metrics.

■ Develop and live by a code of conduct that includes honesty, integrity, and mutual respect.

■ Develop, document, and distribute your organization's vision statement, goals, and performance metrics and results. Distribute those
items by e-mail, posters, Web site ads or articles, company newslet-
ters, and CD-ROMs. When distributing performance metrics and
results, be sure to include information about customer satisfaction,
product and service quality, employee satisfaction, delivery times,
cycle times, budget, and expenses.

■ Recognize and reward individuals and teams for outstanding performance. Tie pay to performance if possible.

Table 3.8 Checklist of 10 Best Practices for Performance-Based Pay System
❑ Align individual performance expectations with organizational goals.
❑ Use performance information to track organizational strategies and goals.
❑ Provide regular and meaningful constructive feedback to employees.
❑ Involve employees in establishing their objectives and pay ranges.
❑ Pay your best performers more money.
❑ Encourage employees to grow and take appropriate risks to improve performance.
❑ Create a grievance system for employees that address their concerns.
❑ Pay poor performers the least amount of money.
❑ Provide individual and team-based education and training appropriate for each employee's role.
❑ Provide sufficient pay incentives to motivate higher levels of performance.

Step 3: Build Leaders at Every Level. One of the best books on leadership is Noel Tichy's *The Leadership Engine*. In the book, Tichy discusses the importance of building leaders at every level of a company
or organization. He provides a simple model that describes typical
situational leadership methods used to obtain results. **Figure 3.6** (See
p. 66), the Leadership Pyramid, illustrates some of Tichy's primary
leadership principles.

Jack Welch, former chairman and CEO of General Electric, in his

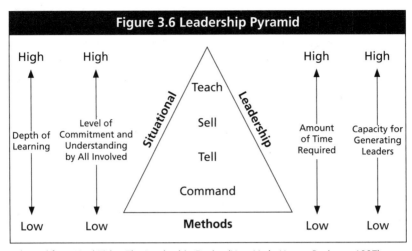

Adapted from Noel Tichy, *The Leadership Engine* (New York: Harper Business, 1997).

book titled *Jack: Straight from the Gut*[6] states how important it is for business leaders to provide frequent feedback to all team members to help them grow and develop their skills. Welch expresses the need for business leaders to evaluate all team members fairly and to rate them A, B, or C. Although all team members are valued, those who are fairly evaluated as A-level (top) performers must be highly cherished, rewarded, trained, and mentored to ensure the organization retains its top talent.

To build project leaders at every level of an organization, senior executives should ensure every project manager has a multiyear professional development plan to achieve the following:

- **Undergraduate-level education**—desired formal educational programs (i.e., a bachelor's degree in business, engineering, science, or other appropriate field);

- **Project management experience**—appropriate number of years of experience managing diverse projects of increasing project value and complexity;

- **Multifunctional business experience**—appropriate number of years of experience in diverse functional areas (such as sales, bid or proposal management, finance, contract management, engineering, manufacturing, quality, purchasing or supply-chain management, accounting);

- **Professional continuing education**—completion of appropriate project management professional development courses, including project planning, project scheduling, risk management, contract management, and quality assurance;

- **Professional certification**—designation as a Project Management Institute Project Management Professional (PMP);

- **Graduate-level education**—completion of an M.B.A. or an M.S. in systems management or project management, or other appropriate master's degree;

- **Portfolio of project results**

  - Number of projects managed,

  - Total value of projects managed,

  - Percentage of projects delivered on time,

  - Percentage of projects completed within budget,

  - Team member feedback, and

  - Customer feedback.

Step 4: Make a Difference. Everyone has encountered people who could be described as leaders—people who really do walk the talk. (See **Table 3.9**, p. 68)

Leadership skills are valued in every profession, not just the most visible or highly paid professions. Thus, being a real IPT leader simply means making a difference—doing the right things at the right time for the right reasons to consistently improve performance results. (See **Table 3.10**, p. 69)

Outputs

Effective teamwork usually achieves the following desired output:

- Exceed customer needs,

- Obtain positive customer feedback,

Table 3.9 Checklist of Best Practices for Real Leaders
Unlike self-proclaimed leaders, real leaders should do the following:
❑ Have ideas, values, energy, passion, and focus.
❑ Lead the team through the tough times.
❑ Hold people accountable.
❑ Get results.
❑ Make decisions.
❑ Successfully draw from their past experience.
❑ Clearly communicate ideas.
❑ Live by a set of values.
❑ Build high-performance teams.
❑ Create energy in others.
❑ Accept blame for team failures and give credit and recognition to others for team successes.
❑ Take the time to teach others to be leaders.

■ Ensure on-time delivery,

■ Provide quality products and services,

■ Exhibit excellent teamwork, and

■ Operate at or below the budget.

Summary

Building a high-performance IPT is a challenge; maintaining a high level of performance for an extended period of time is a great challenge; observing the work and results of a high-performance IPT is a pleasure. Performance-based acquisition is driven by people, and people are driven by leadership. Without the best people and real leadership driving the acquisition (buying and selling) process, there will be late deliveries, cost overruns, poor quality, and upset customers. In both the public and the private sectors, more time and attention must be paid to developing great talent to ensure future success than buying the latest software package or revamping the organizational structure.

In chapters 4, 5, and 6, we discuss the performance-based acquisition essential element of processes. We begin the discussion of processes

Table 3.10 Checklist of Key Best Practices in Acquisition Teamwork to Improve Performance Result for Buyers and Sellers

❑ Communicate the importance and value of teamwork to everyone.

❑ Create true IPTs with buyer, seller, and subcontractor multifunctional team members working together.

❑ Build common customer-focused project goals.

❑ Work together to develop performance-based requirements.

❑ Create a collaborative, performance-based culture.

❑ Spend time to develop high-performance IPTs.

❑ Select the right people.

❑ Remove poor performers.

❑ Honor commitments.

❑ Hold people accountable.

❑ Ensure that the right people serve on executive review boards for project phase control gates.

❑ Understand and mitigate the barriers to teamwork.

❑ Develop leaders at every level of the organization.

❑ Clearly document roles and responsibilities.

❑ Provide team-building training and leadership training to everyone.

❑ Create and follow a code of conduct.

❑ Develop a project charter.

❑ Resolve team conflicts.

❑ Ensure proper team conduct, including compliance with applicable laws, regulations, policies, and contract terms and conditions.

❑ Create a responsibility assignment matrix.

❑ Develop a multiparty participation matrix.

❑ Provide and document team member feedback and assessments.

❑ Develop succession plans.

❑ Recognize and reward individual and team performance.

❑ Use a pay-for-performance system.

❑ Understand that leadership drives people and that people drive everything else.

in chapter 4 with a macro view by examining the 10 key trends that are driving e-business—specifically, how organizations are adapting their systems and processes to evolve with changing customer demands, based on rapid advancements in technology. In chapter 5, we examine how every organization must develop effective processes to manage opportunities and risks. In chapter 6, we provide a detailed discussion of the process to create a supplier value chain that will ensure successful performance results.

Questions to Consider

1. How effective are your IPTs in achieving customer goals?

2. Does your organization formally charter IPTs?

3. How well does your organization establish team members' roles and responsibilities?

4. How effectively does your organization develop teamwork and leadership skills?

Endnotes

1. Bruce T. Barkley and James H. Saylor, *Customer-Driven Project Management* (New York: McGraw-Hill, 1991).

2. Barkley and Saylor, 1991.

3. Gregory A. Garrett, *Managing Complex Outsourced Projects* (Chicago, IL: CCH, Inc., 2004).

4. Gregory A. Garrett and Reginald J. Kipke, *The Capture Management Life Cycle* (Chicago, IL: CCH Inc., 2003).

5. Ross Foti, "CH2M HILL Interview," *PM Network Magazine*, January 2003.

6. Jack Welch, *Jack: Straight from the Gut* (NY: Warner Business Books, 2001).

CHAPTER 04

E-Business: Understanding Key Trends and Applying Best Practices

Introduction

Today, we live in a world focused on and somewhat obsessed with high performance. New performance-oriented trends are driving e-business and new best practices for buying and selling in both the public and the private sectors. Few concepts have so radically changed buying and selling as has the advent of e-business. Simply stated, the streamlining of transactions and interactions between buyers, sellers, and subcontractors as a result of e-business has caused senior executives worldwide to reexamine traditional definitions and customer expectations of speed, service, and execution.

During the past decade, organizations in both the public and the private business sectors have been driven by changing customer expectations as a result of tremendous advancements in technology and societal changes. Organizations have been forced to transform their processes and to develop e-business strategies, thereby focusing on providing speed to the market and an excellent execution of value-added products, services, and integrated solutions. This chapter focuses on the key trends driving e-business and related best practices so they can improve buying and selling in terms of processes, performance, and price. This chapter includes numerous case studies from leading organizations in both the U.S. federal government and industry. Specifically, it examines what they are doing to improve performance results.

Key Trends Driving e-Business

Extensive research shows 10 key trends that drive e-business. They can be divided into four major trend categories: customer, service, technology, and execution. **Table 4.1** (this page) provides a summary of those categories and the 10 key trends driving e-business.

Table 4.1 10 Key Trends Driving E-Business	
Major Trend Category	**Key Trend**
Customer	1. Need for speed
	2. Desire for self-service
	3. Need for best value
Service	4. Desire for increased process visibility
	5. Need for seamless customer service
Technology	6. Focus on integrated enterprise architecture
	7. Desire for wireless Web applications
	8. Need for convergence of infrastructure
Execution	9. Focus on partnering and outsourcing
	10. Desire for virtual distribution

Adapted from Ravi Kalakota and Marcia Robinson, *E-Business 2.0* (Boston: Addison-Wesley, 2004).

The following is a brief discussion of each of the 10 key trends driving e-business and a few of the many best practices and case studies that have improved buying and selling processes, performance, or price.

1. **The Need for Speed**. No, we are not talking about driving a car really fast. Rather, we are focusing on a cultural trend that affects nearly every aspect of life and business. In both the public and the private sectors, customers hate delays; moreover, they hate waiting for delivery of products and services. Both buyers and sellers understand that time is money. For e-business to succeed, all organizations must examine ways to reduce their respective cycle time from quote to delivery or payment.

From a buyer's perspective, it is important to reduce the procurement acquisition lead time (PALT). Buyers are continually assessing their seller's' source selection process, contract negotiation and contract formation process, task ordering process, contract administration process, and contract close-out process—all in an effort to reduce time and money. Remember, the typical buyer's mantra is "I want it better, faster, and cheaper!" **Table 4.2** (See p. 73) contains a

Table 4.2 Checklist of Best Practices for Buyers to Reduce Cycle Time

❑ Conduct continuous process improvement by analyzing each process activity and benchmarking against other organizations in various industries.

❑ Use a simplified purchasing approval process.

❑ Use procurement cards.

❑ Integrate business processes and information systems.

❑ Use prequalified suppliers.

❑ Use supply schedules, frame contracts, and indefinite delivery and indefinite quantity contracts.

❑ Conduct spending analysis.

❑ Make oral presentations.

❑ Use award without discussions.

❑ Use bid and proposal page limitations.

❑ Use e-auctions and reverse auctions.

❑ Transmit electronically all solicitation documents (such as request for quotes, requests for proposals, and invitations for bid)

❑ Use electronic signatures.

❑ Use electronic award of contracts, and contract amendments or modifications.

❑ Use supplier report cards.

❑ Transmit status reports electronically.

❑ Use electronic payment.

❑ Use performance-based contracts, which contain incentives for early delivery and penalties for late delivery.

few of the many buyer best practices that can help buyers to reduce the PALT, or cycle time.

From a seller's perspective, organizations must reduce the PALT, or cycle time, from quote to cash. For companies delivering products, services, and integrated solutions, speed is a must to survive and thrive. Like buyers, sellers must evaluate all their major business processes to seek ways to save time and money. Sellers typically focus their process improvement actions on links in the supply chain, such as order processing, engineering and design, manufacturing, packaging, transportation and distribution, installation, invoicing, and receipt of payment.

For both buyers and sellers, the need for speed is real and accelerating. Delays at any step in the acquisition process are unacceptable. Why do delays occur? Often, delays are caused by poorly designed processes that have excessive hand-offs or too many reviews and approval steps. Sometimes delays are the result of people choosing to run fast and loose—not following the approved processes. Whatever the root cause of delays, buyers and sellers must work together, leveraging e-business tools to reduce cycle time to meet or exceed their customers' need for speed.

2. The Desire for Self-Services. Clearly, one of the key trends driving e-business is that buyers, sellers, and users are looking for real-time access to information that will solve problems and save time. Nearly everyone in the world is embracing 24x7x365 for self-service solutions.[1]

Consumers are able to shop anytime, virtually anywhere, as long as they are connected to the Internet. Given the time demands on people everywhere, nearly everyone is searching for convenience or a time-saver. Self-service has had and continues to have a large effect on the workforce, especially on intermediaries or people who are in the middle from real estate, insurance, travel, stock investments, and car purchases, to auctions, sources that supply parts, and retail organizations. Very few intermediaries have survived. Sellers are using self-service catalogs and self-service Web sites to reduce costs and cycle time and to increase customer satisfaction.

Today, companies such as Dell and Gateway Computer allow customers to access product offerings; to determine their own software and hardware needs; and then to configure, order, and pay online for new systems. In addition, customers get limited technical support without ever talking to a person.[2] The following are a few self-service best practices:

- Provide user-centric, not technology-centric, tools for customers and users on your Web site.

- Keep customer Web sites simple and easy to use.

- Pay attention to the total on-line experience, and try to make it fun and user friendly.

■ Remove distracting clutter on your Web site.

■ Eliminate experience inhibitors, such as Web pages that load slowly.

■ Build a new infrastructure and design new protocols to realize the benefits of self-service.

Case Study: MyPay, Defense Finance and Accounting Services

MyPay is a Web site with a toll-free number, thereby allowing current and former Department of Defense (DOD) employees to access pay accounts from anywhere at any time. MyPay is important because it eliminates paperwork and speeds the process of updating or making adjustments. By modeling myPay after technology developed by the Office of Personnel Management, the Defense Finance and Accounting Services (DFAS) saved money and time.

Straightforward tasks, such as viewing statements of leave and earnings or reallocating pay among bank accounts, should not turn into administrative headaches for military personnel who are stationed overseas. That is the philosophy behind myPay, a DFAS project granting secure, 24-hour-a-day access to pay accounts, tax statements, and travel vouchers on the Web or through a toll-free number to service members worldwide as well as to DOD civilians, annuity recipients, and retirees.

Through myPay, service members and civilians can initiate a range of pay account changes, including address updates and adjustments to taxes withheld without having to visit a DFAS field office or file extensive paperwork. Nearly 3 million people have signed up since its 2000 launch, and DFAS hopes to attract another million in the next year.

As myPay becomes more popular, DFAS continues to add features. One new feature allows family members to view accounts (but blocks them from making changes). The myPay system also offers electronic delivery of leave and earnings statements up to 48 hours before payday, an option that could save the Pentagon millions of dollars annually.[3]

The growth of self-service as a customer requirement means that both buying and selling organizations need to transform and integrate hardware and software applications, systems, and processes to enable self-service to reach its full potential.

3. **Need for Best Value**. Buyers will say that price is always important. However, sometimes buyers are willing to pay more than the lowest price to gain something of perceived higher value. Thus, the real question is how much more than the lowest price of technically

acceptable products, services, or solutions is a buyer willing to pay? The answer, of course, is that it depends. The premium a potential buyer is willing to pay is based on many factors that affect the buyer's perception of value and of what constitutes a fair and reasonable price. Typically, sellers view the best-value pricing strategy as an opportunity to increase profitability. Sellers usually attempt to demonstrate value to buyers by differentiating their products, services, or solutions from those of their competitors in terms of the respective strengths they offer in comparison to their competitors' weaknesses.

Although best-value pricing and best-value source selection sound easy in theory, in fact, they are challenging for many public sector organizations. Local, state, and federal government organizations' purchasing practices often are the subject of intense public scrutiny. Government buying organizations, therefore, are often hesitant to apply best-value source selection to the complete spectrum of purchases. Furthermore, government buying organizations are often uncomfortable simply applying good business judgment because they fear the appearance of subjectivity or the application of good business judgment. Instead, they prefer the appearance of objectivity, which requires excessive documentation, numerical analysis, and color-coding schemes for evaluating factors other than price (such as technical solution, quality, past performance, and use of small businesses as subcontractors).

The growing trend for best-value products, services, and solutions in both the public and the private sectors means sellers must do a better job of providing real value and differentiating their products, services, and solutions from those of their competitors. Likewise, buying organizations, especially in government agencies, must do a better job of training their contract management personnel and of trusting them to use good judgment. Contract managers must be empowered to apply effective business judgment so they can streamline the overly bureaucratic, time-consuming, and expensive source selection processes that still exist in many government agencies. Chapter 9 provides a more detailed discussion of best value.

4. **Desire for Increased Process Visibility**. The growing trend for increased process visibility focuses on providing customers with access to timely and accurate information about a potential or actual product, service, or order. Providing process visibility or "transparency" to products, services, and their respective processes helps create higher levels of customer satisfaction. As organizations in both the public and the private sectors strive to build applications, sys-

tems, and processes that make internal operations truly transparent, they serve both their customers and suppliers better. United Parcel Service, FedEx, Solectron, and other organizations are using greater process visibility to enhance customer contact, and they use high-quality service to increase customer satisfaction and loyalty.[4]

Case Study: e-Access, U.S. Postal Service

The U.S. Postal Service uses a Web-based system for processing employee and contractor requests to access programs and data. The system of e-Access is important because employees and contractors have faster access to systems whereby they can see and learn what is happening and can use better data security. As a result of the system, the Postal Service learned these lessons: Do not simply post forms online. Instead, use e-mail and the Web to standardize procedures, to track information, provide visibility, and build in administrative controls.

Before e-Access, Postal Service employees and contractors waited as long as a month for permission to use management systems they needed to do their jobs. Someone working in accounting, for example, might need permission to enter and view the financial database or the payroll system. Each request for data access or software was made on a piece of paper and was passed to a supervisor and then on to various administrators. With nearly 2 million requests circulating each year, more than a few were lost. And, no one kept track of the permissions granted.

Now such requests take less than a week and are not lost. Users select the applications that they need from the Postal Service's intranet. Then, e-Access automatically routes requests to the right people. Supervisors and administrators receive e-mail messages giving them 24 hours to act on requests. Employees who do not have computers can use e-Access by telephone to update records such as health benefits or home addresses.

Users can check the status of their requests on line without contacting the help desk staff members. Managers can quickly check their staff members' security clearances and can revoke permissions if necessary. And the agency has a centralized record of the applications that each of its 825,000 users can access.[5]

5. **Need for Seamless Customer Service**. The trend is that customer service is no longer one customer dealing with one enterprise. With outsourcing of business functionality and the increasing complexity of products, many service calls require coordinating two or more organizations. To provide the kind of service that guarantees customer

loyalty, organizations need to coordinate with their partners better. Partners should be considered part of an organization's extended enterprise; only then can customer service issues be addressed seamlessly. A cooperative partnership also makes it easier to share customer information, which is vitally important as organizations increasingly depend on third-party support.

Managers need to take a close look at their customer service processes on a regular basis and to determine if those processes are easy to use. Too often, a disconnect occurs as a consequence of the way business processes, including customer service, have been previously established. Customers must be able to call or log on to gain access to and enjoy immediate recognition by any area of an organization and to have their requests or purchases processed smoothly. If not, customers are left with an uneasy sense of apathy and will probably think twice before calling that organization again.

What does the trend toward more consistent and reliable customer service mean for e-business? To achieve their business objectives, all organizations need to adopt integrated customer service applications that address the entire customer relationship rather than focus on departmental solutions that address only one part of the customer account relationship. Implementing integrated applications and the business practices they support will become increasingly critical for ensuring quality processes not only within an organization but also in a firm's relationship with its partners. As a result, organizations should develop customer relationship solutions that go beyond the boundaries of the company to encompass the entire extended enterprise.[6]

6. **Focus on Integrated Enterprise Architecture.** The trend in most organizations is to integrate various functional business areas such as accounting, finance, engineering, manufacturing, order processing, distribution, and customer service and their respective business-application software into an enterprisewide architecture. Companies such as SAP, Oracle, and PeopleSoft have helped many organizations in both government and industry throughout the world so they can connect disparate systems; provide greater access to information; and link buyers, sellers, and subcontractors more closely through the enterprise architecture.

However, creating an integrated enterprise architecture using enterprise software applications is time-consuming, difficult, and expensive. The larger the organization and the more legacy systems it has, the greater the resistance to change and the greater the time and money needed to make such a transformation.

Case Study: Enterprise Architecture—DOD Leads the Charge

While a number of federal agencies have embraced enterprise architecture (EA) as more than just a mandate that must be complied with, many industry observers believe that the DOD is farther along the learning curve in harnessing EA to make strategic operational decisions.

DOD agency executives are increasingly using investments in EA to understand and better manage critical assets—whether those assets are bombers, equipment, or facilities to support the war fighter or whether the assets will allocate resources to help management improve administrative processes like financial reporting and accounting. Within specific mission or program areas, EA is increasingly being leveraged to determine what assets and processes are most suitable in specific situations.

The DOD, in short, is successfully leveraging EA to establish operational objectives, to implement technology, and to define standards. For instance, the DOD has rolled out the Net Centric Enterprise Services (NCES), which is a model that embraces both standards and the reuse of services and processes across the organization. NCES leverages the work of the Defense Information Services Agency, which identifies standards, tests them, and then puts them into mainstream use.[7]

More effectively melding various functional silos into customer-focused integrated project teams through use of enterprise applications will in the long-term save time, reduce expenses, and improve performance results.

7. Desire for Wireless Web Applications. The trend is for all business in both the public and the private sectors to be mobile, integrated, and personal. The growth of wireless infrastructure around the world is continually providing new wireless applications for voice, data, and video. New powerful wireless networks are rapidly providing convenient wireless applications and reduced costs to perform everyday tasks such as organizing business activities, sending e-mail, making phone calls, and conducting meetings.

However, it is important to note that having more information faster is not necessarily better. As information technology allows for rapid communication, managers are under greater pressure to make more informed decisions faster while doing multiple tasks.

Case Study: Emergency Patient Tracking System—City of St. Louis

The city of St. Louis has a tracking system that uses bar-code identification tags and wireless communications to monitor and direct patient care during mass-casualty incidents. The emergency tracking system is important because it provides real-time situational awareness, thus allowing officials to direct resources effectively and potentially saving lives. Routine use of the system ensures that operators will know how to use it in an emergency.

During the anthrax attacks in the fall of 2001, public health officials in St. Louis realized they needed to be able to manage large numbers of casualties in a medical emergency. So they created the Emergency Patient Tracking System. It is essentially a high-end inventory management system, but instead of tracking widgets, it tracks patients.

By using off-the-shelf technology—including radios equipped with Global Positioning System transponders; bar-code readers (patients are given bar-coded bracelets for identification); and a secure, wireless communications network that allows Web-based access—ambulance crews, hospital workers, and public health officials now monitor the flow of patients throughout the urban medical system.

Because the system is used daily for the routine transport of patients there is no need to make special adaptations during an emergency. The technology could be applied easily anywhere satellite communications are available; in remote areas, portable communications towers could be used. This model could be scaled to the entire country.[8]

Wireless Web applications are becoming increasingly popular and more affordable. However, many organizations still do not have the funds to purchase the hardware, software, related infrastructure, and training needed for this time-saving, potentially life-saving technology.

8. **Need for Convergence of Infrastructure.** Globally, telephone, cable, television, wireless, and computer data networks are ceasing to be separate, insolated systems. A key trend in the infrastructure for e-business is the convergence of various voice, data, and video networks into a powerful unified network, which is based on the internet protocol (IP). The packet-switching network layer has demonstrated the capability to serve as a backbone that can transmit any form or kind of information rapidly and inexpensively.[9]

Both buyers and sellers worldwide are pursuing investments in their respective communications infrastructure, through voice, data, and video convergence, as a means to reduce operating costs and to provide greater convenience for users and customers. Increasingly, government agencies and commercial companies are adopting voice over internet protocol (VoIP) technology to provide users with the convenience and the capability of having conversations over the Internet. In addition, VoIP allows organizations to reduce operational costs.

More public institutions—colleges, universities, and local, state, and federal government agencies—are embracing the convergence of voice, data, and video over lower-cost, high-speed networks, often avoiding costly toll or roaming charges. VoIP allows buyers and sellers to communicate better, faster, and cheaper.

9. **Focus on Partnering and Outsourcing.** Traditionally, outsourcing has been used as a cost-control method. However, as performance-based acquisition grows and as communications technology becomes more widespread, organizations will increasingly use outsourcing to create virtual enterprises, to change organizational culture, to gain access to premium partners, and to implement proven best practices or leading-edge technologies. Both buyers and sellers are outsourcing entire business processes and functional areas, including many support functions such as accounting and finance, information technology, human resources, and purchasing, to improve performance and cost-effectiveness.

Business process outsourcing is the delegation of one or more business processes to an external provider to improve overall business performance in a particular area. It offers organizations innovative ways to save money and to enter or create new markets. It also offers organizations flexibility to scale up or ramp down, depending on seasonal cycles and production needs. A single organization working alone is no longer a viable business model.[10]

Case Study: Sun Microsystems Contract Manufacturing

Sun Microsystems decided to focus on designing its hardware and software and to either subcontract or acquire nearly all of its workstations' components. Sun limited its own manufacturing to prototyping, handling final assembly, and testing. By leveraging its partners, Sun was able to rapidly introduce four major new product generations in its first five years of operation, doubling the price-performance ratio with each successive year.[11]

Case Study: Acquisition Center of Excellence for Services

The Acquisition Center of Excellence (ACE) for Services is a partnership among the Office of Federal Procurement Policy, the Defense Acquisition University, and the Federal Acquisition Institute, with participation from federal government agencies, associations, and industry representatives. The ACE for Services offers a collaborative structure that has proven to be extremely effective in the creation and transfer of knowledge. It also provides value to organizations in the following ways:

- It fosters collaborative sharing of knowledge across organizational boundaries.

- It provides a one-stop resource information center to share acquisition-related policies and presentations, e-tools, training, and best practices from both government and industry.

To join the ACE for Services partnership and to contribute to the sharing of information and best practices, contact the following by e-mail: **Julia_wise@omb.eop.gov** or **Jeffrey.birch@dau.mil**.

To suggest a link or to contribute information directly to the ACE site, go to **http://acc.dau.mil/ace**.

Partnering and collaboration are vital to the success of performance-based acquisitions, so buyers, sellers, and subcontractors must work together effectively using improved systems and processes to achieve success.

10. **Desire for Virtual Distribution.** A new trend in many multiseller and multibuyer marketplaces is the use of new intermediaries called virtual distributors. Virtual distributors aggregate buyers and sellers using Web technology. Firms such as Ventro, SciQuest, and hsupply.com are accumulating marketing and product information content to establish more efficient markets in previously fragmented places. By aggregating buyers, sellers, technology, content, and commerce, those new virtual distributors are taking advantage of the Web to create more efficient and cost-effective marketplaces.[12]

Case Study: ChemConnect

ChemConnect is an on-line exchange that connects buyers and sellers. It features the World Chemical Exchange, a commodity transaction service tailored to perform large chemical transactions. Companies listed with the service can place notices for the chemicals they need to buy or want to sell. Buyers submit performance requirements, and qualified suppliers submit bids and offers, including details of delivery, production, letters of credit, and other essentials of large transactions. ChemConnect says that its goal is to bring the market efficiencies of the bid-and-offer process to large-scale chemical trading. Thus, e-business comes to the chemical industry just in time to provide a solution, thereby allowing suppliers to deal directly and cost-effectively with even the smallest customers.[13]

Virtual distribution provides a relatively simple process approach, using Internet technology to reduce costs and to improve performance results. (See **Table 4.3** [p. 83] for a checklist of e-business best practices.)

Table 4.3 Checklist of Key e-Business Best Practices to Improve Performance Results for Buyers and Sellers

❑ Know the four major trend categories driving e-business.

❑ Understand the 10 key trends driving e-business:

1. Need for speed

2. Desire for self-service

3. Need for best value

4. Desire for increased process visibility

5. Need for seamless customer service

6. Focus on integrated enterprise architecture

7. Desire for wireless Web applications

8. Need for convergence of infrastructure

9. Focus on partnering and outsourcing

10. Desire for virtual distribution

❑ Understand the cost, value, and risk associated with information technology investments.

❑ Understand the user hardware, software, infrastructure, and training required to transfer the promise of an e-business technology into improved performance results.

❑ Know what the customer values.

❑ Spend money wisely.

Summary

In the world of e-business, innovation means understanding the 10 key trends and rapidly capitalizing on them to maximize opportunities for buying or selling products, services, or integrated solutions. An organization's success depends on an understanding of its customers' needs and the ability to rapidly innovate and integrate e-business technologies cost-effectively. Most organizations realize that customer and technology trends evolve, sometimes quickly and unexpectedly. Therefore, knowing the 10 key trends that are driving e-business and being able to apply proven best practices appropriately are vital to improving performance and achieving success.

In the next chapter, we will examine the process for managing both the opportunity and the risk in complex acquisitions.

Questions to Consider

1. How well has your organization adapted its software applications, hardware systems, and processes to leverage the power of e-business?

2. How many of the 10 key trends affecting e-business has your organization embraced and used to improve buying and selling?

3. Which of the 10 key trends does your organization need to spend more time and money on to leverage the full potential benefits of e-business?

Endnotes

1. Ravi Kalakota and Marcia Robinson, *E-Business 2.0* (Boston: Addison-Wesley, Boston, 2004).

2. Ibid.

3. Beth Dickey, "Bright Ideas," *Government Executive Magazine*, National Journal Group Inc., Washington, DC, December 2004.

4. Kalakota and Robinson.

5. Dickey.

6. Kalakota and Robinson.

7. Booz Allen Hamilton Study, "Enterprise Architecture," *Government Executive Magazine*, National Journal Group Inc., Washington, DC, December 2004.

8. Dickey.

9. Kalakota and Robinson.

10. Kalakota and Robinson.

11. Kalakota and Robinson.

12. Kalakota and Robinson.

13. Kalakota and Robinson.

The Process for Managing Opportunity and Risk in Complex Acquisitions

Introduction

Managing a complex acquisition in a performance-based acquisition (PBA) environment—which typically involves a buyer, seller, (prime contractor), and numerous subcontractors with a combination of high-technology products and services—is a great challenge. Many books have been written on managing projects within a single organization; however, few publications have tackled what it takes to make complex acquisitions succeed in a PBA environment. This chapter provides a summary of the opportunity and risk management (ORM) process that should be considered when managing complex acquisitions programs and related projects, plus a few of the many tools, techniques, and best practices that should be applied to achieve success.

The concept of managing opportunities and risks is an inherent part of everyone's life and, as such, is a crucial aspect of every project. Many people, including project managers, often assume risks without ever formally assessing or attempting to mitigate them. ORM is an attempt to predict future outcomes on the basis of current knowledge, which means ORM is not a precise science. However, it is possible to increase opportunities and to reduce risks or prevent risk events from occurring by using a process approach to ORM.

ORM is an important element of both contract management and project management because every project contains elements of uncertainty, such as varying amounts of funding, changes in contract delivery dates, changes in technical requirements, and increases or decreases in quantity. ORM should be thought of as a part of the project management methodology. In general, opportunities for outsourcing business are becoming increasingly larger and more complex. In today's systems environment, it is not uncommon for business solutions to consist of numerous product and service components from inside as well as outside an organization. This complexity brings with it new business opportunities and risks.

What Is Opportunity?

Opportunity is the measure of the probability that an opportunity event—a positive desired change—will occur and the desired effect of that event.

What Is Risk?

Risk is the measure of the probability that a risk event—an unwanted change—will occur and the associated effect of that event. In other words, risk consists of three components:

- A risk event (an unwanted change),

- The probability of occurrence (uncertainty), and

- The significance of the negative impact (the amount at stake).

What Is Opportunity and Risk Management?

The primary goal of ORM is to continually seek ways to maximize opportunities and to mitigate risks. ORM is an iterative process approach to managing those opportunities and risks that may occur during the course of business and that could affect the success or failure of the project. Once identified, the probability of each event's occurrence and its potential effect on the project are analyzed and prioritized (ranked from the highest to lowest). Beginning with the events with the highest priority and working down, the project team determines what options or strategies are available and then chooses the best strategy to maximize opportunities and to reduce or prevent the identified risks from occurring. This information is the basis for the ORM plan, which should be continually used and updated during the project's life cycle.

Integration of ORM into Project Management

Some business managers rely solely on their intuitive reasoning (ability to guess correctly) as their basis for decision making. But in today's complex systems environment, an astute business manager understands the importance of using a highly skilled project team to identify both the opportunities and the risk events, to assess the possible effects (positive and negative), and to develop appropriate strategies to increase opportunities and reduce risks. A project work breakdown structure (WBS) is an effective means of relating project tasks to possible opportunities and risks.

To integrate ORM successfully into project management, the project manager must ensure that an ORM plan is included as part of the overall business management planning process. It is vital that ORM become a mindset for all business professionals, especially sales managers, purchasing managers, contract managers, and project managers.

Figure 5.1 (See this page) lists the key inputs, a few of the many proven tools and techniques to increase business opportunities and mitigate project risks, and the desired outputs that should be considered when managing complex projects.

Inputs

The following items are all key inputs to the ORM process, which should be used when managing complex projects:

■ **People**.

Given that multiple parties are typically involved with complex

Figure 5.1 The Opportunity and Risk Management Process

Inputs	Tools and Techniques	Outputs
■ People	■ Opportunity and risk management (ORM) model	■ Successful projects
■ Elements of opportunity		• Maximize opportunities
■ Elements of risk	■ Project complexity assessment tool	• Mitigate risks
■ Organizational culture (risk-taking vs. risk-adverse)	■ Project risk management plan (outline)	• Obtain follow-on projects
■ Training	■ Types of contracts—risk-sharing tools	
	■ Project doability analysis form	
	■ ORM decision-support software matrix	

projects, which usually consist of people from multiple-functional disciplines (sales, engineering, contracts, finance, manufacturing, purchasing and supply-chain management, quality, project management, etc.), the need for effective opportunity and risk management is great.

■ **Elements of Opportunity.**

- *Strategic alignment* refers to how consistent the project opportunity is within your core business or corporate direction so you can acquire new business. Organizations have a much higher probability of being successful during delivery when the project opportunity is consistent with their core business and their strategic direction.

- *Competitive environment* refers to whether you or your competitors are perceived by the buyer as the leader for products, service, and solutions and whether you are favored as the key seller. Opportunities whereby the buyer perceives your company as the leader and as the favored seller (for reasons other than price) are highly desirable. Buyers may have the perception because of technology, reputation, past experience, industry commitment, and so on.

- *Project value* refers to the dollar value of the project. The intent is to distinguish "small" from "large" revenue opportunities. Obviously, this evaluation needs to be assessed in the context of your organization's size.

- *Expected margin* refers to what the likely margins are on the business, given the competitive environment, and what it will take to win.

- *Future business potential* refers to the degree to which this project will effect additional business beyond the scope of this specific opportunity. For example, the opportunity may be a means to win a new project. Consider the degree to which specifically identifiable future business depends on winning and successfully delivering this business.

- *Probability of success* refers to the likelihood that you will win and accomplish the performance-based requirements.

- *Collateral benefit* refers to the degree to which pursuit of this project will improve the existing skill level of your team or will develop new skills that will benefit other projects in the future.

- *Project importance* refers to the overall importance of the project to the buyer, seller, and end customers or users. This evaluation should be based on consideration of all opportunity elements, along with any other tangible or intangible aspects of the opportunity that are considered relevant.

■ **Elements of Risk.**

- *Customer commitment* refers to the degree to which the buyer and end-customer has demonstrated a solid commitment to implement the products, services, and solutions offered in the project. Typically, this type of commitment is demonstrated either through (1) budgeting for the implementation in a current or future business plan, or (2) identifying and assigning resources to support the implementation.

- *Seller's competence* refers to the seller's past experience or core competencies to deliver the products, services, and solutions required in the project. The more past experience the seller has in projects exactly like this one, the lower the risk. Conversely, if this type of project has never been successfully completed by any company in the past, then there is a much higher risk.

- *External obstacles* refers to the degree to which roadblocks exist that are beyond the control of either the buyer or the seller. A good example of an obstacle would be if the buyer were a regulated utility that must obtain approval from a state or federal authority before it can implement the project. Another example might be if the buyer has yet to secure the capital needed to fund the implementation during a period when capital is tightly constrained.

- *Project engagement* refers to the degree to which the seller was involved in establishing the performance-based requirements. The more involved the seller was in establishing the requirements, the better the seller's understanding and the greater the likelihood of success.

- *Solution life-cycle match* refers to the degree to which the seller's solution involves the use of existing mature products versus the use of new products or leading-edge technology. On the one hand, if the solution involves mature products that are available today, the risk level of your solution's working is very low. On the other hand, if the solution involves many new products that have yet to be released or are based on leading-edge technology, you have a risk of encountering development delays or of having the products not work as planned.

- *Period of performance* refers to the length of the project. The longer the project, the greater the chance of significant changes. Personnel, customer environment, and business climate are a few examples of changes that can introduce risks that will negatively impact the project.

- *Delivery schedule* refers to when the delivery is required and who controls the schedule. The ideal situation is if the schedule is realistic and can be mutually agreed to between buyer and seller. Conversely, if the delivery schedule is fixed and has also identified penalties for missing schedules, there will be greater risk associated with missing deliveries.

- *Resource coordination* refers to the number of groups or external suppliers that must be engaged to deliver the solution. The larger the number of internal groups that are required, the more coordination that is required to ensure successful delivery and the higher the risk of having a disconnect and delivery problem. Coordination of outside suppliers typically introduces even more risk because you have more control over internal groups than over external suppliers to resolve problems.

- *Nonperformance penalties* refer to the degree to which the buyer has specified contract penalties for failure to deliver as promised. If the buyer has not specified penalties or if you can negotiate between the buyer and the customer, then you can minimize the risks. If the buyer has specified monetary or other penalties that are non-negotiable, then this arrangement increases risk.

- *Overall feasibility* refers to the degree of feasibility of the project as assessed by a knowledgeable representative who is accountable to deliver the solution and who serves both the buyer and the seller. A major factor to consider when assessing feasibility is your company's past experience and success when addressing unforeseen problems equitably. If the project is extremely complex and either the buyer or seller has a poor track record of supporting complex projects, then there is a high risk that the project will not be successfully implemented.

■ **Organizational Culture.**

An organizational culture is the tendency that an organization has either to promote innovation and risk-taking or to promote status quo and risk aversion.

■ **Training.**

All individuals involved with managing complex outsourced projects need to receive competency-based training on the ORM process and on numerous related tools and techniques, as discussed later in this chapter.

Tools and Techniques

The following are a few of the many tools and techniques that have proven effective to help business professionals who are involved in complex projects so they can maximize the elements of opportunity

Figure 5.2 Opportunity and Risk Management Six-Step Model

1. Identify opportunities and risks.
2. Analyze opportunities and risk.
3. Prioritize opportunities and risk.

Opportunity and Risk Assessment

4. Develop opportunity and risk action plans.
5. Implement opportunity and risk action plans.
6. Evaluate project results.

Opportunity and Risk Action Plans

Table 5.1 Project Complexity Assessment Tools (Project Complexity Continuum)

First, determine where on the continuum each project assessment factor falls, and then determine what is the appropriate level of project management support to achieve success in a cost-effective manner.

Aggregate Weighting:

Level 3 Projects
Level 2 Projects
Level 1 Projects

Project Assessment Factor	Low	Low to Medium	Medium	Medium to High	High
1. Project Value (total revenue in $millions)	Less than $5	$5–$10	$10–$50	$50–$100	More than $100
2. Project Gross Margin (total margin in percentage of revenue)	Less than 10%	10%–15%	16%–25%	26%–40%	More than 40%
3. Project Professional Services (% of revenue)	10% or Less	15%–25%	25%–35%	35%–45%	More than 45%
4. Project Technical Complexity	Very Low	Low	Moderate	High	Very High
5. Technological Maturity	Very High	High	Moderate	Low	Very Low
6. Project Risk (scope, schedule, cost, contract terms, and supplier factors)	Very Low	Low	Moderate	High	Very High
7. Project Duration	6 Months or Less	6 Months - 1 Year	1 year- 18 Months	18 Months- 2 Years	More than 2 years
8. Extent of Outsourcing (% of labor cost)	None or less than 10%	Few or less than 0%	Multiple or less than 50%	Few or more than 50%	Multiple or more than 50%
9. Project Research and Development	None	Minimal	30% or Less	30%–50%	Over 50%
10. Project Importance to Principal Supplier	Very Low	Low	Moderate	High	Very High

This project has been determined to be executed at level _____, and it will need the project management resources, tools, and techniques required for that project level.

and minimize or mitigate the elements of risk.

- **The Opportunity and Risk Management (ORM) Model.** The ORM Model (**Figure 5.2**, p. 91) is an ongoing process model that has two major pieces: first, opportunity and risk assessment and, second, opportunity and risk action plans. The assessment of opportunity and risk is composed of three steps: identify opportunities and risk, analyze them, and prioritize them. The plans for opportunities and risk actions are also composed of three steps: develop opportunity and risk action plan strategies, implement opportunity and risk action plans into the project management plan, and evaluate project results. The following diagram illustrates the suggested six-step ORM model.

- **Project Complexity Assessment Tool (PCAT).** The PCAT shown in **Table 5.1** (See p. 92) is a proven-effective means of assessing 10 key project-related factors to determine the relative difficulty of managing a project. Once the project complexity has been assessed, an organization can then determine the appropriate level of project management support to ensure project success.

- **Project Risk Management Plan Outline.** Every complex project should have a risk management plan that has been created, is being implemented, and will be revised as needed throughout the life of the project. The outline in **Table 5.2** (this page) can be used to prepare a comprehensive project risk management plan for complex projects.

Table 5.2 Outline for Project Risk Management Plan

1.0 Project Scope
    Insert the scope statement or provide a summary of the project, including a description of the work to be accomplished, a description of the customer's goals and objectives for the project, a general description of how the project will be accomplished, and other pertinent information that will provide a good overview of the project.
 	
2.0 Risk Event Descriptions
    For each element of the work breakdown structure (WBS), identify any major risks involved in that element. Complete the risk event descriptions and the risk event results. Reference or include a copy of the WBS in the section.

The process is carried out as follows:

2.1 Identify Risks. For each element of the WBS, identify any major risks associated with that element. Ensure that each risk event refers to a specific WBS element.

2.2 Analyze Risks and Calculate the Effect of the Weighted Cost. In analyzing the risks, make the assumption that the risk event identified will occur. Think in terms of the remedial activity that will need to take place to rectify the occurrence of the risk event. With the same guidelines used in calculating the cost of the WBS elements, calculate the rectification cost (impact) without any form of "padding" or risk adjustment. Analyze the risk event and apply a weighting to the impact on a scale of 1 through 5 as follows:

Weight 1: Has little potential to cause disruption of schedule costs, or performance (quality). Increase the impact by 5 percent.
Weight 2: May cause minor disruption of schedule, costs, or performance (quality). Increase the impact by 10 percent.
Weight 3: May cause some disruption of schedule, costs, or performance (quality). Increase the impact by 15 percent.
Weight 4: May cause major disruption of schedule, costs, or performance (quality). Increase the impact by 20 percent.
Weight 5: Could cause significant serious disruption of schedule, costs, or performance (quality). Increase the impact by 25 percent. Finally, estimate the probability of the event occurring as a percentage (between 0.01 and 0.99), and calculate the weighted cost impact as follows:
(Cost Impact + Cost Impact Increase) x Probability of Occurrence = Weighted Cost Impact
Example: For a risk event with an estimate cost impact of $2,750, a weight of 4, and probability of occurrence at 85 percent: ($2,750 + $550) x 0.85 = $2,805.

2.3 Identify High-Risk Events. If a specific risk event has greater than 75-percent probability, if the weighted cost impact is greater than 10 percent of the total project cost, or both, the risk event is by definition a high-risk event. For each high-risk event, create a separate and unique WBS element that identifies the work required and the weighted cost impact required to rectify the occurrence of the high-risk event. This WBS element must be flagged as a high-risk event element that is distinct from a normal WBS element.

2.4 Develop Mitigation Strategies. Determine potential strategies for mitigating the risk—either avoiding it, controlling it, or transferring it to another party. Assuming the risk consequences is also a potential mitigation strategy, but it is the least desirable. Evaluate the potential cost impact of the mitigation strategy, and reflect that impact in the risk budget.

2.5 Establish the Risk Budget. Each high-risk event will become a line item in the risk budget. The other risk events should be accumulated and used to establish the managerial reserve. An amount for contingency—or those events and circumstances not anticipated in any way—should be calculated according to experience. Those amounts together become the risk budget portion of the project budget. The risk budget should be margined at the same rate as the project budget so you can establish the budget at the selling price. This amount then is presented to the customer in the proposal as the project price.

3.0 Risk Reassessment Plan

Identify the major reassessment points for this project, and ensure that those reassessment points are identified in the project plan. At a minimum, high-risk events should be reassessed at the following times:

- Whenever major changes occur in the project or its environment,

- Before major decision milestones, and

- Periodically, according to some predetermined schedule.

3.1 Risk Management Timetable. Indicate the timetable for risk management activities. Ensure that the key events are also reflected on the project schedule. Major milestones include the following:

- Completion of risk identification and analysis,

- Risk prioritization,

- Completion of mitigation strategy development,

- Incorporation into project plans and WBS,

- Key reassessment points, and

- Documentation of risk results.

- **Contract Type and Risk-Sharing Tools. Tables 5.3** (See p. 97) and **5.4** (See p. 98) provide summaries of the various forms of contractual pricing arrangements, which are often called contract types. The summaries provide a discussion or listing of the essential elements, advantages, disadvantages, and suitability for the various contract types typically used in outsourcing products and services. Most projects that are outsourced in both the public and the private business sectors are typically priced using a firm-fixed-price (FFP) contract type. FFP contracts place 100-percent financial risk on the seller; conversely, cost-type contracts often used on complex U.S. government contracts will place a greater financial risk on the buyer. Numerous types of pricing arrangements are available that can be negotiated to more fairly share risks between the buyer and seller. An additional item of complexity occurs when two or more pricing arrangements are included on the same contract. They are typically separated by specific contract line item numbers (CLINs) or specific performance areas. The contract type and the detailed terms and conditions, that are included in the contract are significant and powerful tools to share or transfer opportunity and risk.

- **Project Doability Analysis.** A number of successful organizations worldwide have found it useful to summarize all of their project-related opportunities and risks into a short simple document—often just a few pages in length—called a project doability analysis. **Table 5.5** (See p. 101) is a suggested project doability analysis form, which can be tailored and used by any organization to summarize the opportunities and risks before or after an organization bids on said project. Of course, it is usually better to conduct a doability analysis before an organization bids on a project. It is better to know what your organization must do to achieve project success before your organization is contractually obligated to perform the work, especially on large, complex projects.

- **Opportunity and Risk Management (ORM) Decision-Support Software Matrix.** As projects become increasingly complex and involve multiple opportunity and risk factors, more and more project stakeholders are seeking help—often from automated tools—to aid their decision-making process. It is important to note that there are numerous decision-support tools available and that those tools, such as the software applications that are contained in the subject software matrix (see **Table 5.6**, p. 102), are merely samples and are not product endorsements.

Table 5.3 Contract Types and Risk-Sharing Tools

Type	Essential Elements and Advantages	Disadvantages	Suitability
Firm-Fixed-Price (FFP)	Reasonably definite design or performance specifications are available. Fair and reasonable price can be established at outset. FFP places least amount of administrative burden on contract manager. Conditions for use include the following: • Adequate competition; • Prior purchase experience of the same, or similar, supplies or services under competitive conditions; • Valid cost or pricing data; • Realistic estimates of proposed cost; • Possible uncertainties in performance that can be identified and priced; • Sellers who are willing to accept contract at a level that causes them to take all financial risks; and • Any other reasonable basis for pricing that can be used to establish fair and reasonable price.	Price is not subject to adjustment regardless of seller performance costs. FFP places 100 percent of financial risk on seller. It is preferred over all other contract types. Price is used with advertised or negotiated procurements.	Commercial products and commercial services for which reasonable prices can be established
Fixed-Price-with-Economic-Price Adjustment-(FP/EPA)	The unstable market or labor conditions during performance period and the contingencies that would otherwise be included in contract price can be identified and made the subject of a separate price adjustment clause. Contingencies must be specifically defined in contract. FP/EPA provides for upward adjustment (with ceiling) in contract price. It may provide for downward adjustment of price if escalated element has potential of failing below contract limits. Three general types of EPAs are based on established prices, actual costs of labor or material, and cost indexes of labor or material.	Price can be adjusted on action of an industry-wide contingency that is beyond seller's control. FP/EPA reduces seller's fixed-price risk. FP/EPA is preferred over any cost-reimbursement-type contract. If contingency manifests, contract administration burden increases. FP/EPA is used with negotiated procurements and, in limited applications, with formal advertising when determined to be feasible. CM must determine if FP/EPA is necessary either to protect seller and buyer against significant fluctuations in labor or material costs or to provide for contract price adjustment in case of changes in seller's established prices.	Commercial products and services for which reasonable prices can be established at time of award

Table 5.3 (cont.)

Type	Essential Elements and Advantages	Disadvantages	Suitability
Fixed-Price-Incentive (FPI)	Cost uncertainties exist, but there is potential for cost reduction or performance improvement by giving seller a degree of cost responsibility and a positive profit incentive.	FPI requires adequate seller accounting system.	Development and production of high-volume, multiyear contracts
	Profit is earned or lost according to the relationship that contract's final negotiated cost bears to total target cost.	Buyer must determine that FPI is least costly and that award of any other type would be impractical.	
	Contract must contain target cost, target profit, ceiling price, and profit-sharing formula.	Buyer and seller administrative effort is more extensive than under other fixed-price contract types.	
	There are two forms of FPI: firm target (FPIF) and successive target (FPIS).	FPI is used only with competitive negotiated contracts.	
	FPIF: Firm target cost, target profit, and profit-sharing formula are negotiated into basic contract; profit is adjusted at contract completion.	Billing prices must be established for interim payment.	
	FPIS: Initial cost and profit targets are negotiated into contract, but final cost target (firm) cannot be negotiated until performance. It contains production points at which either a firm target and final profit formula, or a FFP contract, can be negotiated.		
	Elements that can be incentives are costs, performance, delivery, or quality.		

Table 5.4 Cost-Reimbursement Contracts (Greatest Risk on Buyer)

Cost	Cost is appropriate for research and development work—particularly with nonprofit educational institutions or other nonprofit organizations—and for facilities contracts.	Cost is appropriate for research and development work—particularly with nonprofit educational institutions or other nonprofit organizations—and for facilities contracts.	Research and development; facilities
	Allowable costs of contract performance are reimbursed, but no fee is paid.	Allowable costs of contract performance are reimbursed, but no fee is paid.	

Cost-Sharing (CS)	CS is used when buyer and seller agree to share costs in a research or development project having potential mutual benefits. Because of commercial benefits accruing to the seller, no fee is paid. Seller agrees to absorb a portion of the costs of performance in expectation of compensating benefits to seller's firm or organization. Such benefits might include an enhancement of the seller's capability and expertise or an improvement of its competitive position in the commercial market.	Care must be taken in negotiating cost-share rate so that the cost ratio is proportional to the potential benefit (that is, the party receiving the greatest potential benefit bears the greatest share of the costs).	Care must be taken in negotiating cost-share rate so that the cost ratio is proportional to the potential benefit (that is, the party receiving the greatest potential benefit bears the greatest share of the costs).
Cost-Plus-Incentive-Fee (CPIF)	Development has a high probability that it is feasible, and positive profit incentives for seller management can be negotiated. Performance incentives must be clearly spelled out and objectively measurable. Fee range should be negotiated to give the seller an incentive over various ranges of cost performance. Fee is adjusted by a formula negotiated into the contract in accordance with the relationship that total costs bears to target cost. Contract must contain target cost, target fee, minimum and maximum fees, and fee adjustment formula. Fee adjustment is made at completion of contract.	It is difficult to negotiate range between the maximum and minimum fees so as to provide an incentive over entire range. Performance must be objectively measurable. CPIF is costly to administer; seller must have an adequate accounting system. CPIF is used only with negotiated contracts. Appropriate buyer surveillance is needed during performance to ensure that effective methods and efficient cost controls are used.	Major systems development and other development programs in which it is determined that CPIF is desirable and administratively practical
Cost-Plus-Award-Fee (CPAF)	Contract completion is feasible and incentives are desired, but performance is not susceptible to finite measurement. It provides for subjective evaluation of seller performance. Seller is evaluated at stated times during performance period. Contract must contain clear and unambiguous evaluation criteria to determine award fee. Award fee is earned for excellence in performance, quality, timeliness, ingenuity, and cost-effectiveness and can be earned in whole or in part. Two separate fee pools can be established in contract: base fee and award fee. Award fee earned by seller is determined by the buyer and is often based on recommendations of an award fee evaluation board.	Buyer's determination of amount of award fee earned by the seller is not subject to disputes clause. CPAF cannot be used to avoid either CPIF or CPFF if either is feasible. It should not be used if the amount of money, period of performance, or expected benefits are insufficient to warrant additional administrative efforts. It is very costly to administer. Seller must have an adequate accounting system. It is used only with negotiated contracts.	Level-of-effort services that can be measured only subjectively, and contracts for which work would have been accomplished under another contract type if performance objectives could have been expressed as definite milestones, targets, and goals that could have been measured

Table 5.4 (cont.)

Type	Essential Elements and Advantages	Disadvantages	Suitability
Cost-Plus-Fixed-Fee (CPFF)	Level of effort is unknown, and seller's performance cannot be subjectively evaluated. CPFF provides for payment of a fixed fee. Seller receives fixed fee regardless of the actual costs incurred during performance. It can be constructed in two ways: Completion form: This clearly defined task has a definite goal and specific end product. Buyer can order more work without an increase in fee if the contract estimated costs are increased. Term form: The scope of work is described in general terms. Seller is obligated only for a specific level of effort for a stated period of time. Completion form is preferred over term form. Fee is expressed as percentages of estimated cost at the time the contract is awarded	Seller has minimum incentive to control costs. CPFF is costly to administer. Seller must have an adequate accounting system. Seller assumes no financial risk.	Completion form: advanced development or technical services contracts Term form: research and exploratory development that is used when the level of effort required is known and when there is an inability to measure risk
Time and Material (T&M)	T&M is not possible when placing a contract to estimate extent or duration of the work, or anticipated cost, with any degree of confidence. T&M calls for provision of direct labor hours at specified hourly rate and materials at cost (or some other basis specified in contract). The fixed hourly rates include wages, overhead, general and administrative expenses, and profit. Material cost can include, if appropriate, material handling costs. Ceiling price is established at time of award.	T&M is used only after a determination that no other type will serve purpose. It does not encourage effective cost control. It requires almost constant surveillance by buyer to ensure effective seller management. Ceiling price is required in contract.	Engineering and design services in conjunction with the production of supplies, engineering design and manufacture, repair, maintenance, and overhaul work to be performed on an as-needed basis

Table 5.5 Project Doability Analysis

Project Manager Doability Assessment: Yes ☐   No ☐

Executive Summary

Project Name:	
Customer:	
Location(s):	Estimated Revenue in US$:
Start Date:	Completion Date:
Prepared by:	Phone #:
Fax:	e-Mail:

I.   Describe the project requirements and deliverables.

II. Evaluate the project technical requirements, availability, and research and development (R&D).

III. Evaluate the feasibility of the project schedule (attach milestone schedule).

IV. Evaluate the reasonableness of the project financial commitments (attach the project business case).

V.   Conduct high-level risk assessment. Consider the following risks, if appropriate: pricing, payment terms, acceptance, warranty, liability, R&D, implementation, environmental, etc. (Attach the risk management plan)

VI. Describe significant assumptions implicit in the evaluation of the technical commitments, schedule, and financial commitments.

VII. Assess the skills of the selected project team members (experience, education, training, professional certifications, strengths, and weaknesses).

VIII. Make an executive assessment of project:
      Doable: Yes ☐   No ☐

Table 5.6 Opportunity and Risk Management (IORM) Decision-Support Software Matrix		
Title of Software	Software Manufacturer	Software/Application Features
At Risk	Palisade Corporation	Software allows users to analyze probability distributions; it runs a Monte Carlo simulation program until the software determines that it has produced nearly every possible outcome. It also produces a cumulative probability distribution.
Decide Right	Avantos Performance Systems, Inc.	Software uses an automated approach for assigning evaluation criteria for categorizing information to aid in decision making. Weights for the evaluation criteria can also be developed offline and entered into the Decide Right model, which then assigns them to the proper category.
Expert Choice	Expert Choice, Inc.	Software provides powerful approach to weighting the evaluation criteria used in the decision-making process. It allows decision makers to automatically record results of their comparisons between alternatives and to compute the final weight.
Prime-Choice	LMI	Software is designed to provide a highly structured, effective approach for making decisions involving complex qualitative issues. It creates a summary stacked bar graph with the best alternative on top and the worst on the bottom. The bar graph also shows the contribution of each criterion to the alternatives' overall rating.

Outputs

If you use the ORM six-step process and the numerous related and proven tools and techniques discussed in this chapter, it is possible to significantly improve acquisition programs and the related project results. Clearly, the desired output of the ORM process and of the various tools and techniques discussed is to achieve successful performance-based acquisitions and related project results. (See **Table 5.7** [p. 103] for a checklist of best practices.)

Table 5.7 Checklist of Key Best Practices for Managing Opportunity and Risk to Improve Performance Results

Buyer and Sellers Should

❏ Educate and train your organization regarding opportunity and risk management.

❏ Understand what is an opportunity and what is a risk.

❏ Integrate opportunity and risk management into your organizational and individual culture.

❏ Develop and practice an opportunity and risk management process.

❏ Understand the elements of risk.

❏ Understand the elements of opportunity.

❏ Use the project complexity assessment tool (PCAT) on your complex acquisitions.

❏ Use a risk management plan.

❏ Develop risk mitigation strategies.

❏ Implement selected risk mitigation strategies.

❏ Select the appropriate type of contract.

❏ Conduct a project and acquisition doability analysis.

❏ Use decision support software as appropriate.

Summary

This chapter has provided a summary of the ORM process and the related tools and techniques that should be considered when managing complex performance-based acquisitions. Too many organizations, in both the public and the private business sectors, do not really take the time and effort to thoroughly identify, assess, prioritize, and develop action plans and to implement said plans to maximize business opportunities and to mitigate risks.

In the next chapter, we will dive into the process of creating a supplier value chain, which is a new concept designed to leverage the power of the supply chain and of value-added business partners to improve performance results.

Questions to Consider

1. Has your organization developed an opportunity and risk management process, which is consistently used on all of your major projects?

2. How does your organization evaluate project complexity? What factors are typically considered?

3. List below the proven tools and techniques that your organization uses to maximize opportunities and to mitigate risks.

06

The Process for Creating a Supplier Value Chain: Best Practices and Case Studies

Introduction

In performance-based acquisition (PBA), the buyer should focus on developing an acquisition strategy that will lead to selection of the "right seller." The seller must understand the performance-based approach, must know or develop an understanding of the buyer's requirement, must have a history of performing exceptionally in the field, and must have the processes and resources in place to support the buyer's requirements. This approach goes a long way to successful project accomplishment. In fact, selecting the right seller and developing a partnership will automatically solve many potential performance issues.

Keep in mind that large businesses have not "cornered the market" on good ideas. Small firms can be nimble, quick thinking, and very dedicated to customer service. Although there is a cost in proposing solutions, a small business with a good solution can and should win performance-based awards.

Few people question that today's business environment is increasingly complex. Organizations cannot make it alone. The continued growth of outsourcing and off-shoring and the increased challenges of emerging markets are driving the need for new and deeper strategic alliances among governments, industry, and business often by using expanded distribution channels.

Value creation drives today's business environment in both the public and the private sectors, which then causes organizations to form performance-based partnerships. Creating value for customers over a sustained period of time—at a fair and reasonable market-based price—is why customers stay with a supplier. There are numerous aspects of outsourcing, which are typically linked to creating value for customers, thus resulting in better performance results and in greater customer loyalty.

The supplier value chain concept is the result of developing a seamless link between supply chain management (SCM), customer relationship management (CRM), and supplier relationship management (SRM). Under that wide arc, which is called supplier value chain, are all kinds of best practices, tools, and techniques to improve relationships, processes, and business results.

Figure 6.1 (See this page) illustrates some of the major aspects that affect customers' perception of value, thus either increasing or decreasing their loyalty to a business partner. As is illustrated in Figure 6.1, trust is critical to winning new business and to achieving customer loyalty. Many factors can and do affect how trust is gained or lost. It is important to note that perceptions more than facts will dramatically affect customer loyalty in some cases. Thus, winning new business and achieving customer loyalty is a blend of art and science, which is like demonstrating the concept of rigid flexibility when developing a project plan while the customers continually change their requirements.

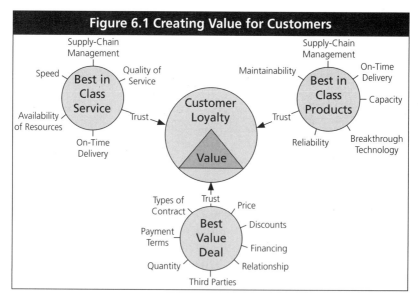

Figure 6.1 Creating Value for Customers

Source: Gregory A. Garrett and Reginald J. Kipke, *The Capture Management Life-Cycle* (Chicago: CCH Incorporated, 2003).

The Economics of Customer Loyalty

Why should you care about customer loyalty? According to numerous business surveys, raising customer retention rates by five percentage points could increase the value of an average customer by 25 to 100 percent.

Figure 6.2 (See this page) shows the increase in the net present value of an average customer in a number of different industries when the customer retention rate increases by five percentage points. For example, if a life insurance company can keep another 5 percent of its customers each year, then total lifetime profits from a typical customer will rise, on average, by 90 percent.

According to the A. T. Kearney's 1997 CEO Global Business Study, when CEOs surveyed were asked to enumerate the key features of a successful partnership with customers, executives repeatedly mentioned trust. "Trust; that's all there is," declared a top ranking U.K. executive. "Trust, honesty, and deliveries made on time," declared a Canadian leader. "Trust and mutual understanding," exclaimed a top U.S. Executive. "Trust, joint understanding, ... and evaluation of performance," stated an Australian business leader.

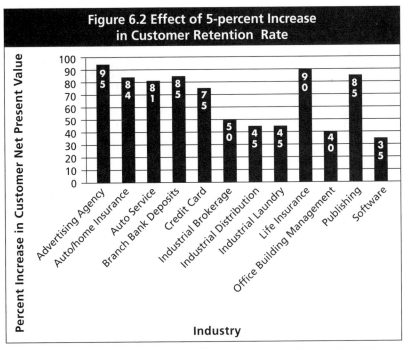

Source: Frederick F. Reichheld, *The Loyalty Effect* (Boston: Harvard Business School Press, 1996).

Supplier Value-Chain Process

By developing a supplier value chain, **Figure 6.3** (See p. 109) lists the key inputs, available tools and techniques, and desired outputs that are essential to ensure acquisition success.

Inputs

The following items are key inputs to creating a successful supplier value chain:

■ Well-defined, performance-based customer needs (requirements);

■ Mutually agreed to (customer and suppliers) joint performance metrics;

■ Positive and professional business relationship (between customer and suppliers);

■ People (all parties involved with the project including customer, supplier, and supply-chain partners; see **Figure 6.4**, p. 110);

■ Processes and information systems (including managing expectations process, supply-chain management process, and related information systems.)

■ Training (including appropriate competency-based education and training in sales management, capture and bid management, contract management, supply-chain management, and all related tools and techniques)

Tools and Techniques
Building Trust

The following is a summary of some of the most effective tools and techniques to develop a supplier value-chain that will ensure complex acquisitions are successful. Each of the following tools and techniques can and should be appropriately tailored to the respective acquisition situation.

The Process of Managing Expectations. In our current dynamic high-speed world of e-business, expectations are incredibly high. Too often, people leap to expect that the impossible can be achieved without knowing all the facts or details. Of course, sometimes companies can create virtual miracles, but, in many cases, those companies fall

Figure 6.3 Supplier Value-Chain Process

Inputs	Tools and Techniques	Outputs
■ Well-defined, performance-based customer needs	**Business Trust** ■ The managing expectations process ■ Checklist of supplier's actions to build customer trust	■ Quality products ■ Quality services ■ Integrated solutions ■ Best-value deal ■ On-time delivery ■ Reduced cycle-time ■ Customer support and service ■ Customer and user satisfaction
■ Mutually agreed to (customer and supplier) Joint performance metrics		
■ Positive and professional business relationship (between customer and suppliers)	**Supply-Chain Management** ■ Supply-chain management best practices and case studies ■ e-Sourcing ■ Supply base benchmarking ■ Supply Management Model	
■ People		
■ Processes and information systems		
■ Supply-chain management		
■ Training	**Customer Relationship Management** ■ Telephone surveys ■ e-Mail surveys ■ Customer visits and interviews ■ Customer focus groups ■ Front-line customer contract	
	Supplier Relationship Management ■ Principal Supplier Key Action Matrix ■ Subcontracting plan outline ■ Spend analysis	

well short of their customers' unrealistic expectations.

No one in business can avoid expectations. Everything companies say or do—or don't say or don't do—sets some form of expectation in the minds of others. Most companies try to set expectations through their advertising and marketing. However, companies' real market expectations are typically set by the companies' actual performance

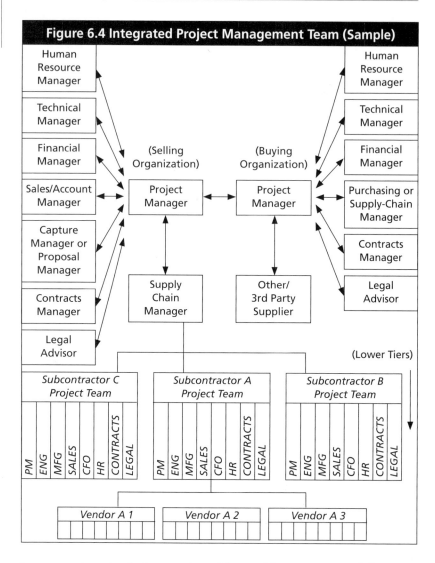

Figure 6.4 Integrated Project Management Team (Sample)

in comparison to their promises. The real key to successfully managing expectations and honoring commitments is understanding the process. (See **Figure 6.5**, p. 111)

Understanding the managing expectations process is good; applying it is even better. Unfortunately, because of the speed of business today, companies frequently react to partial information while using inaccurate assumptions, rather than by truly listening and understanding their customers' needs and goals. Often, suppliers do not properly distinguish the real difference between a customer's needs versus their desires.[1]

Aligning expectations to reality is a critical step in managing the

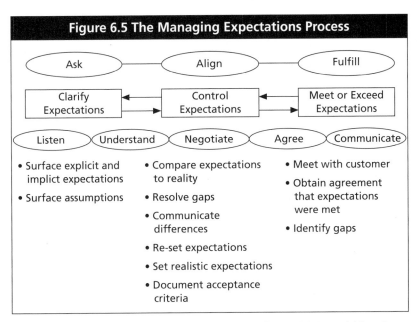

Figure 6.5 The Managing Expectations Process

Ask — Align — Fulfill

| Clarify Expectations | Control Expectations | Meet or Exceed Expectations |

Listen — Understand — Negotiate — Agree — Communicate

- Surface explicit and implict expectations
- Surface assumptions

- Compare expectations to reality
- Resolve gaps
- Communicate differences
- Re-set expectations
- Set realistic expectations
- Document acceptance criteria

- Meet with customer
- Obtain agreement that expectations were met
- Identify gaps

Source: Adapted from Dorothy Kirk, "Managing Expectations," *PM Network Magazine*, August 2000 (Project Management Institute).

expectations process. Aligning expectations does not mean reducing objectives or requirements to the lowest level. Instead, aligning expectations is about negotiating a challenging but achievable set of objectives for all parties on the basis of the realities of the situation (i.e., technology, maturity, schedule, budget, scope of work, mutual priorities, and resource availability).

To meet or exceed customer expectations, a company must first agree upon, preferably in writing, what is required. Those requirements are often referred to as acceptance criteria, including price, schedule, quality, quantity, and like items. It is clearly in the best interest of both parties to ensure that the agreed-to products, services, or solutions will meet or exceed the documented acceptance criteria.

Checklist of Supplier's Actions to Build Customers' Trust. One of the biggest challenges in creating and maintaining a successful long-term business partnership is building trust. Trust is like quality; it is difficult to accurately describe, but you know it when it's there. Trust is typically earned when you do—on a repeated basis—what you say you are going to do; in other words, when you honor commitments. A company can also instill trust when it comes to the rescue of another company in a time of urgent business need. Building trust in business partnerships can take years to accomplish, but sometimes those relationships can be lost very quickly.

It is important to keep your customers well informed about the facts by providing customers with project status reports whether on a contract or program basis. All business professionals must learn to deliver the truth, both good and bad. No business partnership goes perfectly, but communicating the good, the bad, and—at times—the ugly will go a long way to building trust. What a company does to

Table 6.1 Checklist of Supplier's Actions to Build Customer Trust

❑ Listen to the customer.

❑ Understand the customer's needs versus goals.

❑ State the obvious.

❑ Be accessible.

❑ Return phone calls, voice-mails, and e-mails in a timely manner.

❑ Provide regular communication on contract, program, and partnership status.

❑ Develop a project plan for every deal (scope of work, integrated schedule, work breakdown structure, responsibility assignment matrix, and acceptance criteria).

❑ Develop a risk management plan

❑ Disclose problems early, and mitigate negative impacts.

❑ Back up all verbal agreements and conversations with written documentation.

❑ Develop a contract changes management process.

❑ Provide frequent communication using multiple media.

❑ Be prepared to deliver both good and bad news at multiple levels, both internally and with customers.

❑ Be flexible; develop alternatives.

❑ Set challenging but achievable project requirements.

❑ Demonstrate passion in honoring commitments.

❑ Recognize that trust is the most important thing in a successful business relationship.

❑ Learn from mistakes, and openly communicate lessons learned.

Source: Gregory A. Garrett, *World Class Contracting*, 3rd ed. (Chicago: CCH Incorporated, 2003).

overcome business obstacles and to successfully communicate those actions with customers can be vital to building trust, even when the final results are not the best.

Table 6.1 (See p. 112) provides a checklist of actions for building trust between customers and suppliers.[2]

Supply-Chain Management

In the 1980s and 1990s, almost the entire professional procurement community hailed supply-chain management (SCM) as the panacea to solving most purchasing challenges. Supply-chain management (SCM) advocates told customers that they needed to (1) use fewer suppliers instead of many suppliers, (2) negotiate long-term contracts instead of short-term contracts, (3) conduct more-detailed progress or milestone tracking of suppliers and their subcontractors, (4) obtain lower pricing by using preferred terms and conditions, and (5) analyze every action and link in the supply-chain between the customer and lowest-level vendor. SCM has helped many companies worldwide reduce their procurement costs and their procurement cycle time.

Advocates of SCM, such as General Motors, Ford, IBM, Motorola, Proctor & Gamble, Wal-Mart, Raytheon, and many others, typically focus their attention on the following list of best practices to optimize supply-chain performance.

SCM Best Practices and Case Studies. What is supply-chain management? The Institute of Supply Management (ISM) typically defines supply-chain management as "the science of integrating the flow of goods and information from initial sourcing all the way through delivery to the end-user. Key activities within this end-to-end process include purchasing, production planning, order processing and fulfillment, inventory management transportation, distribution, and customer service."

Fortune 1000 corporations are beginning to recognize that untapped potential resides within their supply chains. This potential, when extracted, creates strategic competitive advantage for the corporation, affects the bottom line, and contributes significantly to customer success. One report noted: "A recent survey by Deloitte Consulting revealed that 91 percent of North American manufacturers ranked supply-chain management as very important or critical to overall company success (although only 2 percent said their supply chains were currently world class)."[3] (See **Table 6.2**, p. 114, for a list of 12 best practices.)

However, more and more companies in the new e-business age have

Table 6.2 Checklist of Supply-Chain Management 12 Best Practices
❑ Retain only core work (products, services, and solutions).
❑ Improve supplier selection process.
❑ Reduce the number of suppliers.
❑ Improve demand forecast accuracy.
❑ Increase inventory turns (velocity).
❑ Decrease outsourcing costs per unit by leveraging major suppliers for lower prices.
❑ Increase standardization of products, as much as possible and appropriate.
❑ Increase global sourcing, especially in geographic areas of lower labor costs.
❑ Maximize economies of scale.
❑ Seek global demand for products and services.
❑ Increase automation and database integration between business partners using enterprise resource planning software tools and web-based trade exchanges.
❑ Use technology tools to increase speed to the market, to reduce costs, and to obtain real-time accurate information.

realized that supply-chain management as a procurement concept is good but is not good enough. To create a truly integrated supply-chain network, a new global hub or trade exchange for each industry must be created that will allow all players to connect their internal systems to the internal systems of other companies through the World Wide Web. Real integration means providing enterprise resource planning to all participants in the industry.

Customers can achieve an integrated supply chain only if they develop trusted partnerships with suppliers, who, in turn, will serve as value-added business service providers. Today, large vertical trade exchanges, which have been built cooperatively by industry participants, are changing the nature of competition. Many winning companies have decided that, because the Web is so accessible and so efficient, competing on the basis of connectivity throughout the supply chain is no longer good business. As a result, many competitors are cooperating to build efficient Internet connections and are competing on how they can use those new capabilities to better achieve customer satisfaction.

As discussed in chapter 4, e-business is forcing businesses world-wide to reexamine how they do business. Today, the questions that CEOs have to answer are more about "How do I design, manufacture, or outsource and distribute products, services, and solutions to meet or exceed my customer's needs?" rather than "What quantity of my off-the-shelf products do I have to sell in order to make my quarterly or annual revenue target?" Winning organizations realize that they must help their customers, suppliers, or both reduce their expenses and improve their performance. The following are a few recent case studies from several industry leaders.

Case Study: Toyota and Supplier Partnering

Bullying or bashing suppliers and subcontractors is totally alien to the spirit and practice of the Toyota Production System (TPS). TPS is focused on building long-term relationships that will last for decades and will involve trust and mutual success. At the same time, TPS connotes discipline and the expectation of improvement and growth. One example is Toyota's program of Construction of Cost Competitiveness for the 21st century (CCC21), which aims at a 30-percent reduction in the prices of 170 parts that the company will buy for its next generation of vehicles. Nearly, all of Toyota's suppliers are highly motivated to help achieve its goals because they believe that, with Toyota's help, they will improve their manufacturing processes. Therefore, Toyota will help them to be more efficient, effective, and competitive, thus more profitable in the future.[4]

Case Study: Cisco Systems' Integrated Supply Chain and Virtual Manufacturing

By using its own Internet strategy and solutions, Cisco Systems has successfully maintained its agility, culture of empowerment, and competitive advantage. All of Cisco's business operations, including finance, supply-chain management, and employee communications, are Internet-based. Today, Cisco transacts nearly 90 percent of orders and 82 percent of customer support inquiries over the Web. Using outsourcing and the Internet has allowed Cisco to create a virtual manufacturing system that seamlessly manages 37 global plants as if they were one plant. Cisco's Internet technology and global real-time project-level accounting allow the company to conduct a virtual close on their financial books each fiscal quarter within 24 hours.

Case Study: Hormel Foods' Oracle Internet Procurement

Hormel Foods has recently completed the installation of Oracle Internet Procurement at all of its 50 locations. Employees at those sites are now able to create purchasing requisitions for nonproduction items and to have them automatically routed for approval. Employees can also track and access information on a real-time basis. Self-guiding online catalogs allow workers to search for goods and services from approved suppliers. Most of the savings associated with the implementation of Oracle Internet Procurement result from the fact that Hormel's procurement personnel no longer must spend considerable amounts of time dealing with routine purchases. Additional savings will be realized through the elimination of noncontract purchases. Hormel values the fact that its procurement personnel now have more time to devote to the more professional tasks of creating, managing, and leveraging partnerships with its suppliers.[5]

Case Study: The Limited's Global Sourcing

The Limited is regarded as one of the world's most successful retailers of apparel. Although all of The Limited's retail outlets are located inside the United States, the retailer has successfully established global sourcing practices. The process of going from product design to shipment of garments to the individual stores takes less than 60 days, which is a dramatically reduced cycle time compared to that of its competitors. In addition, superior global supply-chain management allows The Limited to have its garments designed by numerous companies throughout Europe, to have the garments produced in Asian and other countries by local manufacturers, and to have the garments shipped using global logistics networks to Columbus, Ohio, where they are distributed to thousands of retail outlets of the Limited Express, Victoria's Secret, Abercrombie and Fitch, Lerner, Henri Bedel, and others.

Case Study: The Ford Motor Co. and Reducing Lead Time

The Customer Service Division of the Ford Motor Co., which supplied more than 500,000 service parts to more than 10,000 dealerships around the world, faced delivery variables ranging as low as 30 percent (per time period for any given part) up to 400 percent. Yet, the division required virtually on-demand availability for each service or repair. The Ford division partnered with a team from Cap Gemini Ernst & Young to improve legacy systems integration while using distribution resource planning tools that improved forecasting and inventory visibility throughout the supply chain. Tools were developed to measure volatility and to streamline inventory lead time, thereby shortening supply-chain lead times. Customer fill rates from 1999 improved from 93 to 98 percent in the United States and from 93.6 to 96.8 percent in Europe.

SCM and E-Sourcing. Aberdeen Group describes strategic e-sourcing as "the process of utilizing Web-based technologies to support the identification, evaluation, negotiation, and configuration of optimal groups of trading partners into a supply-chain network, which can then respond to changing market demands with greater efficiency." Industry analysts further state that e-sourcing is "one of the most direct and effective ways that an organization can utilize the Internet to control costs, improve profits, and enhance overall responsiveness to changing market dynamics."

In his article titled "Establishing Mutual Equity for Buyers and Sellers with E-Sourcing," which was published in the *NCMA Contract Management Magazine* of March 2005, Jemin Patel, CEO and president of HedgeHog e-Sourcing On Demand, stated there are two primary types of e-sourcing:

1. On-line reverse auctions use forum that has one buyer and many sellers. Reverse auctions are an effective way for buyers to reduce purchasing costs and to streamline procurement when buying capital equipment, materials, and services from local, national, and global suppliers. Buyers initiate reverse auctions by distributing purchasing solicitations, such as request for quotes, and then suppliers compete against each other in Web-based, real-time auctions to win the buyer's business, thus driving down the price in the process.

2. On-line forward auctions use forum that has one seller and many buyers. Forward auctions are an effective way for sellers to obtain the best price for outdated, obsolete, or excess capital equipment and materials and for services they are selling or liquidating. Suppliers notify buyers of the products or services that are available, and buyers compete against each other in Web-based, real-time auctions, thus driving up demand and price as they bid.

Most of today's e-sourcing solutions offer software in a hosted, Web-based, on-demand model. This software allows users to start using systems immediately without costly or time-consuming technology integration. Additionally, many options use a subscription-based or usage-based pricing model. This pricing makes them highly affordable for small businesses and public agencies that have ongoing sourcing needs or for organizations that need an e-sourcing service but will use it only occasionally.

The e-sourcing best practices include the following:

- Provide well-defined requirements for the needed products, services, or both;

- Focus on the quality of products, services, or both;

- Build a collaborative business environment;

- Streamline the negotiation process; and

- Reduce administrative time and expense.

Case Study: The State of Kentucky & E-Sourcing

In late 2004, the Kentucky Council of Area Development Districts (KYCADD) partnered with HedgeHog e-Sourcing On Demand to develop an e-sourcing system that is designed to improve the sourcing process for municipal buyers in 120 counties and to increase business opportunities in Kentucky for suppliers. KYCADD's role is to provide economic planning, area development, and technology services to local government entities by systematically linking the governor's office, local leadership, state and federal agencies, and private organizations. The on-demand e-sourcing system, known as ADD-OPS (Area Development Districts On-line Procurement Systems), is helping KYCADD accomplish its mission quickly and cost-effectively.

While the ADD-OPS program is still in its infancy, it is receiving a warm welcome from Kentucky's public buying community. This community includes public works departments, emergency medical services (police and fire departments), fiscal courts, and housing authorities. Those entities are using this free, on-line purchasing system to accomplish the following:

- Build comprehensive databases of qualified suppliers that reach beyond Kentucky's borders,

- Distribute requests for proposals more efficiently while staying compliant with state procurement regulations,

- Combat Kentucky's funding crisis by consolidating purchasing power through large-scale individual or group buys, and

- Tap into strategic and tactical procurement enterprise.

SCM and Supply Base Benchmarking. On the basis of two benchmarking events that included Cisco, Boeing, Motorola, Unisys, Raytheon, and Tyco, the following findings (see **Table 6.3**, p. 120) were made regarding keys to supply base optimization.[6]

SCM and Supply Management Model. Dr. David Burt in his book *World-Class Supply Management* provides a four-stage continuum toward "world-class," whereby organizations can evaluate their current state of operations. They can draw a comparison to the model (See **Table 6.4**, p. 121) and can determine potential areas of process improvement.

Customer Relationship Management

Various software companies, including SAP, Baan, Oracle, and Deltek (to name a few), have developed a diverse portfolio of enterprise resource planning tools to facilitate customer service 24 hours a day/7 days a week/365 days a year. Customer relationship nanagement (CRM) is the name given to many of those Web-based tools, which facilitate customer interactions. In addition to the ever-expanding software applications available, there are numerous proven-effective, simpler, cost-effective means to facilitate customer feedback, including those listed next.

Telephone Surveys. Phone surveys are excellent methods to use if time is of the essence, if the questions are not intrusive, and if the survey is not too long. Great care must be taken to verify accuracy. Phone surveys are excellent listening tools, but they have limitations because they have no visual aids and because often people do not want to talk on the phone for long periods of time.

E-Mail Surveys. The e-mail surveys can be slightly longer than telephone surveys because respondents fill out the questionnaires at their own pace. Well-crafted questionnaires help eliminate the potential bias of an interviewer. The e-mail surveys allow companies to gather a much greater quantity of information than telephone surveys. Respondents also have more opportunity to think about their answers and to provide more detailed information. In addition, e-mail surveys allow respondents to answer questions anonymously while providing the business opportunity to present itself in a high-quality and more standardized manner to its customers. However, e-mail surveys also have limitations. First, the response rate on e-mail surveys

Table 6.3 Checklist of Supply Base Optimization Key Actions

❏ The process must start with the customer and then work backward to define the supply-chain strategy.

❏ A significant portion of product cost is driven by external sources.

❏ Strategies should be linked to business processes.

❏ A business can measure success through its performance improvement.

❏ The supply chain must own sourcing.

❏ The supply executive leader should report to the business's president.

❏ Process improvements must be driven from the top down to be successful.

❏ Multifunctional senior leadership endorsement is a must.

❏ Tools are used to bring processes upstream into the design process to ensure critical early involvement with engineering.

❏ The strategic approach results in significant reductions in the number of suppliers.

❏ The commodity strategy is prioritized around spend.

❏ Commodity teams are cross-functional.

❏ A business should focus on standardization to reduce complexity.

❏ Involvement of the entire value chain, including customers, produces the greatest success.

❏ Trust and collaboration with suppliers is a key enabler.

❏ Early involvement with the "right" suppliers is key to success.

❏ Process centralization adds to efficiency and focus.

❏ A business should staff for success.

❏ It is important to move resources from tactical to strategic focus.

❏ It is essential to evaluate employee skill sets and to train, develop, and make changes if needed.

❏ A business can create urgency through clear case for action.

Source: Shirley Patterson, "Supply Base Optimization and Integrated Supply-Chain Management," *Contract Management*, (January 2005): 24–35.

is generally lower than on other survey tools. Second, the survey may get lost with other e-mails. Third, respondents may not complete the entire survey.

Customer Visits and Interviews. One of the best ways to gather customer information and to assess customer satisfaction is by going to customer locations so you can interview them. You can ask customers directly what they like and do not like about your company, products, or services and what they perceive to be your company's strengths and weaknesses. A major advantage of customer visits and

Table 6.4 The Progression of World-Class Supply Management			
Stage 1: Clerical	**Stage 2: Mechanical**	**Stage 3: Proactive**	**Stage 4: World Class**
Process paperwork.	Use a transactional focus.	Coordinate the procurement system.	Supply management and core competence.
Confirm actions of others.	React to acquisitions.	Develop suppliers that	Use strategic sourcing.
Put emphasis on convenience.	Do not be involved in key source selections.	■ Have long-term contracts, ■ Are involved in development of requirements, and	Monitor supply environment. ■ Develop and implement. ■ Use commodity strategies.
Make relationships personal.	Put an emphasis on purchase price.	■ Plan for recurring requirements.	■ Use commodity teams. Develop and manage alliances and networks.
Have the major impact be overhead.	Have relationships that are transactional and adversarial.	Remember that procurement adds value.	■ Time-based competition Use virtually defect-free materials and services.
Keep reporting at a very low level.	Be revenue neutral for a bottom-line effect.	■ Be active in source selection. ■ Use near defect-free materials and services.	■ Leverage supplier technology. Use integrated supply strategy.
Remember that data are not available.	Use reporting at a low level. Use data to expedite. Use computers and process paperwork.	■ Put the emphasis on cost, quality, and timeliness. ■ Have relationships that are transactional and collaborative.	Manage risk. Have an emphasis on total cost. Have relationships that are transactional, collaborative, and alliances.
		Use profit contributor for a bottom-line impact. ■ Report to upper management. ■ Use data about facilities sourcing and pricing. ■ Fulfill social responsibilities. ■ Use e-commerce.	Increase the shareholder value for bottom-line effect. ■ Report to the member and executive group. ■ Use data about facilities strategic planning. ■ Understand the key supplier industries. ■ Use e-commerce II.

Source: David Burt, Donald Dolder, and Stephen Starling, *World-Class Supply Management* (New York: McGraw-Hill, 2003).

personal interviews is that the interviewer can gather information by verbal and nonverbal responses to questions. Customer visits are very expensive, especially if your customers are spread over a wide geographic area. **Table 6.5** (this page) provides a checklist of tips for suppliers conducting customer interviews.[7]

Customer Focus Groups. These focus groups consist of individuals who represent a number of your customers and who are brought together to participate in discussions concerning a series of topics, questions, products, or services. Customer focus groups are sometimes referred to as user-groups and can prove to be very effective when dealing with improvements to existing products, product features, and customer support services. Limitations to customer focus groups include the following:

■ A dominant individual who can overly influence discussions,

■ An ineffective moderator who may allow discussions to go off-topic, and

■ Time constraints.

Front-Line Customer Contact. Perhaps the most valuable type of customer feedback is the daily personal discussions, e-mails, telephone calls, conference calls, and actual work that your company

Table 6.5 Checklist of Tips for Suppliers Conducting Customer Interviews
❑ The interviewer must have a professional appearance.
❑ The interviewer must have a thorough knowledge of the specific characteristics and requirements of the customers' projects.
❑ The interviewer should clarify the roles and responsibilities of the suppliers' key personnel who interface with the customer.
❑ The interviewer should seek to understand what the customer perceives as both your companies' strengths and its areas for improvement.
❑ The interviewer should understand what are the customers' key performance areas and metrics.

Table 6.6 Principal Supplier Key Actions Matrix

Plan Element	Type of Plan (see key below)											
	Risk Mgt	Finc	PM	M&S	VM	Q&A	Train	Safety	T&A	Trans	Life Cyc Mgt	Confg Mgt
Customers' relationship management			X	X						X	X	
Customers' responsibilities during implementation			X	X								
Customers' responsibilities for acceptance review			X	X					X			
Customers' responsibilities for change management			X	X								X
Customers' responsibilities over project life cycle			X	X							X	
Deliverables' requirements and testing			X			X			X			
Design and management of the project for a smooth transition			X	X	X					X	X	X
Inclusion of risk management strategies in appropriate plans	X	X	X	X	X	X	X	X	X	X	X	X
Project implementation and management training	X		X				X	X	X	X	X	X
Provisions for customer billings		X		X					X			
Provisions for principal supplier payment		X		X								
Quality of vendors					X	X						
Provisions for vendors' payment		X			X							
Quality training requirements				X		X	X					
Vendors' responsibilities during implementation			X		X	X						

Key for plan type abbreviations: Rsk Mgt = Risk Management, Finc = Finance, PM = Project Management, M&S = Marketing and Sales, VM = Vendor Management, Q&A = Quality Assurance, Train = Training, T&A = Test and Acceptance, Trans = Transition, Life Cyc Mgt = Life Cycle Management, Confg Mgt = Configuration Management.

employees engage in with your customers and the communication they share with each other.[8]

Supplier Relationship Management

Like the topic of CRM, supplier relationship management (SRM) is an area in which numerous software companies have developed a wide-array of database management ERP tools to facilitate communication. In addition to the numerous SRM software applications available, a number of simple cost-effective tools will help manage supply-chain partners.

Principal Supplier Key Actions Matrix. Table 6.6 (p. 123) provides a useful matrix of key actions that principal suppliers (prime contractors) should perform when successfully managing outsourced projects that involve buyers, sellers, and subcontractors.

Subcontracting Plan Outline. Use the outline in **Table 6.7** (See p. 125) to prepare a comprehensive subcontracting plan.

Spend Analysis. Spend analysis is a tool that provides buyers with a better understanding of who their suppliers are, how much money they spend, what products or services they are acquiring, and where the best opportunities are for the buyers to leverage their power to negotiate better deals with their suppliers. Increasingly, during the past five years, private sector companies such as Wal-Mart, IBM, Proctor & Gamble, NCR, Lucent Technologies, and others have been using spend analysis as a tool to reduce their expenses and to improve performance.

Case Study: GAO Report "Using Spend Analysis to Help Agencies Take a More Strategic Approach to Procurement" (September 2004)

Recognizing the potential in the U.S. federal government's buying practices, the General Accounting Office (GAO) examined whether the following departments are using spend analysis to improve their performance:[9]

■ Department of Agriculture (DOA),

■ Health and Human Services (HHS), and

■ Veterans Affairs (VA).

Table 6.7 Outline of Subcontracting Plan

1.0 Overview

The subcontracting plan explains the overall project approach to using third-party suppliers or supply-chain partners on the project. Third-party suppliers may provide hardware, perform services, or develop and provide software used in the system. The principal supplier or prime contractor's responsibility for supplier management is to ensure that all subcontracted elements are fully integrated into the overall system and that they are managed integrally throughout the project. Explain the project's approach to using subcontractors, and generally describe which project elements will be performed by third-party suppliers. Describe generally the process of managing those suppliers.

2.0 Project Elements to Be Subcontracted

Use the work breakdown structure (WBS) to identify which WBS elements will be subcontracted. Describe why those elements will be performed by subcontractors and why the principal supplier cannot or should not do the work internally. For each element, discuss the specific requirements for the subcontractor. Provide a schedule showing when subcontracts will be awarded for each element.

3.0 Identification and Selection of Subcontractors

Discuss the process by which subcontractors will be selected. If subcontractors will be competitively selected, identify which principal supplier organizations will be responsible for preparing statements of work and other requirements documentation. Typically, they will be the organizations that have responsibility for the WBS elements being subcontracted. For each WBS element to be subcontracted, identify the third-party supplier that will perform the work. If that supplier is already known, there is usually no need for a formal procurement procedure.

4.0 Subcontract Management

4.1 Discuss the overall process for managing the subcontracts. What principal supplier organizations will provide legal and contracting support? Who will be responsible for administering subcontract changes and modifications? Who will review progress and approve payment of supplier invoices?

4.2 As each subcontract is awarded, establish a subcontract tracking summary in a file for that subcontract. Use the summary to record the progress of the subcontract throughout its life.

4.3 Assign a project team member or organization the responsibility for managing each subcontract. Identify the responsible parties in this section of the subcontracting plan, as well as on each subcontract tracking summary.

5.0 Supplier Participation in Project Management

Discuss the level of supplier participation in the project management process. Some suppliers may be responsible for major portions of the project. If this is the case, there should be a representative from those suppliers on the project steering committee to facilitate project control and communication. Discuss supplier input to the project management information system. Discuss the level of reporting required from suppliers, and ensure that the input and reports are listed as contractual requirements in the subcontracts.

GAO also assessed the following:

- Whether agencies used spend analysis to obtain knowledge so they could improve buying or products and services, and

- How agencies' buying practices compare to leading companies' best practices.

In analyzing the agencies, GAO compared the five key processes that are shown in **Table 6.8** (See this page). **Tables 6.9** (p. 128), **6.10** (p. 129), and **6.11** (p. 130) summarize GAO's analysis of the various agencies' spend analysis practices.

Table 6.8 Five Key Processes for Spend Analysis
1. Automation: Compile data automatically.
2. Extraction: Cull essential data from accounts payable and other internal systems.
3. Supplemental information: Seek additional data from other internal and external sources.
4. Organization: Review data to ensure accuracy and completeness; organize data into logical, comprehensive commodity and supplier categories.
5. Analysis and strategic goals: Using standard reporting and analytical tools, analyze data on a continual basis to support decisions on strategic-sourcing and procurement management in areas such as cost cutting, streamlining operations, and reducing the number of suppliers. Scope generally covers an organization's entire spending.

Source: GAO Analysis.

Outputs

Clearly, the desired results of a supplier value chain are the following:

- Quality products,

- Quality services,

- Integrated solutions,

- Best-value deal,

■ On-time delivery,

■ Reduced cycle time,

■ Customer support and service, and

■ Customer and user satisfaction.

For a checklist of supplier value-chain bests practices that will improve performance results, see **Table 6.12** (See p. 131).

Summary

In retrospect, a seller or supplier must take the time to do the following: (1) understand a customer's needs and goals, (2) translate those needs into specific project requirements, (3) negotiate a reasonable deal, (4) form a win–win contract, (5) create a successful supply-chain infrastructure, (6) create customer-goal focused projects and related programs, and (7) meet or exceed customer expectations. Without the proactive support of the supplier's executive leadership, it is difficult, if not impossible, to achieve customer loyalty. The supplier's leadership must establish a customer-focused project culture and a strong supply-chain management infrastructure. It is the primary responsibility of the supplier's executive leadership to ensure that the following actions are taken:

■ Hire and retain a highly qualified and diverse team of talented people who are receptive to change.

■ Develop well thought-out business processes and user-friendly customer relationship management (CRM) and supplier relationship management, (SRM) information systems, which provide accurate and real-time data.

■ Conduct appropriate level of spend analysis on a regular basis.

■ Create and provide simple tools and techniques to facilitate rapid knowledge transfer.

■ Facilitate and provide meaningful training programs that are for competency-based contract management and supply-chain management and will build expertise in each respective functional discipline and will improve employees' leadership and teamwork skills

Table 6.9 U.S. Department of Agriculture	
Agriculture Spend Analysis Practices	
Spend Analysis Process	Agency Practice
Automation	In 2001, DOA furnished 2000 data to a spend analysis consultant who used commercially available automation tools to compile the data that would expedite the analysis to fulfill a one-time requirement. DOA plans to create an automated spend analysis tool to extract data from the single acquisition system to begin in October 2006. The data are expected to be compiled into a new shared data warehouse that will extract components' procurement data as the new system goes on line. The warehouse is expected to contain business intelligence and data mining capability so that the spend analysis process can be repeated at the agency or component level.
Extraction	DOA wanted the 2001 spend analysis to cover all products and services procurements other than the nonprocurement-related agricultural commodity purchases. To accomplish this goal, the agency extracted data from three databases: contract actions for $25,000 or less, contract actions of more than $25,000, and the purchase card management system. Spend analysis did not include financial management data such as accounts payable systems.
Supplemental Information	DOA's purchase card management system obtains data from the bankcard vendor on all purchase card transactions with agency cardholders. The agency furnished 2000 purchase card data for the 2001 spend analysis. In 2004, DOA obtained up-to-date purchase card data on agency transactions with high-dollar, high-volume vendors from its bankcard vendor to supplement the 2001 spend analysis.
Organization	DOA's spend analysis consultant cleansed and validated the 2001 data that the agency furnished, on the basis of its spend analysis experience and supply market knowledge. The consultant used federal product and service classification to organize agency spending into 15 categories encompassing 52 more detailed subcategories. Information technology (IT) for example, included telecom equipment, IT equipment, office technology, and IT and telecom services. The spend analysis consultant also proposed a feasibility classification strategy that could be used for more detailed opportunity analyses of high-potential subcategories.
Analysis and Strategic Goals	DOA is not analyzing data on a continual basis. Following the completion of the initial spend analysis in October 2001, the agency used the results to support decisions for an agencywide agreement dealing with an office supply discount agreement from a major supplier. An agreement was awarded in 2003 so that DOA purchase cardholders could use the supplier's Web-based catalog to obtain small purchases of wide range of office supplies at reduced prices. In 2004, DOA created a temporary subcommittee of procurement managers to review the 2001 spend analysis report and more recent purchase card data where available. The agency will identify a few more high-dollar, high-volume product subcategories where purchase card buying power can be leveraged through discount agreements with major suppliers.

Source: GAO analysis of agency information.

Table 6.10 U.S. Department of Health and Human Services	
Health and Human Services Spend Analysis Practices	
Spend Analysis Process	**Agency Practice**
Automation	HHS has furnished services procurement data to one consultant and products procurement data to a second. While both use commercially available automation tools to compile data for more rapid spend analyses, these are one-time or periodic requirements. No automation tool is available to allow HHS to consistently repeat the spend analysis process, but the agency may consider obtaining such a system.
Extraction	HHS wants its acquisition consolidation initiative to cover as many of its services buys as possible; therefore, HHS provided its spend analysis consultant services contract data from one 2002 database (contracts for $25,000 or less were not included).
	For its product-focused strategic sourcing initiative, HHS provided a consultant with data from 2002 on office supplies, office equipment, office furniture, peripheral information technology (IT) equipment, and custodial supplies. Furnished data were extracted from two contract databases: actions for $25,000 or less, and for more than $25,000. This year, the HHS consultant will receive 2003 purchase data for all other products, data extracted from the same two databases, as well as with data from HHS financial management sources, such as accounts payable systems.
Supplemental Information	To identify the top-selling office product suppliers, HHS provided the consultant data from the agency's bankcard vendor on all purchase card transactions, as well as other information from prospective commodity suppliers on estimated sales to agency purchasers. These data enhance awareness of the volume and scope of HHS purchasing. This year, the HHS consultant will receive 2003 purchase card data as well. HHS sought no additional spend analysis data for the services acquisition consolidation.
Organization	In 2003, both consultants cleansed and validated data that HHS furnished on the basis of their spend analysis experience and supply market knowledge. The consultants used the federal product and services classification to organize categories of commodities and suppliers. This organization helped them identify and rank high-dollar, high-volume opportunities to target for office product strategic-sourcing and services acquisition consolidation.
	In 2004, the consultant will analyze new data involving small and larger purchase card and contract buys. The data will be organized into logical, comprehensive categories of products and supplies to identify and rank top categories to target for additional strategic sourcing.
Analysis and Strategic Goals	HHS is not analyzing data on a continual basis. The agency had two consultants analyze data in 2003 and will have one consultant do a second round of product-focused spend analysis in 2004. HHS is using that analysis to support strategic sourcing decisions for national discount agreements with a few major suppliers for office supplies, office equipment, office furniture, IT peripherals, and custodial supplies.
	HHS will use the consultant's spend analysis of services acquisitions to plan areas where existing contracts can be used by agency division purchasers to leverage buying power and to reduce the need for new stand-alone contracts. As of June 2004, HHS is continuing its planning and anticipates shared implementation of at least some of the existing contracts in 2005.

Source: GAO analysis of agency information.

Table 6.11 U.S. Department of Veterans Affairs

Veterans Affairs Spend Analysis Practices

Spend Analysis Process	Agency Practice
Automation	The VA uses an automated compilation of pharmaceutical and prosthetic and sensory aid purchase data into two central databases, which are updated continuously. The automated compilation of medical supply and equipment purchase data, but not clinical care and support services, will be compiled into a central database that will be available in 2006.
Extraction	The VA's pharmaceutical and prosthetics spend analysis covers all veterans' medical facilities purchases. The facilities' pharmaceutical purchase and vendor payment data are extracted from centralized commercial distributors' on-line ordering and delivery systems. The prosthetics data are extracted from multiple medical facilities' procurement and vendor payment systems.
	In 2006, standardized medical supply and equipment data will be extracted from facilities' procurement and vendor payment systems. None will be extracted on facilities' purchases for clinical care and support services.
Supplemental Information	The VA obtains pharmaceutical sales and payment data from centralized commercial distributors' on-line order and delivery systems. The agency's chief logistics office analyzes weekly summaries of bankcard vendors' transactions with the agency. The VA recently required purchase card program managers to consolidate quarterly reviews from the cardholders and to analyze purchases.
Organization	The VA's pharmaceutical and prosthetics spend analysis databases fall into logical comprehensive categories of commodities and suppliers. The agency is organizing and standardizing procurement data on medical supplies and equipment purchases; a spend analysis database is planned for completion in 2006.
	In 2004, a naming standard was [AQ: Past tense for 2004. Did it happen?] developed for each high-technology and high-cost medical product that had been given a national contract. To track compliance with contracted products, the VA will have to use a standard name when buying. The agency will not organize facilities' clinical care and support services procurement data into logical, comprehensive categories or commodities and suppliers.
Analysis and Strategic Goals	Commodity teams are continually analyzing pharmaceutical and prosthetics spending data to make decisions in contracting and procurement management. In 2003, the VA saved $394 million through discounted pharmaceutical national contracts. As of June 2004, prosthetics contract savings were more than $57 million.
	By 2006, standard reporting and analytical tools will be in place for medical supplies and equipment purchases, which new commodity teams will use to help reduce the number of suppliers, cut costs, streamline operations, and address the agency's small business goals. The VA's spend analysis system plan does not, however, include purchased clinical care and support services.

Source: GAO analysis of agency information.

Table 6.12 Checklist of Supplier Value Chain Best Practices to Improve Performance Results

The Buyer Should

❑ Develop an acquisition strategy that will lead to selection of the right seller.

❑ Develop a positive professional business relationship with the seller that is based on trust

❑ Treat the seller with respect at all times.

❑ Develop well-defined, performance-based requirements.

❑ Use e-sourcing as appropriate.

❑ Develop mutually agreed-to performance measures and metrics.

❑ Conduct spend analysis.

The Seller Should

❑ Create value for their buyers and end customers.

❑ Understand the buyer's requirements.

❑ Hold the buyers accountable for their contractual obligations.

❑ Possess a excellent track record.

❑ Have sufficient resources to accomplish agreed-to requirements.

❑ Develop a positive professional business relationship with the buyer that is based on trust.

❑ Treat the buyer and subcontractors with respect at all times.

❑ Flow-down all appropriate performance-based requirements to subcontractors.

❑ Conduct customer visits, interviews, and focus groups.

Buyer and Seller Should

❑ Mutually manage expectations.

❑ Clearly communicate.

❑ Form a true supplier value chain.

❑ Be accessible.

❑ Return phone calls, voice-mails, and e-mail in a timely manner.

❑ Develop a project plan for each deal.

❑ Disclose problems early.

❑ Mitigate negative impacts.

❑ Develop a contract change management process.

❑ Set challenging but achievable project requirements.

❑ Honor commitments.

❑ Celebrate joint successes.

❑ Share best practices.

so they can develop high-performance, integrated project teams.

All of the aforementioned actions are required to maximize a supplier's chances of meeting customer goals and of achieving customer loyalty in today's highly competitive global business environment. The next chapter discusses the five critical components that must be included for a performance-based contract to be successful.

Questions to Consider

1. How effectively does your organization leverage your suppliers so it can help your organization reduce costs and increase performance?

2. How effectively does your organization leverage your supply-chain partners, prime contractors, subcontractors, or all of them to accelerate delivery?

3. How well does your organization manage customers' expectations?

4. How effectively does your organization obtain customer feedback?

5. How effectively does your organization select potential supply-chain partners?

Endnotes

1. Gregory A. Garrett, *World Class Contracting*, 3rd ed. (Chicago: CCH Incorporated, 2005).

2. Ibid.

3. Gregory A. Garrett, *Managing Complex Outsourced Projects* (Chicago: CCH Incorporated, 2004).

4. David Burt, Donald Dolber, and Stephen Starling, *World Class Supply Management* (New York: McGraw-Hill, 2003).

5. Ibid., note 1.

6. Shirley Patterson, "Supply Base Optimization and Integrated Supply-Chain Management," *Contract Management*, (January 2005): pp. 24-35.

7. Gregory A. Garrett and Reginald J. Kipke, *The Capture Management Life Cycle* (Chicago: CCH Incorporated, 2003).

8. Ibid.

9. GAO Report 04-870, "Best Practices: Using Spend Analysis to Help Agencies Take a More Strategic Approach to Procurement," September 2004.

CHAPTER 07

Performance-Based Contracts

Five Critical Components

One of the key aspects of performance-based acquisition (PBA) is the use of performance-based contracts (PBCs). PBCs have been successfully used to buy and sell products, services, or integrated solutions in both the public and the private business sectors for many years. The foundation of PBCs is customers' requirements. The buying organization must determine customers' needs, must be able to communicate their needs in terms of performance-based requirements, and must be able to create challenging yet realistic performance-based metrics to hold sellers accountable. Typically, PBCs contain the following five critical components.

1. Performance work statement (PWS) or statement of objectives (SOO)

2. Quality assurance surveillance plan (QASP)

3. Performance-based metrics

4. Contractual incentives (positive or negative)

5. The right pricing arrangement (type of contract)

Each of the five critical components of PBCs should be developed by the buyer or the buying organization in partnership with the seller and its subcontractors.

First Critical Component: PWS or SOO

There are two ways to develop a specification for a PBA: (1) by using a PWS or (2) by using an emerging methodology built around an SOO.

The PWS process is commonly used in U.S. government contracting and is discussed in numerous guides on performance-based contracting and in the federal acquisition regulation. Among its key processes are the conduct of a job analysis and the development of a PWS and QASP. When people talk about performance-based contracting, this process is typically the model they have in mind.

The alternative process—use of a SOO—is an emerging methodology that turns the acquisition process around and that requires competing sellers to develop the statement of work, performance metrics, and QASP—all of which should be evaluated before contract award.[1]

A PBC does not direct how the work is to be accomplished. The methods for accomplishing the work should be determined by a seller with specialized business knowledge. The PWS should have a mix of objectively and subjectively measurable performance requirements.

There are important reasons to expend the time and effort to analyze the work that must be performed. This analysis is the beginning of the effort to specifically identify needs. It becomes evident as the development of the PWS and the QASP progresses why participants should include the output desired and why functional area representatives should, at this time, eliminate vague, confusing, or incomplete requirements. This opportunity is excellent for the functional managers to ask if particular services are required.

All tasks required of the suppliers should be analyzed for clarity and simplicity to ensure that the seller will understand the requirements. This analysis will improve supplier performance and will reduce friction between the buyer and the seller. Sellers generally use higher costs to hedge against perceived contracting risks. If the buyers eliminate questionable or ambiguous requirements, the sellers' concern about risks is reduced and so are the costs.

Once the buyers have developed a specific list of capabilities they desire, then they need to specify performance requirements for each of the tasks identified as required outputs.[2] A PWS can serve as a powerful tool to inform sellers of the buyers' needs, while allowing the sellers the flexibility to be innovative, creative, and not bound by detailed products or services specifications.

The following are the best practices for PWS and SOO (See **Table 7.1** on p. 137).

Table 7.1 PWS and SOO Best Practices
For PWS:
❏ Conduct an analysis.
❏ Apply the "so what?" test.
❏ Capture the results of the analysis in a matrix.
❏ Write the PWS.
❏ Let the seller solve the problem, including the labor mix.
For SOO:
❏ Begin with the acquisition's "elevator message."
❏ Describe the scope.
❏ Write the performance objectives into the SOO.
❏ Make sure the buyer and the seller share objectives.
❏ Identify the constraints.
❏ Develop the background.
❏ Make the final checks and maintain the perspective.[3]

Source: Appendix A

Second Critical Component: QASP

The QASP establishes the plan that will be followed to ensure that the buyer receives the performance it is paying for. The information developed by this plan provides objective evidence of acceptable performance and also provides the means whereby deductions may properly be taken for unacceptable performance. To accomplish this goal, you should carefully plan the QASP. The make-up and depth of the QASP depends on the size and complexity of the contract. Generally the QASP will contain the following:

■ A statement of the plan's purpose;

■ The names of the technical representative or quality assurance evaluator, including alternates;

■ The specific authority and responsibilities of those individuals;

■ Instructions on how to use the plan;

■ A surveillance schedule;

■ The surveillance methods that will be used;

■ Appropriate documentation for each method (e.g., schedules, checklists, reports);

■ The performance requirements summary;

■ Sampling guides for each task to be sampled; and

■ Deduction and incentive formulas, as appropriate.

The PWS and QASP should be prepared together and should be read together during surveillance. The goal of those documents is to clearly state what the buyer's requirements are and how the buyer will determine acceptable and unacceptable performance.

Properly written, the QASP can be an excellent communications tool. In fact, it is essential to discuss the QASP with the seller so that all surveillance methods are understood. In PBC, the buyer may decide to request that the seller prepare and submit a QASP for the buyer's approval. In PBC, the seller is responsible for the quality of all products, services, and solutions; the buyer is responsible for performance assessment.

Third Critical Component: Performance-Based Measurements and Metrics

Table 7.2 (this page) contains performance-based measurements and metrics best practices:

Table 7.2 Performance-based Measurements & Metrics Best Practices
❑ Review the success determinants.
❑ Rely on commercial quality standards.
❑ Have the seller propose the metrics and the QASP.
❑ Select only a few meaningful measures on which to judge success.
❑ Include contractual language for negotiated changes to the metrics and measures.
❑ Most important, consider the relationship.[4]

Table 7.3 (See p. 139) lists many of the key performance areas and related metrics commonly used on complex contracts, in buying and selling products, in services, or in integrated business solutions in the private sector. No one performance area or metric is more important than the others. In fact, most buying organizations are developing a balanced scorecard, as discussed in Chapter 8. That scorecard is composed of numerous metrics that are designed to evaluate their

performance and the performance of their suppliers. Each organization should decide which performance areas and related metrics are most appropriate for their respective business and related contracts.

Table 7.3 Checklist for Buyers and Sellers	
Key Performance Areas	**Key Performance Metrics**
Financial	❑ Return on investment
	❑ On-budget (planned expenses vs. actual expenses)
	❑ Cost reduction (current costs vs. future costs)
	• Implementation costs
	• Operations costs
	• Maintenance costs
	• Support costs
	❑ Return on assets
	❑ Net present value
	❑ Cost performance index
	❑ Revenue generated (annual and quarterly)
	❑ Days of sales outstanding
	❑ Revenue or expense to headcount
	❑ Inventory turns
Schedule	❑ Number of milestones on-time
	❑ On-time delivery % (mutually agreed-to date)
	❑ Number of days cycle-time (order to delivery)
	❑ Earned value method
	❑ Schedule performance index
Technical	❑ Capacity volume
	❑ Operating time and usage
	❑ Capabilities and features
	❑ Speed
	❑ Number of product failures and outages
Quality	❑ Mean-time-between failure
	❑ Mean-time-to-repair
	❑ Number of complaints
	❑ Number of defects

Fourth Critical Component: Contractual Incentives

The direct relationship between the PWS and the QASP and the care with which the PBC is developed create a vastly improved understanding between the buyer and the seller. The contractual incentives selected by the buyer should seek to accomplish this same goal. Incentives can emphasize areas where superior performance is desired and where inadequate performance is particularly undesirable. Consequently, incentives may be positive, negative, or both. Deductions represent the value of tasks not performed satisfactorily.

The mutual understanding of negative and positive performance incentives is established in the solicitation and may be discussed during source selection. Incentives reflect reasonable value to the buyer; however, those incentives should not be provided to attain the specified minimum requirements of the contract. To be innovative and to perform in a highly satisfactory manner, incentives must be built into the entire PBC process. Discussion with the seller to change values for deductions should be conducted with careful analysis so that incentives are effective for their intended purpose. A more detailed discussion of contractual incentives is provided later in this chapter as part of the discussion of the various pricing arrangements used to form a PBC.

Fifth Critical Component: The Right Pricing Arrangement

The pricing arrangement or contract type will significantly affect the PBC process. When deciding which type of contract to use, the buyer should ask the following:

1. Can the buyer properly describe the requirements in a performance-based statement of work?

2. Can sellers accurately estimate the cost to perform the contract with the information provided in the solicitation?

Procurement planning is necessary to ensure that sufficient workload data are available to accurately describe tasks in the PWS. If the contract is replacing a previous contract for the same product or services, this task is easier. If there are adequate data to develop an effective PWS, a QASP, and the appropriate performance metrics, then in most cases a fixed-price contract should be selected. However, many factors must be considered when selecting the right pricing arrangement to ensure that the seller is properly motivated to achieve mission success.

Both buyers and sellers must be aware of the many types of contract pricing arrangements available so they can choose the right type for each situation. Over time, three general pricing arrangements categories have evolved: fixed-price, cost-reimbursement (CR), and time-and-materials. Those categories and the contract types within each category are described in more detail in chapter 9, along with information on determining contract price and using pricing arrangements to balance the risk between contracting parties. In today's complex business world, a solid understanding of contract pricing options is essential for meeting business objectives.

Assessment of Requirements to Determine Costs

Contract cost is determined by the contract requirements, which fall into two main categories: technical and administrative.

Technical Requirements

The solicitation PWS should contain technical requirements. The PWS describes what the buyer wants to buy—in terms of desired performance results or outputs that must be rendered by the seller. The seller must consume resources—labor, capital, and money—to provide products and services to the buyer.

Administrative Requirements

Contract clauses describe other terms and conditions that will require the seller to consume resources, although the terms and conditions relate only indirectly to the technical requirements. The following clause excerpt provides such an example:

> Company-Furnished Property
> ... orders from ABC Company shall be held at the Seller's risk and shall be kept insured by the Seller at the Seller's expense while in Seller's custody and control in an amount equal to the replacement cost thereof, with loss payable to ABC Company.

The insurance requirement will cost money, but the insurance is only indirectly related to the technical requirements of the project. Contracts contain many such administrative requirements.

Pricing Contracts

Contract pricing begins with determining the cost of performing the contract. To determine contract cost, a business professional who manages contracts must thoroughly analyze a prospective buyer's solicitation and must develop a work breakdown structure that is based on the technical and administrative performance requirements. Next, that professional decides how the work will be implemented—that is, the order in which it will be performed and the methods and procedures that will be used to accomplish it. Using those plans, the business professional estimates performance costs so that a price can be proposed. After the company has agreed on a contract price, it will be obligated to complete the work at that price unless a different arrangement can be negotiated.

To estimate performance costs, you must answer the following four questions: What resources (labor, capital, money) will be needed to do the work? In what quantities will they be needed? When will they be needed? How much will those resources cost in the marketplace?

Estimating techniques will not necessarily require developing detailed answers to those questions. Parametric estimates, for instance, are used at a very high level and do not involve the type of analysis implied by the four questions. Nevertheless, some level of response to those questions is implicit in every cost estimate.

Uncertainty and Risk in Contract Pricing

The business professional's cost estimate will be a judgment, that is, a prediction about the future, rather than a fact. When the project manager says, "I estimate that the contract will cost US$500,000 to complete," that statement really means, "I predict that when I have completed the project according to the specifications, statement of work, and other contract terms and conditions, I will have consumed US$500,000 worth of labor, capital, and money."

The problem with such a prediction, as with all predictions, is that no one will know whether it is true until all the events have occurred. Predictions are based largely on history; they assume that cause-and-effect relationships in the future will be similar to those in the past. However, people frequently have an incorrect or incomplete understanding of the past. In addition, they may carry out even the best-laid plans imperfectly because of error or unexpected events. All those factors can cause the future to materialize different from the way it was predicted.

Thus, the business professional's estimate may be incorrect. If it is too high, the company's proposal may not be competitive. If it is too low, the contract price may not be high enough to cover the project costs, and the company will suffer a financial loss.

However sound the cost estimate, the contract *price* must be negotiated. Every negotiated price is a compromise between the extremes of an optimistic and a pessimistic prediction about future costs. The range between those two extremes is called the *range of possible costs*. The compromise results from negotiation between a risk-avoiding buyer and a risk-avoiding seller.

The risk-avoiding buyer wants to minimize the risk of agreeing to a price that is higher than necessary to cover the seller's costs plus a reasonable profit. Thus, the buyer tends to push the price toward the more optimistic end of the range of possible costs. The risk-avoiding seller wants to avoid the risk of agreeing to a price that may not cover its actual performance costs or allow a reasonable profit. Thus, the seller tends to push the price toward the more pessimistic end of the range of possible costs.

The consequence of uncertainty about the future is either risk or the possibility of injury. A seller who undertakes a contractual obligation to complete a project for a fixed price but who has estimated too low will suffer financial loss, unless the seller can shift the excess costs to the buyer or can avoid them altogether. The effort made to avoid the injury will be proportional to its magnitude and related to its cause and direction.

Classification of Contract Incentives

The fundamental purpose of contract incentives is to motivate desired performance in one or more specific areas. Contract incentives are generally classified as either objectively based and evaluated or subjectively based and evaluated. Further, both classifications of contract incentives are typically categorized as positive incentives (rewards—get more money) or as negative incentives (penalties—get less money) or as some combination thereof.

Those incentives that use predetermined formula-based methods to calculate the amount of incentive, either positive or negative, in one or more designated areas are objectively based and evaluated. Facts and actual events are used as a basis for determination; individual judgment and opinions are not considered in an evaluation of performance.

Objectively based and evaluated contract incentives commonly include the following designated performance areas:

- Cost performance,

- Schedule or delivery performance, and

■ Quality performance.

Subjectively based and evaluated contract incentives are those incentives that use individual judgment, opinions, and informed impressions as the basis for determining the amount of incentive, either positive or negative, in one or more designated areas. Those incentives can and often do contain some objective aspects or factors. However, subjective contract incentives are ultimately determined by one or more individuals who make a decision according to their experience, their knowledge, and the available information—a total judgment.

Subjectively-based and evaluated contract incentives typically include the following:

■ Award fees,

■ Award term, and

■ Other special incentives
  • Value engineering changes
  • Share-in-savings.

Objective Incentives

Figure 7.1 (See p. 145) summarizes the link between the rewards and penalties and the contract incentives that are described in the paragraphs within this section.

Incentives That Are Based on Cost Performance

Cost is the most commonly chosen performance variable. For fixed-price cost incentive contracts, the parties negotiate a *target cost* and a *target profit* (which equals the target price), plus a *sharing formula* for cost overruns and cost underruns. The parties also negotiate a *ceiling price*, which is the buyer's maximum dollar liability. When performance is complete, the parties determine the final actual costs and apply the sharing formula to any overrun or underrun. Application of the sharing formula determines the seller's final profit, if any.

Consider an example in which the parties agree to the following arrangement:

Target cost: US$10 million

Figure 7.1 Contract Incentives			
Types of Incentives	**Postive (rewards)**	**No Reward or Penalty**	**Negative (penalties)**
Objective Incentives			
Cost Performance	Under Budget ◄───►	On Budget	Over Budget ◄───►
Schedule or Delivery Performance	Early Delivery ◄───►	On-Time Delivery	Late Delivery ◄───►
Quality Performance	Exceed Requirements ◄───►	Achieve Contract Requirements	Do Not Achieve Requirements ◄───►
Subjective Incentives			
Award Fee Award Terms Other Special Incentives	Exceed Requirements ◄───►	Achieve Award Fee Award Term Plan	Do Not Achieve Requirements ◄───►

Target profit: US$850,000

Target price: US$10.85 million

Sharing formula: 70/30 (buyer 70 percent, seller 30 percent)

Ceiling price: US$11.5 million

Assume that the seller completes the work at an actual cost of US$10,050,000, overrunning the target cost by US$50,000. The seller's share of the overrun is 30 percent of US$50,000, which is US$15,000. The target profit will be reduced by that amount (US$850,000 – 15,000 = US$835,000). The seller will then receive the US$10,050,000 cost of performance plus an earned profit of US$835,000. Thus, the price to the buyer will be US$10,885,000, which is US$615,000 below the ceiling price. The US$35,000 increase over the target price of US$10,850,000 represents the buyer's 70-percent share of the cost overrun.

Had the seller overrun the target cost by US$100,000, thereby raising the actual cost to US$10.1 million, then the seller's share of the overrun would have been 30 percent, or US$30,000. That amount would have reduced the seller's profit to US$820,000.

Basically, at some point before reaching the ceiling price, the sharing arrangement effectively changes to 0/100, with the seller assuming 100 percent of the cost risk. This effect is implicit in fixed-price incentive arrangements because of the ceiling price and is not an explicit element of the formula. The point at which sharing changes to 0/100 is called the *point of total assumption (PTA)*, which represents a cost figure. Indeed, the PTA is often appropriately referred to as the high-cost estimate.

Figure 7.2 (See p. 147) depicts the relationships and outcomes in graphical form. (Note that the graph describes a first-degree linear equation of the form $Y = A - BX$, with cost as the independent variable X, and profit as the dependent variable Y. B, the coefficient of X, is equal to the seller's share.)

$$PTA = \left[\frac{\text{Ceiling price} - \text{Target price}}{\text{Buyer Share Ratio}} \right] + \text{Target Cost}$$

The PTA can be determined by applying the following formula:

In the event of an underrun, the seller would enjoy greater profit. If the final cost is US$9 million (a US$1 million underrun), the seller's share of the underrun is 30 percent, which is US$300,000. Thus, the price to the buyer would include the US$9 million cost and the US$850,000 target profit, plus the seller's US$300,000 underrun share (total profit of US$1,150,000). Thus, US$9 million actual cost plus US$1,150,000 actual profit equals- US$10,150,000 actual price, reflecting precisely the buyer's 70-percent share of the US$1 million underrun [US$10,850,000 target price – 70 percent of the US$1 million underrun (US$700,000) = US$10,150,000]. [AQ: Note that I changed some of the dollar figures to "million" instead of "000,000" per Chicago style.]

Incentives That Are Based on Schedule or Delivery Performance

For many years, construction, aerospace, and numerous service industries have used schedule or delivery performance incentives to motivate sellers to provide either early or on-time delivery of products and services.

The term *liquidated damages* represents a negative incentive designed to mitigate the consequences for poor performance (i.e., for late delivery). Typically, a liquidated damages clause stated in the contract terms and conditions designates how much money one party (usually the seller) must pay the other party (usually the buyer) for not meeting the contract schedule. Often the amount of liquidated damages payable is specified as an amount of money for a specific

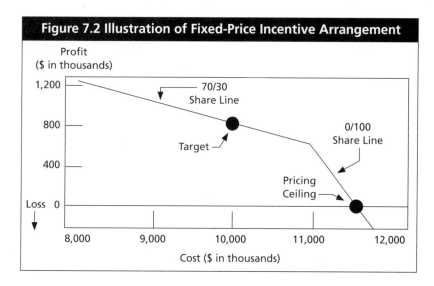

Figure 7.2 Illustration of Fixed-Price Incentive Arrangement

Profit
($ in thousands)

70/30 Share Line

0/100 Share Line

Target

Pricing Ceiling

Loss 0

8,000   9,000   10,000   11,000   12,000

Cost ($ in thousands)

period of time (day, week, month). A key aspect of liquidated damages is that the amount of damages is to be based on the amount of damages incurred or compensable in nature, not on an excessive or punitive amount.

A proven best practice for buyers is to require negative incentives for late delivery and late schedule performance. Likewise, a proven best practice for sellers is to limit their liability on liquidated damages by agreeing to a cap or maximum amount and by seeking positive incentives (or rewards) for early delivery and early schedule performance.

Incentives That Are Based on Quality Performance

The term quality performance incentives represents one of the most common topics in government and commercial contracting. Surveys in both government and industry have revealed widespread service contracting problems, including deficient statements of work, poor contract administration, performance delays, and quality shortcomings.

When a contract is based on performance, all aspects of the contract are structured around the purpose of the work to be performed rather than around the manner in which it is to be done. The buyer seeks to elicit the best performance that the seller has to offer—at a reasonable price or cost—by stating its objectives and by giving sellers both latitude in determining how to achieve them and incentives for achieving them. In source selection, for example, the buyer might publish a draft solicitation for comment, might use quality-related evaluation factors, or both. The statement of work will provide performance standards rather than spelling out what the seller is to do.

The contract normally contains a plan for quality assurance surveillance. And the contract typically includes positive and negative performance incentives.

Few people disagree with the concept that buyers, who collectively spend billions of dollars on services annually, should look to the performance-based approach and should focus more on results and less on detailed requirements. However, implementing performance-based contracting (using cost, schedule, or quality performance variables) is far easier said than done. The sound use of performance incentives is key to the success of the performance-based contracting approach.

Problems with Applying Objective Incentives

The schemes for objective incentives that are described do have some merit, but they also involve some serious practical problems. First, they assume a level of buyer and seller competence that may not exist. Second, they assume effects that may not occur. Third, they create serious challenges for contract administration.

To negotiate objective incentives intelligently, the parties must have some knowledge of the range of possible costs for a project. They also must have some knowledge of the likely causes and probabilities of different cost outcomes. If both parties do not have sufficient information on those issues, then they will not be able to structure an effective incentive formula.

It is important that the parties share their information. If one party has superior knowledge and does not share that knowledge with the other, that first party will be able to skew the formula in its favor during negotiation. If that skewing happens, the whole point of the arrangement, which is to equitably balance the risks of performance, will be lost. The result will be that the buyer is usually at a disadvantage with respect to the seller.

An objective incentive assumes that the seller can effect a performance outcome along the entire range of the independent variable. However, such may not be true. For instance, the seller may actually exercise control along only a short sector of the range of possible costs. Some possible cost outcomes may be entirely outside the seller's control because of factors such as market performance. In reality, the seller's project manager may have little control over important factors, such as overhead costs, that may determine the cost outcome. In addition, short-term companywide factors, especially those involving overhead, may, on some contracts, make incurring additional cost rather than earning additional profit more advantageous for the seller.

In addition, objective cost incentives are complicated and costly to administer, with all the cost definition, measurement, allocation, and confirmation problems of CR contracts. The parties must be particularly careful to segregate the target cost effects of cost growth from those of cost overruns; otherwise, the parties may lose money for the wrong reasons. As a practical matter, segregating such costs is often quite difficult.

When using other performance incentives, the parties may find themselves disputing the causes of various performance outcomes. The seller may argue that schedule delays are a result of actions of the buyer. Quality problems, such as poor reliability, may have been caused by improper buyer operation rather than by seller performance. The causes of performance failures may be difficult to determine.

One reason for using such contracts is to reduce the deleterious effects of risk on the behavior of the parties. Thus, if a pricing arrangement increases the likelihood of trouble, it should not be used. The decision to apply objective incentives should be made only after careful analysis.

Best Practices: 15 Actions to Improve Your Use of Contract Incentives

The following best practices should be followed when using incentives:

- Think creatively. Creativity is a critical aspect in the success of performance-based incentive contracting.

- Avoid rewarding sellers for simply meeting contract requirements.

- Recognize that developing clear, concise, objectively measurable performance incentives will be a challenge. Plan appropriately.

- Create a proper balance of incentives—cost, schedule, and quality performance.

- Ensure that performance incentives focus the seller's efforts on the buyer's desired objectives.

- Make all forms of performance incentives challenging yet attainable.

- Ensure that incentives motivate quality control and that the results of the seller's quality control efforts can be measured.

■ Consider tying on-time delivery to costs or to quality performance criteria.

■ Recognize that not everything can be measured objectively. Consider using a combination of objectively measured standards and subjectively determined incentives.

■ Encourage open communication and ongoing involvement with potential sellers in developing the PWS or SOO and the incentive plan—both before and after issuing the formal request for proposals.

■ Consider including socioeconomic incentives (non-statement-of-work related) in the incentive plan.

■ Use clear, objective formulas for determining performance incentives.

■ Use a combination of positive and negative incentives.

■ Include incentives for discounts that are based on early payments.

■ Ensure that all incentives, both positive and negative, have limits.

Subjective Incentives
Award-Fee Plans
In an award-fee plan, the parties negotiate an estimated cost, just as for cost-plus-fixed-fee contracts. Then the parties negotiate an agreement on the amount of money to be included in an *award-fee pool.* Finally, they agree on a set of criteria and procedures to be applied by the buyer in determining how well the seller has performed and how much fee the seller has earned. In some cases, the parties also negotiate a *base fee,* which is a fixed fee that the seller will earn, no matter how its performance is evaluated.

The contract performance period is then divided into equal *award-fee periods.* A part of the award-fee pool is allocated to each period proportionate to the percentage of the work that is scheduled to be completed. All this information is included in the award-fee plan, which becomes part of the contract. In some cases, the contract allows the buyer to change the award fee plan unilaterally before the start of a new award-fee period.

During each award-fee period, the buyer observes and documents the seller's performance achievements or failures. At the end of each period, the buyer evaluates the seller's performance according to the award-fee plan and then decides how much fee to award from the portion allocated to that period. Under some contracts, the seller has an opportunity to present its own evaluation of its performance along with a specific request for award fee. The buyer then informs the seller how much of the available award fee it has earned and how its performance could be improved during ensuing award-fee periods. This arrangement invariably involves subjectivity on the part of the buyer; precisely how much subjectivity will depend on how the award-fee plan is written.

Pros and Cons of the Award-Fee Arrangement

The cost-plus-award-fee (CPAF) contract is a cost-reimbursement contract with all its requirements for cost definition, measurement, allocation, and confirmation. For the buyer, the CPAF contract requires the additional administrative investment associated with observing, documenting, and evaluating seller performance. However, this disadvantage may sometimes be overemphasized, because the buyer should already be performing many of those activities under a CR contract.

The disadvantages for the buyer are offset by the extraordinary power that the buyer obtains from the ability to make subjective determinations about how much fee the seller has earned. The buyer may have difficulty establishing objective criteria for satisfactory service performance.

The power of subjective fee determination tends to make sellers extraordinarily responsive to the buyer's demands. However, the buyer must be careful, because that very responsiveness can be the cause of cost overruns and unintended cost growth.

The buyer's advantages are almost entirely disadvantages from the viewpoint of the seller, because the seller will have placed itself within the power of the buyer to an exceptional degree. Subjectivity can approach arbitrariness or even cross the line. The seller may find itself dealing with a buyer that is impossible to please or that believes that the seller cannot earn all the award fee because no one can achieve "perfect" performance.

Consideration of "Award Term"

"Award term" is a contract performance incentive feature that ties the length of a contract's term to the performance of the seller. The contract can be extended for "good" performance or reduced for "poor" performance.

Award term is a contracting tool used to promote efficient and quality seller performance. In itself, it is not an acquisition strategy, nor is it a performance solution. As with any tool, its use requires careful planning, implementation, and management or measurement to ensure its success in incentivizing sellers and in improving performance.

The award-term feature is similar to award-fee contracting where contract performance goals, plans, assessments, and awards are made regularly during the life of a contract. Award-term solicitations and contracts should include base period (e.g., 3 years) and a maximum term (e.g., 10 years), which is similar to quantity estimates that are used in indefinite quantity and indefinite delivery contracts for supplies.

When applying the award-term feature, buyers need to identify and understand the project or task:

■ Conditions, constraints, assumptions, and complexities;

■ Schedule, performance, and cost critical success factors; and

■ Schedule, performance, and cost risks.

Buyers also need to understand marketplace conditions and pricing realities. Only then can buyers establish meaningful and appropriate schedule, performance, and cost measures or parameters for a specific contract. Those measures must be meaningful, accurate, and quantifiable to provide the right incentives and contract performance results. Specifics need to be incorporated and integrated in an award-term plan.[5]

Award term is best applied when using performance or solution-based requirements where a SOW or SOO describes the buyer's required outcomes or results (the "what" and "when" of the buyer's requirement) and where the seller has the freedom to apply its own management and best performance practices (the "how" of the requirement) toward performing the contract. The award-term plan must specify success measurement criteria, regarding how performance will be measured (i.e., defines what is "good" or "poor" performance) and how the award-term decision will be made.

There should also be a clear indication of the consequences of various levels of performance in terms of the contract's minimum, estimated, and maximum terms—and the buyer needs to be prepared to follow up with those consequences. If seller performance is below the standard set, the contract ends at the completion of the base period.[6]

Other Special Incentives

There is a growing recognition by buyers and sellers worldwide, in both the public and private sectors, that contract incentives can be expanded and that they are indeed valuable tools to motivate the desired performance. Increasingly, when outsourcing, buyers are motivating sellers to subcontract with local companies, often with special rewards for subcontracting with designated small businesses.

Likewise, many sellers are providing buyers with special incentives for early payment, such as product or services discounts or even additional specified services at no charge. See **Table 7.4** (this page) for a checklist of things to remember about successful performance-based contracts.

Table 7.4 Checklist of Key Best Practices in Performance-Based Contracting to Improve Business Results
Buyers and sellers should do the following:
❑ Work together to develop an appropriate performance work statement (PWS) or statement of objectives (SOO).
❑ Think creatively.
❑ Jointly develop an appropriate quality assurance surveillance plan (QASP).
❑ Jointly develop appropriate performance-based measures, metrics, and incentives.
❑ Make incentives challenging yet attainable.
❑ Negotiate a fair and reasonable pricing arrangement to achieve high performance results.
❑ Identify constraints.
❑ Develop a surveillance schedule.
❑ Review and agree on success determinants.
❑ Select only a few meaningful measures on which to judge success.

Summary

In this chapter, we have discussed the five critical components to forming and documenting a performance-based contract (PBC). In addition, the U.S. federal government has developed a detailed guide specifically for acquiring professional services using PBCs, called "The Seven Steps to Performance-Based Services Acquisition." For a full version, go to **www.acqnet.gov/library/OFPP/BestPractices/pbsc**. Plus, we have included a copy of the "Seven Steps to Performance-

Based Services Acquisition—Executive Summary" (see Appendix A, on p. 273).

In the next chapter, we will discuss the need for developing and successfully using performance-based scorecards, both internally and externally, to help organizations improve their performance results.

Questions to Consider

1. How well does your organization understand, agree to, and document your customer's requirements?

2. How effectively does your organization translate customer requirements into performance-based contracts?

3. Which performance-based metrics does your organization typically use in your business to evaluate or measure performance?

4. Which pricing arrangements and contractual incentives does your organization use most frequently on your contracts to buy or sell products and services?

Endnotes

1. Seven Steps to Performance-Based Acquisition—Executive Summary; this material in Appendix A.

2. Gerard Jones, Michael Mickaliger, and Joseph Witzgtall, "Performance Sunrise: Blending Contract Management with Project Management," *Contract Management*, (April 2004): 20

3. Ibid.

4. Ibid., Note 1.

5. Ibid.

6. Ibid.

CHAPTER 08

Performance and Balanced Scorecards: Best Practices and Case Studies

Introduction

Performance-based acquisition (PBA) is all about getting results—through innovation, collaboration, improved communications, and enhanced teamwork. Performance-oriented or balanced scorecards are important tools to help organizations stay focused on what is most important to achieve high performance results.

Nearly everyone has at some time been evaluated by a teacher or supervisor using a report card or scorecard to assess that person's performance. During the past decade, organizations in both the public and private sectors have become increasingly performance oriented. Thus, more and more organizations have created report cards or performance scorecards. Some organizations create report cards to assess their performance, and they design other report cards to evaluate the performance of their sellers, subcontractors, or both.

The most common term used today is the balanced scorecard (BSC). In this chapter, we will examine the following:

■ What is the BSC?

■ How does one create a BSC program?

■ What are some pros and cons of the BSC approach to improve performance?

- What are a few of the best practices and case studies from organizations that have successfully applied balanced scorecards and other performance scorecards?

- What are some guidelines for a successful subcontractor performance-based program?

What Is the Balanced Scorecard?

The BSC is a method that translates strategic themes into actionable and measurable objectives that are ready for execution at all levels of an organization.[1]

More than 50 percent of the Fortune 1,000 and 40 percent of companies in Europe use a form of the BSC, according to Bain & Co.[2] The BSC helps organizations build a bridge between several other dichotomous elements of strategy. Increasingly, organizations are realizing the importance of creating a balanced approach to their diverse strategic objectives and their overall higher levels of performance.

Michael Tracy and Fred Wiersema, authors of the best-selling book titled *Discipline of Market Leaders*, list three strategic objectives or thrusts to market leaders:[3]

1. Operational excellence,

2. Product leadership, and

3. Customer intimacy.

The BSC serves the needs of many worldwide organizations that are in need of making strategy actionable. The BSC ensures that performance areas, related metrics, and strategic themes are balanced with financial and nonfinancial (customer satisfaction, quality, on-time-delivery, etc.) leading and lagging indicators.[4]

A properly developed BSC has the following characteristics:[5]

- Its methodology is suited for managing business strategy.

- It uses a common language at all levels of the organization.

- It uses a common set of principles to manage day-to-day operations, as well as to framework the organization's strategy.

- It is designed to identify and manage business purposes.

■ It provides a balance between relatively opposing forces in strategy.

■ It aligns strategic goals with objectives, targets, and metrics.

■ It cascades to all levels of the organization.

How Does One Create a BSC Program?

In their book titled *Balanced Scorecard*, Professors Robert Kaplan and David Norton declared that strategy is a set of hypotheses about cause and effect. Kaplan and Norton also declared four perspectives that can guide organizations as they translate strategy into actionable terms.[6]

1. Financial perspective

   ■ What are the financial targets?

   ■ What drives those targets?

   ■ What kind of profit and revenue will you achieve?

   ■ In a nonprofit organization, what budget guides you?

2. Customer perspective

   ■ Who are the customers?

   ■ How do you delight them?

   ■ What segments do you wish to address?

   ■ What goals do you wish to achieve with partners?

   ■ What are your goals for the distribution channels?

3. Internal perspective

   ■ Which processes must we be the best at to win customers?

   ■ What internal activities do we need to sustain competencies?

4. Learning and growth perspective

■ What must we be great in performing?

■ How do we train our people to improve their performance?

■ What climate and culture will nurture growth?

■ In developing our people, what do we have to do to achieve organization objectives?

Simply stated, a BSC program should integrate an organization's vision, mission, values, and goals to its strategies, performance areas, and metrics,—for each individual and team within an organization. **Figure 8.1** (this page) illustrates how the various components of the BSC should be linked or mapped.

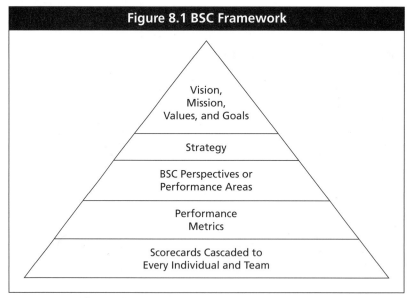

Source: Adapted from Mohan Nair, *Essentials of Balanced Scorecard* (New York: John Wiley & Sons, 2004).

What Are Some Pros and Cons of the BSC Approach to Improve Performance?

There are numerous advantages or pros of using the BSC approach to improve performance, including the following:

■ It facilitates communication.

■ It helps the organization gain greater self-knowledge.

■ It focuses the organizational leadership on what's most important.

■ It provides a common communications tool to inform everyone in the organization of the vision, mission, values, goals, strategies, key performance areas, metrics, and performance targets to achieve success.

■ It provides a roadmap whereby every individual or team can map its respective performance responsibilities to the organization's BSC program.

■ It helps translate strategy into action at every level of an organization.

Likewise, there are several disadvantages or cons when developing and implementing the BSC approach, including the following:

■ It can include contested performance metrics.

■ It can have contested performance measurements.

■ It can demonstrate resistance to change.

■ It can seek a quick and easy solution.

■ It can enlarge the extent of time required to inform, educate, and train people in the proper use of the BSC program.

■ It can involve getting caught-up in the process and losing sight on what is most important.

■ It may assume that people really get it.

■ It can underestimate the total cost of implementing the BSC program, especially if one or more software applications are deployed to facilitate the BSC program.

What Are a Few of the Best Practices and Case Studies from Organizations That Have Successfully Applied Balanced Scorecards and Other Performance Scorecards?

Table 8.1 (See p. 160) provides a summary of a few of the many proven-effective best practices for creating performance and bal-

Table 8.1 Checklist of Best Practices for Creating Performance and Balanced Scorecards

❑ Identify the organization's

- Vision

- Mission

- Values

- Goals or objectives

❑ Choose three to five organizational goals or objectives.

❑ Clarify strategies to achieve goals.

❑ Divide or break down strategies into performance areas and metrics.

❑ Develop a map or weave a golden thread among the key actions, performance areas and metrics, and strategy.

❑ Select performance metrics for each performance area to achieve organizational goals or objectives.

❑ Choose three to five performance areas and related metrics.

❑ Communicate all aspects of the performance and balanced scorecard to all organizational team members.

❑ Tie each individual's performance plan to the performance and balanced scorecards.

anced scorecards.

The following are a few of the many well-documented case studies from organizations that have developed performance and balanced scorecards—either to internally evaluate their own organizational performance or to externally evaluate the performance of their sellers or subcontractors.

Case Study: Starbucks Corporation Balanced Scorecard Approach

Starbucks Corporation is hiring 200 employees per day and building four stores per day.[7] This phenomenal growth could not have been achieved without the key ingredient of people. Employees at Starbucks strive to make their products—primarily, gourmet coffee—taste identical anywhere that customers visit.

People come to Starbucks for the experience as much as for the coffee. Although Starbucks has based its strategy on the learning and growth of the team, it has not forgotten that it must balance all other perspectives if it is to gain market share. Starbucks has recognized the value of learning and growth as a strategic theme and has created a unique recipe of activities that has linked to a unique relationship with their people (employees). Those people are linked to a special relationship to the customers.[8]

Case Study: Honda Supplier Report Cards

Honda uses a report card to monitor its core subcontractors. Unlike most Fortune 500 companies, which send report cards to suppliers once or twice a year, Honda sends report cards to its suppliers' senior executives every month. A typical report card has six sections:

1. Quality

2. Delivery

3. Quantity

4. Performance

5. Incidents

6. Comments

Honda expects its key subcontractors to meet all of their performance metrics. Honda holds subcontractors accountable if they fall short. If the subcontractor cannot quickly resolve any performance failures, then Honda sends in a team to help the subcontractor resolve the problem to achieve desired performance.[9]

Table 8.2 (See p. 162), which is a subcontractor evaluation form, provides a simple, but effective, means of evaluating important aspects of a potential subcontractor's capabilities.

What Are Some Guidelines for a Successful Subcontractor Performance-Based Program?

According to Sharon Horton, in her September 2004 article, it is essential for the relationship between the buyer and seller that the scorecard not be "sprung" on the seller. Buyers should actually develop the scorecard with the input of the seller or subcontractor, thus building commitment to both the process and the ratings. During the development period, the buyer and seller will need to determine an appropriate frequency of usage—monthly, quarterly, yearly—and to have procedures for the role of the scorecard in the overall rela-

	Low ◄——► High					Not Req uired	Description
Level	**1**	**2**	**3**	**4**	**5**		**Description**
Access to Equipment							Owns or can acquire required equipment for the job
Condition of Equipment							Has equipment in good repair; has maintenance ability
Adequate Insurance							Has adequate insurance, is bonded, etc.
Access to Staffing							Has ability to staff and manage require workforce
Dependability and Reputation							Knows prior work record of contractor
Flexibility							Shows adaptability to work methods
Job Knowledge							Has knowledge of required work processes
Job Knowledge (Ability to Learn)							Has capacity to learn new work processes
Earlier Job Experience							Gained prior experience with similar jobs and technology
Quality Process							Displays documented question and answer (Q/A) process
Quality Performance							Documents existence of results of Q/A inspections
Safety Performance							Uses safety processes or equipment and shares reports (if available)
Local Country National							Knows that the subcontractor is based in or has a tie to the country or region of work site
Supervision Experience							Has experience as work supervisor
Timeliness of Billing Reports							Has a process for billing; needs close supervision by project manager
Willingness to Compromise							Has adaptability to work with
Delivery Performance							Has ability to deliver on-time

Table 8.2 Subcontractor Evaluation Form

Note: Rate the subcontractor on each of the above characteristics from 1 (least desirable) to 5 (most desirable). If a particular characteristic does not apply, mark the "Not Req." box (for Not Required) instead. Use the ratings to compare subcontractors.

tionship in the management program.

Table 8.3 (this page) illustrates a complete sample scorecard—after the performance actuals are entered. It is usually desirable to have multiple people rate sellers or subcontractors so you can get a broader view of performance. In such a case, scorecards are sent to all the internal reviewers, who will each complete an individual scorecard. Upon their return, the scorecards are consolidated across all reviewers by summing and averaging.[10]

Although the raw total is sometimes used, it is also frequent to assign a letter "grade" to sellers or subcontractors after a total score is calculated. This scale is common:

A = 90–100
B = 80–89
C = 70–79
D = 60–69
F = <59

After the rating is put on the scorecard, the results should be

Table 8.3 Sample Scorecard						
Performance Indicator Description	Target	Weight	Actual	Rating	Score	Comments
On-Time Deliveries	95% 90% 85% 80% <75%	20%	92%			
Price	Lowest	10%				
Product Availability	99.9% 99.6% 99.4% 99.1% <99.0%	10%	99.7%			
Customer Support		20%				
Meets All Service Levels	95% 92% 90% 85% 75%	20%	86%			
Overall Customer Satisfaction		20%				
		100%				

reviewed with the seller or subcontractor. This discussion keeps the seller or subcontractor informed on its performance, allows for midreview period (or midcontract) corrections, eliminates excuses, and, in many cases, provides incentives for improved performance. A comparison to last period's scorecards also identifies performance trends, such as these: How did the seller or subcontractor do in each of the performance indicators, as well as overall? Is the performance getting better or worse?

The outcome of the scorecard review with the seller or subcontractor should identify any required corrective actions, remedial programs, and continuous improvement programs. Corrective actions, which represent the first-level problem resolution processes, are used to improve the results of one or more individual poor performance scores.

Usually, the seller or subcontractor prepares a plan that will address specific actions and will implement that plan with a timetable for deliverables or results. Remedial programs are used for sellers or subcontractors whose overall results are failing. Now, more actions are needed to bring the scorecard up to a satisfactory performance level. Finally, continuous improvement programs are for satisfactorily performing sellers or subcontractors and are used to raise the standard of performance.

For the buyer, the scorecard use should go beyond grading an individual's move into comparing sellers or subcontractors both within categories and across categories. There are many opportunities to produce charts and reports identifying performance trends and poor performers. The scorecard should also feed into seller or subcontractor replacement—a nonperformer should either be eliminated entirely or not used. The buyer can repeat the RFP (request for proposal) to add new sellers or subcontractors to its category as failing companies are "let go."

The use of scorecards is critical in the relationship with a seller or subcontractor as part of the management program in the same way that report cards are used in school systems. Providing quantitative metrics for performance improves relationships and can increase incentive to perform. More important, focus is shifted onto the goals of the buyer and the end customer, rather than being misaligned or actually looking at lazy performance.

A scorecard with well-developed performance indicators works to keep the seller or subcontractor focused on the customer's goals because those goals are reflected in the ratings. If on-time deliveries and responsiveness to buyer support requests are important, they become part of the scorecard, and the sellers or subcontractors' performance with the buyer is evaluated on the basis of those goals. Other buyers may have different goals, such as low cost and low error rates. In addition, because the scorecard identifies problem areas, the seller or subcontractor will now focus on areas for improvement and innovation.[11]

Performance Measurement Case Studies: On the Web

The right information can make it easier to understand the concepts behind performance measurement and to initiate it into your organization. The following are three Web sites that will help you become better informed about performance measurement and about the use of balanced scorecards specifically in government organizations. You will find case studies, contact information, and discussion groups that will help you implement a performance measurement and a reporting system in your organization.

Performance Measurement for Government

This site **http://accounting.rutgers.edu/raw/seagov/pmg/main.html**, gives a comprehensive look at performance measurement and reporting within a government institution. Part of the Rutgers site, this section is run by the Governmental Accounting Standards Board and includes case studies, discussion forums, and research by the Standards Board on performance measurement. Probably one of the most useful sections for some people is the "Citizen's Guide," which looks at performance measurement without all of the jargon, thereby explaining the basics for those new to the concept. This Web address is a one-stop destination for anyone looking for information on performance measurement in the government or looking for contacts in the field.

Performance Measure Management

This site **www.sao.state.tx.us/Resources/Manuals/prfmguide.html**, is managed by the Texas State Auditor's Office and is based on the knowledge that office has gained by implementing a successful performance measurement initiative. The site offers a range of features that public sector managers who are initiating performance measurement into their organization will find useful. As well as explaining the importance of performance measurement and reporting in government, the site provides basic information on measures and explains when and how they should be changed. Additionally, the site looks at strategic planning and performance budgeting systems, at what they are, and at how performance measurement can be used within a system.

The Performance Management Association

This United Kingdom site **www.performanceportal.org**, was organized by the Performance Measurement Association, a multidisciplinary organization that is headed by a group of academics from business schools across the globe. The site offers a list of relevant links, plus performance measurement conferences and a discussion forum for performance measurement professionals. A newsletter is posted on the site, which offers updates in the field of performance measurement.[12]

See **Table 8.4** (this page) for a list of best practices about performance and balanced scorecards that will improve business results.

Table 8.4 Checklist of Key Best Practices for Performance and Balanced Scorecards to Improve Business Results

Buyers and sellers should do the following:

❑ Understand the value and importance of using a performance report card or a balanced scorecard for your organization.

❑ Develop a balanced scorecard program.

❑ Understand the four perspectives that can guide organizations as they translate strategy into improved performance results.

❑ Be able to link organizational vision, mission, values, and individual goals.

❑ Understand the pros and cons of a BSC program.

❑ Know and be able to apply the best practices for creating performance and balanced scorecards.

❑ Use performance reports cards for sellers and subcontractors to ensure higher performance results.

❑ Understand the guidelines for a successful subcontractor performance program.

Summary

As previously stated, PBA is all about improving performance results through innovation, collaboration, improved communications, and enhanced teamwork.

In this chapter, we have provided a detailed discussion of how to create and apply performance and balanced scorecards within your organization or with your sellers or subcontractors. Said simply, creating and applying a performance and balanced scorecard program is all about developing and implementing a plan to improve an organization's performance results. The BSC approach is simple and effective and has been used worldwide in both the public and private sectors to help organizations improve performance. If your organization does not have a BSC program, ask yourself why, and then work with others within your organization to create a BSC. Every buyer, seller, and subcontractor involved in PBA should have an internal balanced scorecard for their organization and should jointly develop a BSC for each of their respective sellers or subcontractors. A BSC program is all about understanding, communicating, and doing what is most important to improve performance results.

In the next chapter, we will thoroughly discuss the fourth essential element of PBA: price. While price is always an important factor, there are many factors that should be considered and effectively managed to achieve true success in complex acquisitions.

Questions to Consider

1. Does your organization have a balanced scorecard (BSC) program?

2. Does your organization apply any type of internal performance or report card program?

3. Does your organization effectively link or map organizational vision, mission, values, and goals to your individual and team objectives?

4. Does your organization apply a report card approach with your sellers or subcontractors? If so, how well are your sellers or subcontractors doing?

Endnotes

1. Mohan Nair, *Essentials of Balanced Scorecard* (New York: John Wiley & Sons, 2004).

2. Bain & Co., *Benchmarking Study: Use of Balanced Scorecards* (London: Bain & Co., 2003).

3. Michael Tracy and Fred Wiersema, *Discipline of Market Leaders* (Boston: HBS Press, 2003).

4. Ibid.

5. Ibid., Note 1.

6. Robert Kaplan and David Norton, *Balanced Scorecard* (Boston: HBS Press, 2001).

7. "Not a Johnny-Come-Latte," *USA Today*, (September 9, 2003): p. 3B.

8. Ibid.

9. Jeffrey K. Liker and Thomas Y. Choi, "Building Deep Supplier Relationships," *Harvard Business Review* (December 2004): 104–13.

10. Sharon Horton, "Successful Supplier Performance Programs," *Contract Management* (September 2004): 22.

11. Ibid.

12. Performance Management Association, Newsletter, 2004.

CHAPTER 09

Price: Strategies, Methods, Arrangements, and Analysis

Introduction

So, what is price? What constitutes a fair and reasonable price? How do you develop the right price? The answer to all three questions is: "It depends." No, I am not trying to be difficult; rather, price is a flexible item that depends on numerous factors. Price should be a derivative of your people, processes, and performance. Price should be adjusted by your business strategy, given the marketplace your organization is operating in as either a buyer or a seller.

This chapter is focused on the performance-based acquisition (PBA) essential element of price. In this chapter, we will examine the following aspects of price: (1) the two most common pricing strategies, which are lowest-price technically acceptable (LPTA) and best value; (2) the three major methods for determining price, which are cost-based pricing, value-based pricing, and activity-based pricing; and (3) the various pricing arrangements or types of contracts and how to properly analyze a price.

In PBA, price is an essential element for both buyers and sellers. Buyers care about price because they have a limited budget and want to ensure that their selected seller is sufficiently motivated to achieve excellence. Likewise, sellers care about price because they want to ensure they are able to cover their actual costs, achieve a reasonable profit, and ensure customer satisfaction. Let us first discuss how organizations develop the right price.

Two Most Common Pricing Strategies

Clearly, in both the public and the private sectors the two most common pricing strategies are the LPTA strategy and the best-value strategy.

LPTA Pricing Strategy

Simply stated, the LPTA strategy is typically used by buyers when there are multiple sellers, usually those who are providing commercially available off-the-shelf products and services. LPTA is the right pricing strategy if there is no real differentiator other than price. Said differently, if all of the products or services being considered for purchase are basically the same in terms of quality, schedule, reputation, technical capability, and technical features, then price should be the key attribute for source selection and contract award.

From a seller's perspective, LPTA is the appropriate pricing strategy in most markets when their products or services offer no real value differentiator from those of their competitors' products or services. LPTA is based on this simple strategy: the lowest price wins the deal. However, LPTA does not necessarily ensure either party of a fair and reasonable price.

In reality, sometimes all of the sellers in the marketplace have overly high prices that are based on supply and demand, and even the lowest price can still be perceived by the buyer as being too expensive. Likewise, sellers may at times feel they are being squeezed by their competitors and customers to drive their prices so low—so they can get the deal—that they are forced to lose money. Both buyers and sellers must properly evaluate the market to ensure when it is truly appropriate to use the LPTA pricing strategy. For both buyers and sellers, it is important to remember that the lowest price is not always the best deal or the right price.

Best-Value Pricing Strategy

The term best value can have several meanings, depending on one's particular perspective. The U.S. federal government defines best value as the expected outcome of an acquisition that—in the government's estimation—provides the greatest overall benefit in response to the requirement. Best value is usually associated with the source selection process. However, the concept can also be applied to other situations.

In all situations, best value is intended to serve as a tool for the buyer and seller to establish a proper balance among factors such as price, quality, technical capabilities, and past performance. Best value applies to products and services already developed, as opposed to value analysis, which examines tradeoffs during the design or production process.

Perhaps it would be more helpful to define best value in terms of what it is and what it is not. Best value is a disciplined and balanced approach, an assessment of tradeoffs between price and performance, a team effort, an evaluation of qualitative and quantitative factors, and an integrated risk assessment. Best value is not price cutting, uncompensated overtime, accounting gimmicks, specials, one-time discounts, the shifting of all price and performance risk to the supplier, or an excuse not to properly define requirements.[1]

For our purposes, best value is a determination of which offer presents the best tradeoff between price and performance, when quality is considered an integral performance factor. The best-value decision can be made using a variety of qualitative and quantitative management tools.

Best-value contracting is intrinsically tied to the process of contract negotiations for several reasons. First of all, if you are to be successful, negotiations must focus on some specific quantifiable objective. Best value offers a meaningful objective to each negotiation party. In addition, contract negotiation typically requires tradeoffs among a variety of interrelated factors. Using best-value techniques helps contract management professionals assess the effect of those tradeoffs to ensure a successful negotiation session. The techniques also help determine the range of values (e.g., cost, production, quality requirements, and lifecycle cost) where tradeoffs can be made while preserving the optimal balance between price, performance, and quality. Finally, best value establishes realistic negotiation objectives up front. For example, best-value contracting techniques can discourage the use of unrealistic initial negotiation positions by suppliers who seek to win a contract with practices such as uncompensated overtime or unrealistically low initial prices.

If you are to be successful, best-value contracting must be an integral part of the acquisition strategy planning process, which means early planning must occur. Best-value contracting also requires a team effort among various disciplines such as engineering, accounting, legal, manufacturing, and contracts so you can clearly identify all acquisition requirements and can determine the optimum tradeoffs among various factors.

Tradeoffs in Decision-Making

Tradeoffs in making a best-value decision should always consider the objectives of both the buyer and seller, which we discussed previously. Tradeoffs may have to be revisited as negotiations progress because the needs of the buyer and seller will be revealed (usually incrementally) during the course of negotiations.

The level of analysis in best-value tradeoff decision depends on the complexity of the particular procurement. Low-technology procurements usually require a simple, straightforward tradeoff approach, because price is normally the primary factor. However, high-technology procurements normally require more sophisticated tradeoff analysis tools, because price is usually secondary to technical and quality concerns.[2]

As a result of the many types of contracting situations, there is no single preferred way to determine best value. Rather, a combination of techniques should be used, preferably integrating quantitative and qualitative factors. The use of a team approach helps with rationally making the necessary tradeoffs rationally (see **Figure 9.1**, this page).

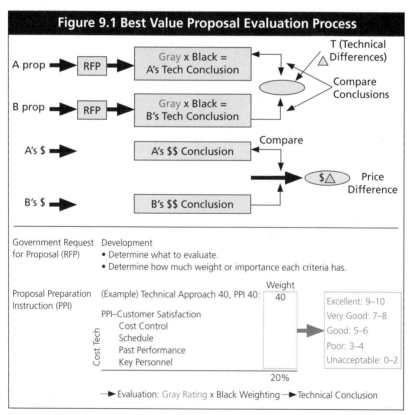

Figure 9.1 Best Value Proposal Evaluation Process

Source: Adapted from Salameri 2004.

The Evolution of Best-Value Pricing

The practice of best-value pricing has continued to grow in importance over the past decade in both the public and the private sectors. First, the federal regulatory environment has continually evolved, gradually allowing for increased best-value pricing techniques. Government contractors have responded to those changes by offering best-value pricing as a part of an overall value-based cost and technical approach. This approach has helped make governments contractors more efficient and competitive. Second, the items and services to be purchased have continued to become more technical and complex (e.g., sophisticated consulting, advanced hardware, software, and professional services). This complexity has often made quality and past performance factors more important than price-related factors. Third, the emphasis on making best-value purchasing decisions will increase as the government refines its attempts to obtain more value for its money. Finally, the continual improvement in increasing the professional qualifications and credentials of both government and industry acquisition workforce personnel has fostered the use of best value on both sides.

The commercial sector has long used best-value contracting techniques as a means to remain competitive and profitable. The federal government has not had the same degree of flexibility to use best-value techniques because it must comply with various requirements that have no material bearing on the business aspects of the contract but are mandated by law to be included in all federal acquisitions as a matter of public policy. As a result, best-value pricing implementation has not achieved its full potential in the government-contracting arena.[3] Too often, best-value pricing really becomes a modified version of LPTA, where the buyer will agree to pay just slightly more than the LPTA for higher overall value. (See **Tables 9.1**, p. 174, and **9.2**, p. 175, for checklists of best value do's and don'ts.)

Major Methods for Determining Price

There are three major methods for determining price: cost-based pricing, value-based pricing, and activity-based pricing.

Cost-Based Pricing

Cost-based pricing (CBP) is a relatively straightforward method of pricing. Using CBP, a seller must have an accurate and acceptable cost-estimating and accounting system whereby the sellers can estimate their future costs, then apply a desired margin, profit, or fee to yield a fair and reasonable price. The two most-common challenges

Table 9.1 Checklist of Best-Value "Do's"

Do:

❏ Develop or obtain proven best-value pricing tools.

❏ Select best-value measurement tools that are easy to understand and use.

❏ Ensure quality factors do not become secondary to cost issues, except for noncomplex acquisitions.

❏ Consider using automation tools for best-value decision making.

❏ Tailor best-value measurement tools to specific procurement situations, realizing that complexity increases with the size and scope of the acquisition.

❏ Use a contract type that fairly allocates risks.

❏ Provide contract incentives for superior (quality) performance.

❏ Implement guidance throughout the agency or company.

❏ Continue to improve techniques.

❏ Make each best-value decision a team effort between contracts, finance, engineering, production, quality assurance, and other related offices.

❏ Ensure that a best-value approach supports the overall negotiation strategy.

❏ Realize that the best-value approach works only if you know what you're buying.

❏ Allow flexibility for tradeoffs.

Source: Richard J. Hernandez and Delane F. Moeller "Negotiating a Quality Contract," NES Manual (Vienna, VA: NCMA, 1992).

faced by sellers when using CBP are creating an adequate cost-estimating and accounting system and applying an appropriate profit or fee structure, which properly balances opportunity versus risk. In the private sector, there are generally accepted accounting practices (GAAP), that are followed and audited to ensure that companies have adequate cost-estimating and accounting systems. There are no real stringent rules for commercial companies on applying an appropriate profit or fee structure.

However, when dealing in the public sector, the U.S. federal government has numerous rules and regulations to ensure that companies doing business with the government (1) have adequate cost-estimating and accounting systems, especially when using cost-type contracts, (2) apply appropriate profit or fee structures, and (3) practice truth in negotiations.

Table 9.2 Checklist of Best-Value "Don'ts"

Don't:

❑ Don't use (1) the low bid or (2) the lowest-cost, technically acceptable offer as a substitute for best value, when best value is applicable.

❑ Don't expect to make a good best-value decision without clearly defining your approach up front.

❑ Don't attempt to implement best-value contracting without properly training acquisition personnel.

❑ Don't forget to research all relevant issues, especially technical factors.

❑ Don't make best-value decision tools unnecessarily complex.

❑ Don't allow for such practices as a "buy-in" or uncompensated overtime.

❑ Don't use auctioning, technical leveling, or technical transfusion techniques as a substitute for best-value contracting.

❑ Don't forget to formalize the elements of the best-value agreement as soon as possible after contract negotiations.

❑ Don't forget to formalize the elements of the best-value agreement as soon as possible after contract negotiations.

❑ Don't expect to obtain the maximum level of economy when buying noncommercial off-the-shelf items.

Source: Hernandez and Moeller, "Negotiating a Quality Contract," 1992.

The primary goal of the cost-estimating and accounting system is to ensure that costs are appropriately, equitably, and consistently estimated and are then allocated to all final cost objectives (i.e., individual contracts, jobs, or products). The U.S. federal government essentially requires a company to maintain and consistently apply any GAAP method that is adequate, efficient, reliable, and equitable, but that is not necessarily exact and specific and is not biased against the government. The government does not require companies to adopt separate or necessarily complex accounting systems. Consequently, contractors are free to develop and use the type of cost-estimating and accounting system that is most appropriate for their businesses. However, consistent application of this approach is vital.

Although the use and design of certain specific cost-estimating accounting records and practices may vary from company to company, the record-keeping system for all companies doing business with the government must, at a minimum, include a general ledger, a job-cost ledger, a set of labor distribution records and time records, a set of subsidiary journals, a chart of accounts, and all the appropriate

Table 9.3 Government Auditor Accounting System Questionnaire

	Yes	No
1. Is the system in accord with generally accepted accounting principles (GAAP)?	❏	❏
2. Will the system be able to identify and segregate direct costs from indirect costs and to allocate the costs equitably to specific contracts on a consistent basis?	❏	❏
3. Is the system that accumulates costs integrated with, and reconcilable to, the general ledger?	❏	❏
4. Do the timekeeping and labor distribution systems appropriately identify direct and indirect labor charges to intermediate and final cost objectives?	❏	❏
5. Will the system be able to determine the cost of work performed at interim points (at least monthly) because of routine posting of costs to the books of account?	❏	❏
6. Will the system be able to identify and segregate unallowable costs as required by FAR Part 31 and any contract terms?	❏	❏
7. If required by the contract, will the system be able to identify costs by contract line item or by unit?	❏	❏
8. Will the system be able to segregate preproduction costs from production costs?	❏	❏
9. Is the system capable of provided the necessary information required by FAR 52.232-20, Limitation of Cost (Also -21 and -22), or FAR 52.216-16, Incentive Price Revision-Firm Target?	❏	❏
10. Is the system able to provide the necessary data for recovery of costs, using progress payments?	❏	❏
11. Is the accounting system designed? Are the records maintained in such a manner, that adequate, reliable data are developed for use in pricing follow-on contracts?	❏	❏
12. Is the accounting system currently in full operation?	❏	❏

Source: Lubeck 2004.

financial statements.[4]

To determine whether a company's accounting system is acceptable, a government auditor will generally go through a checklist, asking questions similar to those found in the accounting system questionnaire (see **Table 9.3**, p. 176).

Accounting information can—and should—be used in more ways than merely to produce financial statements and job-cost reports. Only after identifying activities that are important to your business and beginning to measure them can you encourage the rest of your team to support your goals. A business that provides clear expectations and real-time performance feedback can be managed on a real-time basis and, therefore, has greater control over its destiny.[5]

Adequate Cost Estimating

Developing a sound cost estimate requires a coordinated effort by a team of qualified seller personnel who understand how to extract and price requirements presented in the buyer's request for proposal (RFP). At a minimum, the team should consist of a program manager, technical manager, contract manager, accounting or finance manager, and senior executive who is responsible for final review and submission of the proposal to the buyer. Depending on the company's size, the magnitude of the proposal, and the types of costs being estimated, the estimating team also may include representatives of purchasing, legal, human resources, operations, and others.

All personnel with any responsibility for preparing a proposal to the U.S. federal government should be well versed in the guidelines contained in the *Federal Acquisition Regulation* (especially FAR 15.4,, Contract Pricing). All team members should have adequate experience and knowledge of the particular requirements of pricing function to which they have been assigned. Responsible personnel should know where to obtain the most relevant and current data and should be aware of the turnaround time allowed for submission of the proposal.[6]

A proposal preparation system that entrusts one person with the sole authority for translating the RFP into requirements, pricing those requirements, and reviewing and submitting the final proposal is an accident waiting to happen. Omission of key personnel in the estimating process can result in cost and delivery projections that do not consider current and future business decisions and company plans. In other words, the proposal may not realistically represent the company's ability to deliver the product or services within the estimated cost or required delivery timelines.

Including personnel who are familiar with various components of the business operations will reduce the risk that a proposal will be over-stated or understated. Even in small companies that have few employees and in which officials wear several hats of responsibility, it is just as important that the estimating system involve at least two or three qualified persons to better ensure an accurately priced final product.

In summary, a forward-pricing proposal should minimize the use of judgmental estimates and should maximize the use of factual data when such data are available and relevant. Developing extensively priced requirements with judgmental estimates does not provide the visibility required by the government to evaluate the reasonableness of a proposal. Judgmental estimates add time to the government audit and cost analysis and sometimes even result in adverse audit opinions because of a lack of verifiable data. The typical cost elements in **Table 9.4** (this page) are examples of verifiable proposal supporting data.

In selecting the proposal resources for developing and pricing RFP requirements, the supplier must be careful to use the most current, accurate, and complete information, especially if the government requires submission of cost or pricing data. This approach means selecting the data most relevant to the proposal being prepared and ensuring that the source information is as current as possible. Even if the proposal is not specifically subject to the Truth in Negotiations Act, companies have an obligation to prepare reasonable estimates and, in that pursuit, should rely on up-to-date, relevant, factual data when possible.

It goes without saying that estimating techniques must be relevant

Table 9.4 Government Auditor Accounting System Questionnaire	
Direct Labor Hours	Labor-hour history of the same or similar projects Company or industry standards
Bill of Direct Materials	Material panning documents Engineering blueprints
Direct Labor Rates	Labor cost history for the same or similar project Average labor rates from payroll data Market wage or salary survey information
Direct Materials	Purchase history of same or similar items Vendor quotations Vendor catalogues
Indirect Rate	Historical annual indirect rates Budgetary or provisional rates

Source: Walker 2004.

to the specific RFP requirements. Supplier techniques should be consistent among all bids and proposals, except in cases in which those techniques clearly will not produce the most accurate cost estimate for the RFP's scope of work.[7]

Cost Proposal Package: Information Required for U.S. Federal Government Prime Contracts

A prime contract cost proposal that is from the U.S. federal government and that requires cost or pricing data must follow the format shown in FAR 15.408, Table 15.2. This information may be helpful in assessing the adequacy of a proposal.

1. 1st Page of Proposal, Table 15.2, Item I.A, lists 11 separate informational requirements.
   a. Solicitation or Contract No.
   b. Offeror name and address
   c. Contact point and phone number
   d. Name of contract administration office
   e. Type of contract option (i.e., new contract, change order, letter contract, etc.)
   f. Date of submission
   g. Name, title, and signature of authorized representative
   h. Proposed cost, fee, and total
   i. What government property is required
   j. Cost accounting standards (CAS)
      i. Whether organization is subject to CAS
      ii. Whether disclosure statement is submitted and determined adequate
      iii. Any notifications of material noncompliance with CAS or disclosure statement and whether proposal is consistent with CAS and disclosed practices; no need to disclose "technical" noncompliances
   k. Statement that proposal reflects estimated or actual costs and that contracting officer or authorized representatives have access to records
2. Summary of Cost and Detailed Support, Table 15.2, Items I.C-G, II, and III
3. Disclosure Narrative, Table 15.2, Items C-G
   a. Helps protect against defective pricing allegations
   b. Describes the basis of estimates
      i. Has specific discussion by cost category (direct materials, direct labor, other direct costs, overhead, etc.)

  ii. Discusses assumptions made and the rationale such as the judgmental factors, the applied and mathematical methods, or the other methods used in the estimate

  iii. Includes method used in projecting from known data

  iv. Includes the nature and amount of contingencies in the proposed price

 c. Discloses significant cost or pricing data in narrative form

  i. Discusses key data used in cost estimating

  ii. Discloses cost date not used in cost estimating and states why it was not used

4. Disclosure Index, Table 15.2, Item I B

 a. Helps protect against defective pricing claims by listing all available cost or pricing data, or listing other information accompanying the proposal or identified in the proposal, appropriately referenced

 b. Index should specifically identify all reports and documents; it should include the following:

  i. Specific report name, number, or both

  ii. Date of most recent report

  iii. Physical location of data

 c. Includes items such as the following:

  i. General ledger

  ii. Payroll register

  iii. Vendor invoice

  iv. A/P history, etc.

 d. Future addition or revisions that—up to the date of agreement on price—must be annotated on a supplemental index

Department of Defense: Weighted Guidelines for Profit or Fee

The Department of Defense's structured approach to profit or fee analysis is known as the weighted guidelines. Those guidelines are implemented using DD Form 1547, Record of Weighted Guidelines Application, which provides the structure of profit or fee objectives and reports the amount negotiated. Several organizations have developed computerized versions of the form to ensure accurate calculation and reporting. The most widely circulated software is the U.S. Air Force Material Command WGM (Weighted Guidance Method). The National Contract Management Association currently markets the WGM software.

The DD Form 1547 is divided into nine sections, as listed below (and as described in further detail in the Contract Pricing Reference Guide, Volume III, Chapter 12.3):

- Identification information,

- Contractor effort cost category,

- Performance risk,

- Contract type risk,

- Working capital adjustment,

- Facilities capital employed,

- Total profit objective,

- Negotiation summary, and

- Contracting officer approval.

In lieu of the WGM, contracting officers may use an alternative structured approach for the following:

- Architect-engineering contracts,

- Construction contracts,

- Termination settlements,

- Contracts smaller than $500,000, and

- Contracts primarily for delivery of materials from subcontractors.

Finally, FAR Subpart 15.5 covers the notification process and procedures for handling mistakes made during this entire process.[8]

Understand the Truth in Negotiations Act

Congress enacted the Truth in Negotiations Act (TINA) as Public Law 87-653 (10 U.S.C. 2306) in December 1962. The TINA has been viewed as one of the most significant pieces of procurement legislation. The original act covered only those contracts entered into by the Department of Defense (DOD) and the National Aeronautics and Space Administration (NASA). Civilian agencies subsequently adopted the same statutory provisions under their own regulations.

The statutory disparity between the various government agencies was addressed by the 1984 Competition in Contracting Act (CICA), which required that the TINA apply to all government contracts. This remedy has significantly decreased the number of disputes brought before the various boards of contract appeals.

The TINA requires prime contractors and subcontractors of U.S. federal government to submit to the government the data related to the basis of estimated contract costs and certify data accuracy. The objective is to provide the government with all necessary and relevant information so everyone is able to negotiate a fair and reasonable price for a contract. The TINA requires that such information is "current, accurate, and complete" at the time the negotiating parties reach such an agreement.[9]

The TINA requires contractors to disclose factual data that prudent buyers and sellers would reasonable expect to significantly affect the contract price negotiation. Some typical data that are disclosed under TINA include the following:

- Historical costs, such as material costs, labor hours expanded, labor rates paid, or labor union settlements;

- "Make or buy" program decisions;

- Subcontractor and vendor quotations;

- Learning curve projections; and

- Other business base projections.

Although the TINA requires disclosure of those types of information to the government, the contractor is not required to rely on the data in developing its proposal. A contractor is not constrained in exercising its best judgment when developing the estimated cost of a contract. The key to compliance with TINA is disclosure of relevant factual data. If current, accurate, and complete cost or pricing data have been disclosed, then one can assume that the government or prime contractor negotiators have the necessary information to reach an informed agreement and a fair and reasonable contract price.[10]

To ensure that government contractors are providing data in compliance with TINA, contractors are required to certify that such disclosures are accurate (i.e., current, accurate, and complete) for contracts or modifications to existing contracts with a value greater than certain dollar thresholds. Exceptions to disclosure and certification are provided in the following cases:

■ The contract price is based on adequate price competition.

■ An established catalog or market price exists, and the item is sold in substantial quantities to the general public.

■ The prices are set by law or regulation.

■ If it is an exceptional case, then such cases must be approved after determinations by the agency's head.

Of course, the government negotiator must likewise spend considerable time analyzing and using such information when negotiating the best deal for the government. Accordingly, after the final "handshake," but before the contractor signs the certification, the contractor generally performs a final review to be sure that all of the cost and pricing data that may affect the final, agreed-to price have been disclosed.

If the certified cost or pricing data are not current, accurate, or complete on the effective date of the certificate, the government is entitled to a downward adjustment to the contract price. Such a situation is known as "defective pricing" under TINA. In addition to an adjustment to the contract price (if warranted), the contractor may be subject to further investigation for fraud. In cases where fraud is determined, criminal penalties may be imposed.

TINA Documentation Requirements

Common sense would dictate that any businessperson would "document" the results of a business negotiation. For government negotiators, the regulations require extensive and specific documentation. The *FAR* requires government contracting officers to establish and document written prenegotiation objectives before entering negotiations in accordance with FAR 15.406-1:

■ A record of significant events in the acquisition,

■ A list of attendees at the briefing,

■ The current acquisition situation,

■ The previous price history,

- A synopsis of offer submitted or received,

- The analytical methods used to establish price objectives,

- The delivery objectives,

- The negotiation plan, and

- The signature blocks for the signature(s) of the approving official(s).

For a completed contract negotiation, the government contracting officer shall use a price negotiation memorandum (PNM), in accordance with FAR 15.406-3. Understanding the many federal regulations are a part of the negotiation process is a major step toward improving the resulting agreements for the buying and selling of products and services for the American public, although having such knowledge is not in itself enough to ensure that negotiations reach a fair and reasonable price.

Value-Based Pricing

Value-based pricing (VBP) is the opposite of cost-based pricing. VBP is all about determining the value of a product or service from the customer's or buyer's perspective. Clearly, the determination of value varies dramatically in certain products or services. For example, the pricing of works of art is certainly not based on the cost of clay, paint, or canvas, plus a reasonable profit or fee structure.

From a seller's perspective, VBP allows the supplier to research the marketplace and to assess the intrinsic and extrinsic value, which a product or service may be deemed to possess by one or more buyers. Thus, VBP is a blend of art and science, where traditional buying and selling that uses cost-based methods do not apply. VBP is like the best-value pricing strategy on steroids. VBP provides the seller with the maximum potential opportunity for the highest possible profit and for the maximum price paid by a buyer. If you are a seller, then VBP is a beautiful thing!

Activity-Based Pricing

Activity-based pricing (ABP) is basically a modified version of cost-based pricing. ABP seeks to determine a fair and reasonable price on the basis of the estimated or actual costs for the accomplishment of activities or processes, plus an appropriate profit, fee, or both. ABP seeks to continuously improve business's activities and processes through internal and external benchmarking, thus reducing costs and increasing profit or fee margins for sellers. Likewise, the ABP method can benefit buyers, because sellers may be able to accelerate price reductions as a result of their continual focus on business activity and process improvement.

ABP has evolved over the past decade as a result of research into activity-based cost and performance (ABC&P), which is a methodology to identify and measure the costs and to evaluate the performance of an organization's business processes. ABC&P provides insights into areas and causes for poor performance, and it helps target efforts on improvement opportunities. Understanding the cost of activities and products helps organizations focus on high payback areas and target investments for improvement of performance. The real key of ABC&P is to develop performance measures for each activity, then to evaluate the actual performance results versus the plan.

Table 9.5 (See p. 186) contains the typical ABC&P model and principal components.

Developing Pricing Arrangements or Contract Types

Over the years, some standard pricing arrangements have evolved. Those arrangements fall into three categories: fixed-price, cost-reimbursement, and time-and-materials contracts. (The Project Management Institute also designates unit-price contracts as a separate category.) The contract categories have developed as practical responses to cost risk, and they have become fairly standard formal arrangements. Incentives can be added to any of the contract types in the three categories and are discussed in detail later in this chapter. **Table 9.6** (See p. 187) lists several common contract types in the categories.[11]

The pricing arrangements, however, are manifested in the specific terms and conditions of contracts (that is, in the contract clauses). No standard clauses for their implementation exist. Therefore, the contracting parties must write clauses that describe their specific agreement.

Fixed-Price Category

Fixed-price contracts are the standard arrangement for business pricing. The two basic types of fixed-price contracts are firm-fixed-price (FFP) and fixed-price with economic price adjustment (FP/EPA). FFP contracts are further divided into lump-sum and unit-price arrangements.

Table 9.5 Activity-Based Cost & Performance (ABC&P) Principal Components		
ABC&P Component	Definition	Examples
Resources	The elements (e.g., labor, materials, and facilities) used to perform work	• Facilities • Supplies • Hardware and software
Resource Driver	A measure of the consumption of a resource, used to determine the portion of the total resource cost assigned to each activity that uses the resource	• Number of hours to perform the activity • Number of square feet occupied • Percentage of time spent
Activity	One step within a process that uses resources to perform work. It occurs over time and has recognizable results	• Test equipment • Teach training classes • Enter data
Activity Driver	A measure of the frequency of activity performance and the effort required to achieve the necessary result	• Number of classes required • Number of forms processed • Number of lines of data
Products	Any object that you wish to gain financial and nonfinancial information about through cost and performance measurement	• Repaired ship • Trained soldier • Processed travel voucher • Army base
Cost Driver	An indicator of why an activity is performed and what causes the cost of performing the activity to change	• Proposed work package for a ship • Yield rate of the activity • Characteristic of a product
Performance Measure	An indicator of the work performed and the results achieved in a activity; a measure of how well an activity meets the needs of its customers	• Cycle time • Number of errors • Customer satisfaction • Inventory fill rates

Source: Burk and Webster 1994.

Table 9.6 Contract Categories and Types			
Contracts Types	Fixed-Price Contracts	Cost-Reimbursement or Unit Price Contracts*	Time-and-Materials Contracts
	Firm-fixed-price Fixed-price with economic price adjustment Fixed-price incentive	Cost-reimbursement Cost-plus-a-percentage-of-cost Cost-plus-fixed fee Cost-plus-incentive fee Cost-plus-award fee	Time-and-materials Unit price

Firm-Fixed-Price Contracts

The simplest and most common business pricing arrangement is the FFP contract. The seller agrees to supply specified goods or deliverables in a specified quantity or to render a specified service or level of effort in return for a specified price, either a lump sum or a unit price. The price is fixed, that is, not subject to change on the basis of the seller's actual cost experience. However, it may be subject to change if the parties modify the contract. This pricing arrangement is used for the sale of commercial goods and services.

Some companies include a complex clause in their FFP contracts. Such a clause may read in part as follows:

Prices and Taxes

The price of products shall be ABC Company's published list prices on the date that ABC Company accepts your order, less any applicable discount. If ABC Company announces a price increase for equipment or software that was licensed for a one-time fee, and after it accepts your order but before shipment, ABC Company shall invoice you at the increased price only if delivery occurs more than 120 days after the effective date of the price increase. If ABC Company announces a price increase for services, rentals, or software that was licensed for a periodic fee, the price increase shall apply to billing periods beginning after its effective date.

Note that the seller, not the buyer, wrote this clause, and it reflects the seller's point of view and concerns. Nevertheless, the pricing arrangement it describes is firm-fixed-price because the contract price will not be subject to adjustment on the basis of ABC Company's actual performance costs.

Clauses such as "Prices and Taxes" frequently form part of a document known as a universal agreement. Such a document is not a contract, it is a precontract agreement that merely communicates any agreed-to terms and conditions (Ts and Cs) that will apply when the buyer places an order. After the seller accepts an order, the company's published or announced list prices become the basis for the contract price according to the terms of the universal agreement. This agreement is discussed later in this chapter in "Purchase Agreements."

FFP contracts are appropriate for most commercial transactions when cost uncertainty is within commercially acceptable limits. Those limits depend on the industry and the market.

Fixed-Price with Economic Price Adjustment

Fixed-price contracts sometimes include various clauses that provide for adjusting prices on the basis of specified contingencies. The clauses may provide for upward or downward adjustments or both. Economic price adjustments are usually limited to factors beyond the seller's immediate control, such as market forces.

This pricing arrangement is not firm-fixed-price because the contract provides for a price adjustment that is based on the seller's actual performance costs. Thus, the seller is protected from the risk of certain labor or material cost increases. The EPA clause can provide for price increases that are based on the seller's costs but not on the seller's decision to increase the prices of its products or services. Thus, there can be a significant difference between this clause and the "Prices and Taxes" clause discussed previously.

The shift of risk to the buyer creates greater buyer intrusion into the affairs of the seller. This intrusion typically takes the form of an audit provision at the end of the clause, particularly when the buyer is a government.

EPA clauses are appropriate in times of market instability, when great uncertainty exists regarding labor and material costs. The risk of cost fluctuations is more balanced between the parties than would be the case under an FFP contract.

Fixed-Price Incentive Contracts

In an FPI contract, seller profit is linked to another aspect of performance: cost, schedule, quality, or a combination of all three. The objective is to give the seller a monetary incentive to optimize cost performance.

FPI contracts may be useful for initial production of complex new products or systems, although the parties may have difficulty agreeing on labor and material costs for such projects because of a lack of production experience. However, the cost uncertainty may not be great enough to warrant use of a CR contract.

Cost-Reimbursement Category

Cost-reimbursement (CR) contracts usually include an estimate of project cost, a provision for reimbursing the seller's expenses, and a provision for paying a fee as profit. Normally, CR contracts also include a limitation on the buyer's cost liability.

A common perception is that CR contracts are to be avoided. However, if uncertainty about costs is great enough, a buyer may be unable to find a seller willing to accept a fixed price, even with adjustment clauses, or a seller may insist on extraordinary contingencies within that price. In the latter case, the buyer may find the demands unreasonable. Such high levels of cost uncertainty are often found in research and development, large-scale construction, and systems integration projects. In such circumstances, the best solution may be a CR contract—but only if the buyer is confident that the seller has a highly accurate and reliable cost accounting system.

The parties to a CR contract will find themselves confronting some challenging issues, especially concerning the definition, measurement, allocation, and confirmation of costs. First, the parties must agree on a definition for acceptable cost. For instance, the buyer may decide that the cost of air travel should be limited to the price of a coach or business-class ticket and should not include a first-class ticket. The buyer will specify other cost limitations, and the parties will negotiate until they agree on what constitutes a reimbursable cost.

Next, the parties must decide who will measure costs and what accounting rules will be used to do so. For example, several depreciation techniques are in use, some of which would be less advantageous to the buyer than others. Which technique will the buyer consider acceptable? How will labor costs be calculated? Will standard costs be acceptable, or must the seller determine and invoice actual costs? What methods of allocating overhead will be acceptable to the buyer? How will the buyer know that the seller's reimbursement invoices are accurate? Will the buyer have the right to obtain an independent audit? If the buyer is also a competitor of the seller, should the seller be willing to open its books to the buyer?

If those issues remain unsettled, the buyer is accepting the risk of having to reimburse costs that it may later find to be unreasonable. This issue is the central problem with cost-reimbursement contracting, and the problem has never been resolved entirely.

Clearly, the CR contract presents the parties with difficulties that they would not face under a fixed-price contract. The parties must define costs and must establish acceptable procedures for cost measurement and allocation, the buyer takes on greater cost risk and must incur greater administrative costs to protect its interests, and the seller faces greater intrusion by the buyer into its affairs. Nevertheless, many contracting parties have found a CR contract to be a better arrangement than a fixed-price contract for undertakings with high cost uncertainty.

Types of CR contracts include those dealing with cost, cost-sharing, cost-plus-a-percentage-of-cost (CPPC), and cos-plus-fixed-fee (CPFF).

Cost Contracts

The cost contract is the simplest type of CR contract. Governments commonly use this type when contracting with universities and non-profit organizations for research projects. The contract provides for reimbursing contractually allowable costs, with no allowance given for profit.

Cost-Sharing Contracts

The cost-sharing contract provides for only partial reimbursement of the seller's costs. The parties share the cost liability, with no allowance for profit. The cost-sharing contract is appropriate when the seller will enjoy some benefit from the results of the project and when that benefit is sufficient to encourage the seller to undertake the work for only a portion of its costs and without fee.

Cost-Plus-a-Percentage-of-Cost Contracts

The CPPC contract provides for the seller to receive reimbursement for its costs and a profit component, called a fee, which is equal to some predetermined percentage of its actual costs. Thus, as costs go up, so does profit. This arrangement is a poor one from the buyer's standpoint; it provides no incentive to control costs, because the fee gets bigger as the costs go up. This type of contract was used extensively by the U.S. government during World War I but has since been made illegal for U.S. government contracts—for good reason. It is still occasionally used for construction projects and some service contracts in the private sector.

The rationale for this pricing arrangement was probably "the bigger the job, the bigger the fee," that is, as the job grows, so should the fee. This arrangement is similar to a professional fee, such as an attorney's fee, which grows as the professional puts more time into the project. This arrangement may have developed as a response to the cost-growth phenomenon in projects that were initially ill defined. As a seller proceeded with the work, the buyer's needs became better defined and grew, until the seller felt that the fees initially agreed to were not enough for the expanded scope of work.

Cost-Plus-Fixed-Fee Contracts

Cost-plus-fixed-fee is the most common type of CR contract. As with other CR contracts, the seller is reimbursed for its costs, but the contract also provides for payment of a fixed fee that does not change in response to the seller's actual cost experience. The seller is paid the fixed fee on successful completion of the contract, whether its actual costs were higher or lower than the estimated costs.

If the seller completes the work for less than the estimated cost, it receives the entire fixed fee. If the seller incurs the estimated cost without completing the work and if the buyer decides not to pay for the overrun costs necessary for completion, the seller receives a portion of the fixed fee that is equal to the percentage of work completed. If the buyer decides to pay cost overrun, the seller must complete the work without any increase in the fixed fee. The only adjustment to the fee would be a result of cost growth, when the buyer requires the seller to do more work than initially specified.

This type of contract is on the opposite end of the spectrum from the FFP contract, because cost risk rests entirely on the shoulders of the buyer. Under a CR contract, a buyer might have to reimburse the seller for the entire estimated cost and part of the fee but have nothing to show for it but bits and pieces of the work.

Incentive Contracts: Cost-Plus-Incentive-Fee Contracts

Cost-plus-incentive-fee (CPIF) contracts allow sharing of cost overruns or underruns through a predetermined formula for fee adjustments that apply to incentives for cost category contracts. Within the basic concept of the buyer's paying all costs for a cost contract, the limits for a CPIF contract become those of maximum and minimum fees.

The necessary elements for a CPIF contract are maximum fee, minimum fee, target cost, target fee, and share ratio(s).

Incentive Contracts: Cost-Plus-Award-Fee Contracts

Cost-plus-award-fee contracts include subjective incentives in which the profit a seller earns depends on how well the seller satisfies a buyer's subjective desires. This type of contract has been used for a long time in both government and commercial contracts worldwide. The U.S. Army Corps of Engineers developed an evaluated fee contract for use in construction during the early 1930s, when it used its contracting experience from World War I. NASA has used CPAF contracts to procure services since the 1950s. Other U.S. government agencies, including the Department of Energy and the DOD, have also used those contracts extensively. A small but growing number of commercial companies now use award fees to motivate their suppliers to achieve exceptional performance.

Cost-plus-award fee contracts are used primarily to procure services, particularly those that involve an ongoing, long-term relationship between buyer and seller, such as maintenance and systems engineering support. Objective criteria for determining the acceptability of the performance of such services are inherently difficult to establish. The award fee arrangement is particularly well suited to such circumstances, at least from the buyer's point of view. However, this type of contract also is used to procure architecture and engineering, research and development, hardware and software systems design and development, construction, and many other services.

Time-and-Materials (T&M) Category

In T&M contracts, the parties negotiate hourly rates for specified types of labor, and they agree that the seller will be reimbursed for parts and materials at cost. Each hourly rate includes labor costs, overhead, and profit. The seller performs the work, documenting the types and quantities of labor used and the costs for parts and materials. When the work is finished, the seller bills the buyer (a) for the number of labor hours at the agreed-on hourly rates and (b) for the costs of materials and parts.

T&M contracts are most often used to procure equipment repair and maintenance services when the cost to repair or overhaul a piece of equipment is uncertain. However, such contracts are also used to procure other support services.

Although T&M contracts appear to be straightforward, they may create some difficulties. This type of contract must be negotiated carefully, because each hourly rate includes a component for overhead costs, which will include both fixed and variable costs. Fixed costs are the costs that will be incurred during a given period of operation, despite the number of work hours performed. To recover its fixed costs, the seller must estimate how many hours will be sold during the contract performance period and must allocate a share to each hour. If the parties overestimate how many hours will be sold during the period of performance, the seller will not recover all its fixed costs. If the parties underestimate how many hours will be sold, the seller will enjoy a windfall profit.

Although the hourly labor rates are fixed, the number of hours delivered and the cost of materials and parts are not. Therefore, the buyer faces the problems of confirming the number of hours delivered and the cost of materials claimed by the seller. These problems are not as great as those under CR contracts, but they are not insignificant.

Other Pricing Methods

In addition to the variety of pricing arrangements already discussed, buyers and sellers use other kinds of agreements to deal with uncertainty and to reduce the administrative costs of contracting. Those arrangements include other transaction authority (OTAs) purchase agreements, memorandums of understanding (MOUs), and letters of intent (LOIs).

Case Study: Defense Advanced Research Projects Agency (DARPA)—OTAs

Other transaction authorities (OTAs) were originally authorized in 1989 to attract commercial companies that were unfamiliar with the U.S. federal government's complex acquisition process. The purpose of OTAs is to streamline the procurement process and to eliminate requirements for detailed accounting systems. Between 1990 and 1998, 75 percent of the contractors using OTA contracts to participate in research projects were traditional defense companies or non-profit universities or other not-for-profit organizations.

In 2002, Secretary of Defense Donald H. Rumsfeld encouraged the use of OTAs to encourage flexible acquisition practices in the development of the missile defense system. The Pentagon has promoted the use of OTAs hoping that commercial companies would sell their technology and would develop new products for the military faster and for less than the costs used by traditional defense contractors. Clearly, OTAs have helped streamline the contracting process and have reduced the costs for developing new technologies and products. However, OTAs have not grown to be as popular with commercial companies as was envisioned or desired by the government.

Purchase Agreements

When two parties expect to deal with one another repeatedly for the purchase and sale of goods and services, they may decide to enter a long-term purchase agreement. Rather than negotiating a new contract for every transaction, the parties agree to the terms and conditions that will apply to any transaction between them of a specified type. This arrangement reduces the time required to obtain products and services once the buyer releases a purchase order to the seller.

Commercially, the purchase agreements are known by a variety of names, including frame contracts, universal agreements, and general purchase agreements. Within the U.S. federal government, the most popular of the more-flexible purchase agreements is the indefinite delivery/indefinite quantity (IDIQ) contracts.

The critical business aspect is to select the appropriate pricing arrangement or combination of pricing arrangements for the contractual situation. The parties must carefully consider the following factors:

■ Technical difficulty,

■ Urgency of requirements,

■ Administrative costs for both parties,

■ Accuracy of seller's cost estimating and cost accounting systems,

■ Product/service/solution maturity, and

■ Overall risk assessment (e.g., technical, schedule, cost, quality).

Price Analysis Best Practices

Price analysis is the process of examining and evaluating a proposed price to determine if it is fair and reasonable without evaluating its separate cost elements and proposed profit. Price analysis always involves some form of comparison with other prices. Adequate price competition is normally considered one of the best bases for price analysis.

Price analysis may involve a number of comparisons. The comparison process is typically described using five steps:

1. Select prices for comparison:

   • Competitive proposal prices,

   • Catalog prices,

   • Historical prices,

   • Price estimates that are based on parametric analysis, or

• Independent company estimates.

2. Identify factors that affect comparability.

3. Determine the effect of identified factors.

4. Adjust prices selected for comparison.

5. Compare adjusted prices.

Select Prices for Comparison

The types of comparisons used typically depend on the estimated dollar value of the contract. Evidence of price reasonableness might include previous prices paid for same or similar items purchased competitively or for knowledge of the supply or service gained from published price catalogs, newspapers, and other sources of market information. If you believe the quoted price is unreasonable, it will be necessary to solicit additional quotes.

Competitive Proposal Prices. Price competition is generally considered to be one of the best bases for price analysis. Competitive prices are offers received from sellers under conditions of adequate price competition. Adequate price competition exists when two or more responsible sellers, competing independently, submit priced offers that satisfy the expressed requirement. The award will be made to a responsible seller whose proposal offers either the greatest value or the lowest evaluated price, especially if you have not found that the price of the otherwise successful seller is unreasonable.

When comparing competitive offers, never use and offer from a seller that you have determined is not responsible. Never use a nonresponsive bid. Also, never use a price from a proposal that is technically outside the competitive range. Although price competition is considered to be one of the best bases for price analysis, you should normally place less reliance on competition when you find the solicitation was made under conditions that unreasonably denied one or more known and qualified sellers an opportunity to compete. In assessing reasonableness, you need to make sure that the offers are comparable.

Catalog Prices. Catalog prices are prices taken from a catalog, price list, schedule, or other verifiable and established record that is regularly maintained by a manufacturer or vendor and is published or otherwise available for customer inspection.

Historical Prices. Historical prices are previous prices paid by the buyer for the same or similar items. Important factors to think about when considering historical price analysis are whether the product or service has been purchased before (by your office or another office within the company), what the historical price was and whether it can be obtained, and whether the historical price was fair and reasonable (make sure the circumstances are comparable).

Price Estimates Based on Parametric Analysis

Parametric analysis uses cost estimating relationships, often referred to as pricing yardsticks. They are formulas for estimating prices on the basis of the relationship of past prices with a product's physical or performance characteristics (e.g, dollars per pound, dollars per horsepower, or dollars per square foot). When you consider a yardstick for price analysis, it is important to determine whether the yardstick has been widely accepted in the marketplace (do both buyers and sellers agree on the validity and reasonableness of the values obtained by a particular yardstick), whether the yardstick has been properly developed (the developer of the yardstick should be able to produce data and calculations used in developing the estimate), and whether the yardstick is accurate (some yardsticks provide rough estimates and not precise prices).

Independent Company Estimates

The buyer itself makes independent company estimates. The most common estimate is the material requisition where a blind estimate is made on the approximate price of the item. A value analysis estimate is another type of buyer estimate. This analysis takes into account the apparent value of one proposed item over another. While the prices may not be comparable, the value of the item to the company may be.

Individuals familiar with the product or service and its use should perform the estimates independent of the requisition and solicitation process. They should determine what the product must do, establish what the total costs related to purchasing the product or service are, identify other ways in which the function can be performed, and document the total costs related to purchasing an alternative produce or service.

Identification of Factors That Affect Comparability

When comparing prices, you must attempt to account for any factors that affect comparability. The following factors affect many price analysis comparisons:

■ Market conditions,

■ Quantity or size,

■ Geographic location,

■ Extent of competition, and

■ Technology.

Market Conditions. The passage of time usually is accompanied by changes in supply, demand, technology, product designs, pricing strategies, laws and regulations that affect supplier costs, and other such factors. As a general rule, select the most recent prices available. The less recent the price, the greater the likelihood and effect of differences in market conditions. However, do not select a price for comparison merely because it is the most recent; look instead for prices that were established under similar market conditions.

Quantity or Size. Variations in quantity can have a significant effect on unit price. Economies of scale do not always apply. For example, increases in order size beyond a certain point may tax seller's capacity and may result in higher prices.

Geographic Location. Geography can have a range of effects on comparability. In major urban centers, you will be able to rely on data from within that geographic region; in more remote, less-urban areas, you must often get data from beyond the immediate area. When you must compare prices across geographic boundaries, take the following steps to enhance comparability:

■ Check the extent of competition.

■ Determine the extent to which variations in the price of labor must be neutralized.

■ Check the freight requirements and accompanying costs.

■ Identify geographic anomalies or trends (for example, many items are more expensive in one region than in another).

Extent of Competition. When comparing one price with another, assess the competitive environment shaping the prices. For example, you can compare last year's competitive price with a current offer for the same item. However, if last year's procurement was made without competition (for example, it was based on urgency), it may not have been a good price with which to compare the current offer.

Technology. Prices from declining industries can rise because the technologies don't keep pace with rising costs. However, technological advances have been made so fast that a comparison of prices separated by a single year must account for those advances. Engineering or design changes must also be taken into account, which means you must identify the new or modified features and estimate their effect on price.

Determination of Effect of Identified Factors
Once you have identified the factors that may affect comparability, you must determine the effect on each specific comparison with the offered price. Questions to keep in mind are as follows:

■ What factors affect this specific comparison?

■ How do the factors affect the comparison?

■ Does this comparison, even with its limitations, contribute to the price analysis?

Adjustment of Prices Selected for Comparison
If you have a price analysis comparison base that does not require adjustment, use it. If you must make an adjustment, try to make the adjustment as objectively as possible. Remember, to establish price comparability, you must do the following:

■ Identify and document price-related differences while taking into account the factors affecting comparability.

■ Factor out price-related differences.

Restoring comparability by establishing a common basis for comparison requires that you assign a monetary value to each identified difference. The cost of terms and conditions peculiar to certain contracts is hard to estimate, so exercise discretion. The challenge is to use the available information and to estimate the price that should be paid. If you cannot objectively adjust the prices for the factor involved, you may need to make a subjective adjustment such as when estimating the effect on price of special or unique contract terms and conditions.

Comparison of Adjusted Prices

After adjusting prices for comparison, determine the weight to give each price comparison. Then establish a should-pay price. If the should-pay price departs significantly from the apparently successful offer, analyze and document any differences. (See the information in **Table 9.7**, p. 200.)

Summary

In retrospect, this chapter has provided a comprehensive discussion of the performance-based acquisition essential element of price. We have also examined the following aspects of price:

■ The two most common pricing strategies —

  • Lowest-price technically acceptable (LPTA)

  • Best value

■ The three major methods for determining price—

  • Cost-based pricing (CBP)

  • Value-based pricing (VBP)

  • Activity-based pricing (ABP)

■ The various pricing arrangements or contract types

■ The numerous means to properly analyze price

As previously stated, price should be a derivative of your people, processes, and performance. Price should be adjusted by your business strategy, given the marketplace your organization is operating in as either a buyer or a seller. Price should always be an important point of discussion, not the beginning nor the totality of the business relationship.

Table 9.7 Checklist of Key Pricing Best Practices to Improve Performance Results

Buyers and sellers should

❑ Understand why price is important to all parties involved in PBA.

❑ Be able to effectively apply or evaluate lowest-price technically acceptable (LPTA) pricing.

❑ Be able to effectively apply or evaluate best-value pricing.

❑ Be able to effectively conduct tradeoff decision making when evaluating price.

❑ Realize the evolution of best-value pricing.

❑ Use a contract type that fairly allocates risk.

❑ Properly train all team members about how to properly use pricing strategies, pricing methods, pricing arrangements, and pricing analysis techniques.

❑ Understand and apply generally accepted accounting practices.

❑ Ensure adequate cost estimating and accounting systems and practices

❑ Understand and comply with all applicable U.S. government contracting laws, regulations, and policies.

Buyers should

❑ Select prices for comparison.
- Competitive proposal prices
- Catalog prices
- Historical prices

❑ Develop prices that are based on parametric analysis.

❑ Use independent estimates for price.

❑ Identify factors that affect price.

❑ Determine the effect of identified factors.

❑ Adjust prices on the basis of price analysis comparisons.

❑ Compare adjusted prices.

❑ Do not force an unfair transfer of risk to the seller.

❑ Do not encourage buy-in pricing.

Sellers should

❑ Use best-value pricing strategy to the maximum extend practicable.

❑ Create value-added differentiators.

❑ Use the value-based pricing method, when appropriate

❑ Hire, train, and retain the best contract negotiators.

❑ Understand the buyer's source selection process and key source selection criteria.

❑ Do not agree to or sign a bad deal.

❑ Ensure a reasonable profit is obtainable.

Questions to Consider

1. Which pricing strategy does your organization use most frequently? How well is it working?

2. What are the disadvantages to using cost-based pricing?

3. What are the advantages to using value-based pricing?

4. Do pricing arrangements or types of contracts really transfer risk between buyers and sellers?

5. How effectively does your organization analyze price?

Endnotes

1. Gregory A. Garrett, *World Class Contracting*, 3rded. (Chicago, IL: CCH Inc., 2003).
2. Darryl L. Walker, "Is Your Estimating System Asking for Trouble," *Contract Management* (NCMA, May 2004): 30.
3. Ibid.
4. Jeffrey A. Lubeck, "Beyond an Adequate Accounting System," *Contract Management*, (NCMA, May 2004): 6.
5. Ibid.
6. Ibid.
7. Ibid.
8. Ibid.
9. Ibid.
10. Ibid. Note 1.

CHAPTER 10

Beyond Performance-Based Acquisition

In his best-selling book titled *The World In 2020: Power, Culture, and Prosperity*, Hamish McRae stated:

> The success of the U.S. economy over the next generation will depend on the efficiency with which the country runs its whole society, not just its industrial sector. It is reasonable to expect U.S. industry to perform rather well; it has both high productivity and a ready supply of labor. It will, however, continue to shed labor, as will the manufacturing sector in every industrial country.
>
> U.S. traded services—things like banking, retailing, distribution—will have increased their share of gross national product still further. Both the production and the export of entertainment products and software will rise sharply, and new services will spring up and provide employment and generate wealth. It seems reasonable to expect that many of the existing service industries will continue to be as productive as any in the world, while new industries will quickly learn to operate to world-class standards of efficiency.[1]

For the above-stated vision of the U.S. economy in 2020 to become reality, performance-based acquisition (PBA) must evolve from inconsistent commercial practices and partially implemented government agency mandates to a true U.S. performance-based culture that is inculcated throughout the public and the private sectors. Experience shows that both U.S. government agencies and commercial industry will take their lead from the true world-class organizations, irrespective of whether the world-class organizations exist in the public or the private sector.

The Emergence of the HPO

We are beginning to see the emergence of a new class of organization, which I refer to as the high-performance organization (HPO). The HPO is the evolution and integration of three key components: (1) performance-based culture, (2) extended-enterprise value chain, and (3) high-performance project discipline.

Figure 10.1 (this page) illustrates the three key aspects of the HPO and how those organizations must be both overlayed and integrated with the 4Ps: people, processes, performance, and price. HPOs help customers meet or exceed their goals, while simultaneously achieving internal organizational performance targets.

HPO: Performance-Based Culture

In a true high-performance organization (HPO), the term performance-based is never used, because everything is based on performance by the very nature of the organizational culture. Said differently, in an

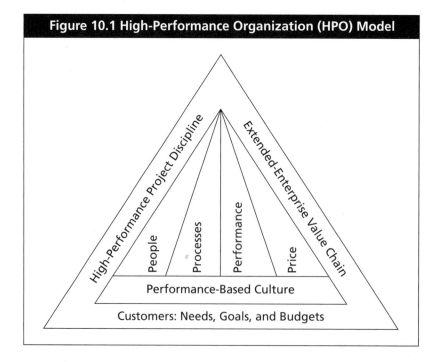

Figure 10.1 High-Performance Organization (HPO) Model

organization that has a performance-based culture, everything is done in a performance-based manner, such as

- "Performance-based" vision, mission, and goals,

- "Performance-based" budgets,

- "Performance-based" payment,

- "Performance-based" promotion,

- "Performance-based" selection of people,

- "Performance-based" selection of suppliers, and

- "Performance-based" organizational, team, and individual objectives and goals.

A performance-based culture is based on a working environment where performance matters most, not what your seniority is, what diversity quotas you have, whom you know, or where you went to school. In a performance-based culture, the organization would be a true meritocracy united with common goals, common objectives, a spirit of knowledge sharing, and respect. In an organization with a performance-based culture, everyone is focused on helping each individual, the individual's team, and the organization reach the highest levels of performance possible.

By its very nature, an organization with a performance-based culture would routinely conduct internal and external benchmarking of its processes, information systems, performance assessment methods, training or professional development programs, and knowledge-sharing practices, so each could continually seek to improve performance.

Today, you probably know a few people who are truly performance-based individuals. You may also know of one or two teams (groups of individuals) who have developed a performance-based culture. And if you are lucky, you may know one organization—typically a small business—that possesses a real performance-based culture. The problem is a real performance-based culture is the exception, not the rule, in both the public and the private sectors.

So, how do you create a performance-based culture? Well, you begin creating that culture by placing the concept in people's mind, then by getting people at all levels of the organization to talk about what it takes to create such a culture. Next, you develop specific action plans from the top to the bottom of the organization. Clearly, creating a performance-based culture does not happen overnight or even in a short span of time. The larger the organization, the more time it will take to inculcate the concept and institute performance-based practices.

Years ago, the late quality guru Dr. W. Edwards Deming was known for stating in his seminars that changing an organization's culture takes both time and a commitment from the top down. When asked how long it takes to change or transform an organization's culture, Dr. Deming would usually respond, "It depends." Dr. Deming would then typically give some general guidelines.[2] Drawing on Dr. Deming's teachings and further research, I have concluded the following guidelines that provide a roughly right view of how long it takes to fully transform an organization's culture:

■ Small organization (100 people or less)—6 months to 1 year;

■ Medium organization (101 to 1,000 people)—1 to 3 years;

■ Large organization (1,000 to 100,000 people)—3 to 5 years; and

■ Super-sized organization (100,000+)—5 to 7 years.

Clearly, many organization's senior executives, especially in the United States, are driven primarily by short-term goals, usually on a quarterly or annual basis. Some U.S. organization's senior executives do develop longer-term strategic plans, typically one to three years, and a few organizations develop three- to five-year strategic plans. However, in our U.S. economy, it is the exception rather than the rule to see an organization conducting any real in depth planning more than five years in advance.

Thus, most senior executives who attempt to evolve their organization into an HPO, by creating a performance-based culture, will likely fail or fall short. Senior executives often fail to achieve a full transformation, because they do not truly plan or commit the resources—both time and money—to complete the organizational transformation. Often, after one or two years, sometimes sooner, senior executives will declare victory while stating that their organization has achieved a full transformation. However, in most cases, only a partial acceptance of the cultural change has occurred within the organization. A performance-based culture is the foundation for a true HPO, which is easy to say, but hard to create and maintain.

HPO: Extended-Enterprise Value Chain (EEVC)

Outsourcing is here to stay. In fact, most experts expect outsourcing to increase in both the public and the private sectors worldwide. Thus, the need to build strong and deep business relationships between government and industry and within business to business will certainly increase during the next five to 10 years. Increasingly, organizations are forming strategic alliances or partnerships between or with a smaller number of suppliers, distributors, resellers, or a combination of all.

Organizations that are involved in buying or selling products, services, and solutions are seeking to leverage their relationships to achieve greater discounts, expanded sales, reduced inventories, reduced cycle times, and enhanced capabilities. Today, more organizations are providing or sharing information with their business partners through extended enterprises databases. Often, organizations are electronically sharing products and services information, forecast or demand information, and a wide variety of other confidential information through Internet or secure Web portals in order to reduce expenses and to maximize performance results.

Information is power, and enterprise software applications, which link multifunctional businesses, departments, and organizations, are being integrated to form new EEVCs. As outsourcing grows, so does the value and power of the supply chain. Thus, by linking supply chains of different organizations together, business partners can create a super-integrated or extended-enterprise value chain. A few organizations such as Honda, UPS, Dell, Cisco Systems, Wal-Mart, and others have learned the importance of creating and mastering the EEVC. Organizations that have created EEVCs have learned the value of building an agile and adaptable supply chain.

Wal-Mart, for example, has further empowered its EEVC by using rather simple but effective technology such as radio frequency identification (RFID) of products through simple, unique bar coding requirements for all of their suppliers. Likewise, the U.S. Department of Defense (DOD) is following Wal-Mart's lead and is now beginning to require a similar unique item identification (UID) program for critical products, items, and components that are typically valued at $5,000 or more on all of its new contracts. These simple examples are just the tip of the iceberg of potential enhancements to propel the power of emerging EEVCs.

In the new world of HPOs, the EEVC will be a key differentiator between competitors. The new business paradigm is—and will increasingly become—the battle of the EEVCs. Said differently, the EEVC, which can do the work—better, faster, and cheaper—will win! When in doubt, just ask Dell.

HPO: High Performance Project Discipline (HPPD)

The performance-based culture is the foundation or heart of the HPO. The EEVC is the body, arms, and legs of the HPO. However, the use of high-performance project discipline is the real brainpower and driving force that operates the HPO. High-performance project discipline (HPPD) is really an organizational blend of art and science. The art of HPPD involves the organization as a whole developing and mastering soft skill areas, including leadership, conflict management, communications, and ethics or integrity. The science of HPPD involves the organization as a whole developing and mastering hard skill areas, including computer literacy, product or technical expertise, project planning and scheduling, risk management, analytical or financial, contract management, supply chain management, and others.

It is not enough to have one or two people within your organization with mastery of HPPD. If you are to achieve a true HPO status, the leadership of the organization must become the driving force or force multiplier of HPPD by enlightening and motivating the entire organization. Leaders must walk the talk by speaking and practicing the appropriate actions each day. HPPD requires extensive, multifunctional, team-based training whereby responsibility, authority, and accountability are cornerstones to organizational behavior.

Some people and organizations like to operate in a fast and loose environment with little to no processes or discipline. Those fast and loose organizations often fail, because they have inconsistent results, high costs, little knowledge transfer, and a lack of scalability. However, some people and organizations are far too rigid, never wanting to change or deviate from how or what they have done in the past. Like most things in life and in business, a little compromise or flexibility can go a long way.

The simple, yet effective concept of rigid flexibility is really the basis for a successful HPPD. Said differently, every organization needs a somewhat flexible project-based methodology, integrated processes, information systems, and proven best practices that well-educated and trained people execute in a highly consistent manner. People need to be held responsible and accountable; HPPD ensures it is done. Allowing everyone to do whatever, whenever, creates chaos, not consistent high-performance results.

Despite, what some people think, discipline is a good word and is the backbone of consistent high-performance execution. Realizing the general demise of multiple-layers of middle management, organizations worldwide are embracing the project management discipline. The project management discipline helps to ensure on-time delivery of quality products, services, and solutions, which meet or exceed customer requirements, while achieving the budget or profitability goals desired. The fastest-growing professional association in the world is the Project Management Institute (PMI), which has grown at an annual rate of over 24 percent for more than a decade. PMI now boasts more than 170,000+ members from more than 100 countries globally.[3]

Numerous industries, including aerospace, automotive, banking, construction, defense, electronics, information technology, telecommunications, and others have all embraced the value proposition of the project management discipline. Likewise, numerous U.S. government agencies, including DOD, DOE, GSA, and NASA have equally endorsed the value of project or program management to help their organizations achieve greater performance results.[4] HPPD is merely taking and applying the PMI proven best practices and appropriately tailoring them to the specific acquisition situation. HPPD achieves consistent excellence in execution through implementing the concept of rigid flexibility to the art and science of project management.

The Rise of HPOs

Today, we see the emergence of a small number of future HPOs (Dell, General Electric, IBM, Microsoft, Toyota, and others). The future HPOs have not fully mastered all three aspects of the HPO: (1) performance-based culture, (2) extended-enterprise value chain, and (3) high-performance project discipline, but those organizations have mastered at least two of the three aspects required to be considered an HPO. Drawing on my experience and research, I find that it is reasonable to assume that over the next 5 to 10 years the HPOs will grow in number and in dominance of their respective industries. Likewise, it is reasonable to expect public sector organizations will attempt to mirror the best practices of the powerful industry HPOs, in an effort to benefit both the public they serve and their respective national economics.

It is also inevitable that some of the emerging HPOs will rise and fall, while others will rise and grow to unprecedented levels of public or private sector dominance. Creating the HPO is the next major paradigm shift in public and private sector business excellence.

Summary

In retrospect, this chapter has discussed the world beyond PBA—to the emergence and rise of the HPOs.

The HPOs will comprise public or private sector organizations that have learned to create and master three key aspects of business: (1) performance-based culture, (2) extended-enterprise value chain, and (3) high-performance project discipline. Understanding and mastering PBA is a key step in the organizational evolution toward a higher level of business performance. The creation of the HPO will serve as the next major paradigm shift—in both the public and the private sector—to achieve excellence in execution. So, the real question is: "How well prepared is your organization to compete and thrive in a world of HPOs?"

Endnotes

1. Hamish McRae, *The World in 2020: Power, Culture, and Prosperity*, (Boston: HBS Press,).

2. W. Edwards Deming, Total Quality Management Seminar (Columbus, Ohio: Ohio State University, 1987).

3. Project Management Institute (PMI) Newsletter, Newtown Square, PA, April 2005.

4. Ibid.

Appendix A
Seven Steps to Performance-Based Services Acquisition

For the full version of the appendix, please visit **www.acqnet.gov.**

Introduction
A Performance-Based Preference
Over the last decade, innovators in Congress and the executive branch have reformed the laws and policies that govern federal acquisition. Among the most important of these reforms are the Government Performance and Results Act of 1993, the Federal Acquisition Streamlining Act of 1994 (FASA), and the Clinger-Cohen Act of 1996. All of these laws send an important message about performance in federal programs and acquisitions.

As is evident from the dates above, performance-based service acquisition is not new. Office of Federal Procurement Policy Pamphlet #4, "A Guide for Writing and Administering Performance Statements of Work for Service Contracts," (now rescinded) described "how to write performance into statements of work" and addressed job analysis, surveillance plans, and quality control in 1980. Eleven years later, OFPP Policy Letter 91-2, Service Contracting, established that:

> It is the policy of the Federal Government that (1) agencies use performance-based contracting methods to the maximum extent practicable when acquiring services, and (2) agencies carefully select acquisition and contract administration strategies, methods, and techniques that

best accommodate the requirements.

The intent is for agencies to describe their needs in terms of what is to be achieved, not how it is to be done. These policies have been incorporated in the Federal Acquisition Regulation Subpart 37.6 (Performance-Based Contracting), and additional guidance is in the OFPP document, "A Guide to Best Practices for Performance-Based Service Contracting." (OFPP Policy Letter 91-2 was rescinded effective March 30, 2000.)

Law and regulation establish a preference for performance-based service acquisition. The new Administration continues a long line of support for this acquisition approach, as demonstrated in OMB Memorandum M-01-15 on performance goals and management initiatives. As cited in the Procurement Executives Council's Strategic Plan:

> ...over the next five years, a majority of the service contracts offered throughout the federal government will be performance-based. In other words, rather than micromanaging the details of how contractors operate, the government must set the standards, set the results and give the contractor the freedom to achieve it in the best way.
>
> —Presidential Candidate George W. Bush
> on June 9, 2000

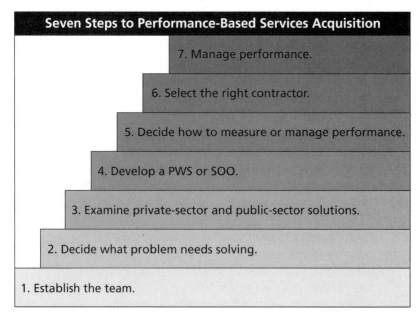

Seven Steps to Performance-Based Services Acquisition

7. Manage performance.

6. Select the right contractor.

5. Decide how to measure or manage performance.

4. Develop a PWS or SOO.

3. Examine private-sector and public-sector solutions.

2. Decide what problem needs solving.

1. Establish the team.

Benefits of Performance-Based Acquisition

Performance-based service acquisition has many benefits, such as:

- Increased likelihood of meeting mission needs;

- Focus on intended results, not process;

- Better value and enhanced performance;

- Less performance risk;

- No detailed specification or process description needed;

- Contractor flexibility in proposing solution;

- Better competition: not just contractors, but solutions;

- Contractor buy-in and shared interests;

- Shared incentives permit innovation and cost effectiveness;

- Less likelihood of a successful protest;

- Surveillance: less frequent, more meaningful;

- Results documented for Government Performance and Results Act reporting, as by-product of acquisition; and

- Variety of solutions from which to choose.

Moving Toward Performance-Based Competency

The federal acquisition workforce has not, to date, fully embraced performance-based acquisition. There are many reasons, such as workload demands, but more fundamentally, traditional "acquisition think" is entrenched in a workforce of dwindling numbers. The situation is complicated by lack of "push" from the program offices who have the mission needs and who fund the acquisitions—because there is where the true key to performance-based acquisition lies. It is not the procurement analyst, the contracting officer, or even the contracting office itself. Performance-based acquisition is a collective responsibility that involves representatives from budget, technical, contracting, logistics, legal, and program offices.

While there are leaders among us who understand the concept and its potential, it is difficult for an agency to assemble a team of people who together have the knowledge to drive such an acquisition through to successful contract performance. This is especially true today because many more types of people play a role in acquisition teams. These people add fresh perspective, insight, energy, and innovation to the process—but they may lack some of the rich contractual background and experience that acquisition often requires.

Performance-based service acquisition can be daunting, with its discussion of work breakdown structures, quality assurance plans, and contractor surveillance. Guides on the subject can easily run to and over 50, 75, or even 100 pages. This makes learning something new appear more complicated than it really is. The foundation for a successful acquisition involves a clear answer to three questions: *what do I need, when do I need it, and how do I know it's good when I get it?*

The virtual guide on which this downloadable guide is based breaks down performance-based service acquisition into seven easy steps, complete with "stories" (case studies). It is intended to make the subject of PBSC accessible for all and shift the paradigm from traditional "acquisition think" into one of collaborative performance-oriented teamwork with a focus on program performance and improvement, not simply contract compliance. Once the shift is made, the library and links sections interwoven in the virtual guide will lead you into the rich web of federal performance-based guidance.

Have a good journey!

Executive Summary

One of the most important challenges facing agencies today is the need for widespread adoption of performance-based acquisition to meet mission and program needs. This administration has set a goal for FY 2002 in OMB Memorandum M-01-15 to "award contracts over $25,000 using PBSC techniques for not less than 20 percent of the total eligible service contracting dollars," increasing to 50 percent by FY 2005.

Although policies supporting performance-based contracting have been in place for more than 20 years, progress has been slow. The single most important reason for this is that the acquisition community is not the sole owner of the problem, nor can the acquisition community implement performance-based contracting on its own.

Laws, policies, and regulations have dramatically changed the acquisition process into one that must operate with a mission-based and program-based focus. Because of this, many more types of people must play a role in acquisition teams today. In addition to technical and contracting staff, for example, there is "value added" by including those from program and financial offices. These people add fresh perspective, insight, energy, and innovation to the process—but they may lack some of the rich contractual background and experience that acquisition often requires.

This guide, geared to the greater acquisition community (especially program offices), breaks down performance-based service acquisition into seven simple steps.

1. Establish an integrated solutions team.

2. Describe the problem that needs solving.

3. Examine private-sector and public-sector solutions.

4. Develop a performance work statement (PWS) or statement of objectives (SOO).

5. Decide how to measure and manage performance.

6. Select the right contractor.

7. Manage performance.

The intent is to make the subject of performance-based acquisition accessible and logical for all and shift the paradigm from traditional "acquisition think" into one of collaborative, performance-oriented teamwork with a focus on program performance, improvement, and innovation, not simply contract compliance. Performance-based acquisition offers the potential to dramatically transform the nature of service delivery, and permit the federal government to tap the enormous creative energy and innovative nature of private industry.

Let the acquisitions begin!

Step 1:
Establish an Integrated
Solutions Team

The trend today, given the statutory, policy, and regulatory mandates discussed in the introduction, is that acquisitions are conducted by teams of people working cooperatively toward a common goal. This is the model used by leading or breakthrough organizations, which have come to recognize the limitations of clearly defined roles, responsibilities, and organizational boundaries, and have adopted the use of acquisition teams that integrate all stakeholders' efforts toward one goal: mission accomplishment. It is also the model that the Office of Management and Budget is seeking when it asks this question of agencies in their budget submissions: "Is there an Integrated Project Team?"

Tasks, Features, and Best Practices

- Ensure senior management involvement and support.
- Tap multi-disciplinary expertise.
- Define roles and responsibilities.
- Develop rules of conduct.
- Empower team members.
- Identify stakeholders and nurture consensus.
- Develop and maintain the knowledge base over the project life.
- "Incent" the team: Establish link between program mission and team members' performance.

See Web site for additional information: www.acqnet.gov.

These principles are also reflected in the *Federal Acquisition Regulation (FAR)*, which (1) recognizes that teams begin with the customer and end with the contractor, and (2) outlines procurement policies and procedures that are used by members of the acquisition team. Note also that the *FAR* specifically provides that contracting officers "should take the lead in encouraging business process innovations and ensuring that business decisions are sound."

In this guide, we call such acquisition teams "integrated solutions teams" in acknowledgment of the fundamental purpose of performance-based acquisition—to find solutions to agency mission and program needs.

Ensure senior management involvement and support.

Most best-practice studies agree: Senior management involvement and support is a predictor of success. For example, the CIO Council document, "Implementing Best Practices: Strategies at Work," cited "strong leadership at the top" as a "success factor" in the selection, evaluation and control processes associated with acquisition investment review. By its very nature, an integrated solutions team has members whose affiliations cut across organizational boundaries. "Turf" can become an issue, unless there is strong, effective senior management support and a shared vision. Program decision-makers should be on the team. Creating "buy-in" from leadership and establishing the realms of authority are essential to project success.

Tap multidisciplinary expertise.

Because of the mission-based and program-based focus of acquisition that has resulted from acquisition reform, many more types of people play a role in acquisition teams today. In addition to contracting staff, for example, are those from the program, financial, user, and even legal offices. All of these skills and more can be required to create a true performance-based approach to an agency's needs.

It is important to recognize that integrated solution teams are not a "training ground." They're a field of operation for not just four, six, or eight people, but four, six, or eight people who are among the best in their fields and grounded or trained in acquisition. Team composition is a critical success factor in performance-based acquisition—so much so, in fact, that the Office of Management and Budget asks about team approach during the budget review process for acquisition funding.

Define roles and responsibilities.

It is important that the members of the team understand what their roles and responsibilities are. Regardless of its representation, the team is responsible for ensuring that the acquisition:

■ Satisfies legal and regulatory requirements,

■ Has performance and investment objectives consistent with the agency's strategic goals,

■ Successfully meets the agency's needs and intended results, and

■ Remains on schedule and within budget.

Successful teams typically have a number of features: shared leadership roles, individual as well as mutual accountability, collective work-products, performance measures related to the collective work-product, and other ingredients.

In a team environment, the roles and responsibilities of the members blur and merge, often with striking results.

Develop rules of conduct.

Seasoned facilitators and team leaders know this: It is important to develop rules of conduct for groups of people. Setting the rules and then insisting on their use is a key to effective team operation. Given a clear purpose and defined approach for working together, teams are much more likely to move quickly through the early phases of team performance and achieve the desired result.

The Monash University's Learning Centre has a Web site on teamwork, which puts the importance of the rules in perspective. It suggests that groups "pass through a sequence of five stages of development:

■ **Forming**, or coming together,

■ **Storming**, or conflict,

■ **Norming**, or working out the rules, and

■ **Performing**, or getting the job done,

While the length of time different groups take to pass through each of these developmental stages varies, high team performance is usually not achieved until the group has passed through the first three stages."

Empower team members.

The "Statement of Guiding Principles for the Federal Acquisition System," says it most simply: *"Participants in the acquisition process should work together as a team and should be empowered to make decisions within their area of responsibility"* (FAR 1.102(a)). Clearly defined levels of empowerment are critical to success.

The Department of Commerce, in its CONOPS (Concept of Operations) acquisition program, has examined the concept of what "empowerment" means in detail. The department believes that empowerment is tied to responsibility, authority, and autonomy. In the agency's project planning tool are the life-cycle tasks of an acquisition and an identification of where responsibility for the performance of that task typically resides.

Identify stakeholders and nurture consensus.

Stakeholders may include customers, the public, oversight organizations, and members and staff of Congress. It is important for the team to know who the stakeholders are and the nature of their interests, objectives, and possible objections. At a minimum, stakeholders should be consulted and, at times, may participate on the team.

In developing the acquisition, the key tools the team should use are consensus and compromise, without losing sight of the three key questions:

1. What do I need?

2. When do I need it?

3. How do I know it's good when I get it?

Develop and maintain the knowledge base over the project life.

"How do you predict the future...you create it."

—Peter Drucker

An emerging concern in the acquisition community is "knowledge management." There are many definitions, but the simplest may well be "the right knowledge in the right place at the right time and in the right context." Knowledge management is a people issue, not a technology issue.

Consider the need to manage the project's knowledge base in this light: Acquisitions often take months, and the contracts that are awarded are often performed over years. People join the team and people leave, taking their knowledge with them.

Further, those people that began the project and those that oversee the project are often different. All too often, when a contract is awarded, the acquisition team "pats itself on the back" and walks away. The project is passed into the care of a contract administrator who doesn't know the history of the project, why decisions were made, and why the contract is structured or worded the way it is. Modification may begin right away. And we wonder why contract performance is sometimes a problem?

The approach needs to shift from a focus on contracting to a focus on both acquisition and project management. Where possible, the same key members of the team (program manager, project manager, and contracting officer) should be part of the integrated solutions team from the initial discussions of mission-based need, through contract performance, and indeed to contract closeout. With this continuity and a focus on maintaining the project's knowledge base, the likelihood of success is exponentially greater.

"Incent" the team: Link program mission and team members' performance.

If continuity is important, what can be done to keep a team together? Added to empowerment and a shared vision, incentives are key. The most fundamental incentives are those that link program mission and team members' performance, and then tie performance to pay. If the acquisition has performance objectives, and the contractor has performance objectives, then the government team should also have performance objectives. Like contractor incentives, the team's objectives should carry a value in terms of pay, recognition, and awards.

Keep in mind that these performance objectives should be program-based, not acquisition-based. Who cares if the contract is awarded in two months if it takes two years to get deliverables in the hands of the users? Make sure the incentives are tied to the "right" results.

Step 2:
Describe the Problem
That Needs Solving

Because a clearer, performance-based picture of the acquisition should be the team's first step, it is not yet time to retrieve the requirement's former solicitation, search for templates, think about contract type or incentives, and decide on the contractor or the solution.

Planning for an acquisition should begin with business planning that focuses on the desired improvement. The first consideration is, what is the problem the agency needs to solve? What results are needed? Will it meet the organizational and mission objectives?

The Government Performance and Results Act of 1993 requires that agencies establish and "manage to" mission-related performance goals and objectives. It stands to reason that any significant, mission-critical acquisition should relate in some way to the Results Act objectives. Although many acquisitions do not make this link, performance-based acquisitions must make this connection to the agency's strategic plan and to employees' performance plans.

Tasks, Features, and Best Practices

- Link acquisition to mission and performance objectives.
- Define (at a high level) desired results.
- Decide what constitutes success.
- Determine the currect level of performance.

See Web site for additional information: www.acqnet.gov.

Link acquisition to mission and performance objectives.

The most effective foundation for an acquisition is the intended effect of the contract in supporting and improving an agency's mission and performance goals and objectives (reported to OMB and Congress under the Results Act's strategic and annual performance planning processes). Describing an acquisition in terms of how it supports these mission-based performance goals allows an agency to establish clearly the relationship of the acquisition to its business, and it sets the stage for crafting an acquisition, in which the performance goals of the contractor and the government are in sync.

In addition to the Government Performance and Results Act, the President's Management Agenda has added the requirement for performance-based budgeting. This links funding to performance, and ensures that programs making progress towards achieving their goals will continue to receive funding. Conversely, programs unable to show adequate progress may lose option-year funding.

This mission-based foundation normally must be established by or in cooperation with people who work in the program area that the resources will support when they are acquired. (This is why assembling the team is the first step in a performance-based acquisition.) Again, note that the focus is not what resources are required; the focus is what outcome is required.

With this foundation, when the planning process is complete, an agency should be able to demonstrate clearly how an individual acquisition's performance objectives will assist in achieving the agency's mission and goals.

Define (at a high level) desired results.

Once the acquisition is linked to the agency's mission needs, the thoughts of the team should turn to what, specifically, are the desired results (outcomes) of contract performance? Is it a lower level of defaults on federal loans? Is it a reduction in benefit processing time? Is it broader dissemination of federal information? Is it a reduction in the average time it takes to get relief checks to victims? What is the ultimate intended result of the contract and how does it relate to the agency's strategic plan?

Note that these are questions that a former solicitation—or someone else's solicitation—cannot answer. This is one of the tough tasks that the integrated solutions team must face.

These answers can normally be found, not with an exhaustive analysis, but through facilitated work sessions with program staff, customers, and stakeholders. By taking the process away from a review of paper or an examination of the status quo, greater innovation and insight is possible. Once aired, those thoughts need to be captured in the performance work statement (PWS) or statement of objectives (SOO).

Note also that to do this well, the team will need to plan to seek information from the private sector during market research (step three). Industry benchmarks and best practices from the "best in the business" may help sharpen the team's focus on what the performance objectives should be.

Decide what constitutes success.

Just as important as a clear vision of desired results is a clear vision of what will constitute success for the project. These are two distinct questions: Where do I want to go, and how will I know when I get there?

In the Joint Direct Attack Munitions (JDAM) research and development acquisition, for example, affordability (in terms of average unit production price) was a key element, along with "how well the product met the live-or-die criteria." Affordability was communicated in no uncertain terms from top-level management to the acquisition team, and from the acquisition team to the competing contractors. As the project manager recalled, "I had a strong sense of empowerment...from the Air Force Chief of Staff who said basically, 'Do what you have to do to get the products under $40,000'."

With that clear a mandate and the benefits of head-to-head contractor competition, the final, winning proposal included an average unit production price between $14,000 and $15,000—far lower than the original cost target of $40,000 and the original cost estimate of $68,000 per unit.

So it is important to establish a clear target for success, which will then serve to focus the efforts of the integrated solutions team in crafting the acquisition, the contractors in competing for award, and the government-industry team throughout contract performance.

Determine the current level of performance.

The main reason to determine the current level of performance is to establish the baseline against which future performance can be measured. If you don't know where you started, you can't tell how far you've come.

In order to think about taking measurements of current performance, think about what happens when you rent a car. The company will give you a piece of paper with an outline of a car on it. You're asked to go outside, and mark on the diagram every nick and scratch you see, so that when you return the car, the baseline is clear. This is precisely what we need to do with our current contracts or operations.

Keep in mind that the government doesn't necessarily have to do the baseline measurement. Another approach is to require a set of metrics as a deliverable under a current contract. Even if there were no existing provision, this could easily be done through contract modification. New solicitations can be written with provision for delivery of baseline and/or current performance levels, either annually, at the end of the contract, or both. The integrated solutions team must determine the adequacy of the baseline data for the new contract, to ensure they achieve the best results.

Step 3:
Examine Private-Sector
& Public-Sector Solutions

Once the acquisition's intended results have been identified, the integrated solutions team should begin to examine both private-sector and public-sector solutions. This is called "market research," and it is a vital means of arming the team with the expertise needed to conduct an effective performance-based acquisition.

Market research is the continuous process of collecting information to maximize reliance on the commercial marketplace and to benefit from its capabilities, technologies, and competitive forces in meeting an agency need. Market research is essential to the government's ability to buy best-value products and services that solve mission-critical problems. Acquisition reform has opened the door to effective new approaches to market research that should be undertaken by the integrated solutions team long before attempting to write a perfor-

---

Tasks, Features, and Best Practices

- Take a team approach to market research.
- Spend time learning from public-sector counterparts.
- Talk to private-sector companies before structuring the acquisition.
- Consider one-on-one meetings with industry.
- Look for existing contracts.
- Document market research.

See Web site for additional information: www.acqnet.gov.

mance work statement.

Take a team approach to market research.

In the past, it was not unusual for technical staff to conduct market research about marketplace offerings, while contracting staff conducted market research more focused on industry practices and pricing. A better approach is for the entire integrated solutions team to be a part of the market research effort. This enables the members of the team to share an understanding and knowledge of the marketplace—an important factor in the development of the acquisition strategy—and a common understanding of what features, schedules, terms, and conditions are key.

Spend time learning from public-sector counterparts.

While many are familiar with examining private-sector sources and solutions as part of market research, looking to the public-sector is not as common a practice. Yet, it makes a great deal of sense on several levels.

First, there is an increased interest in cross-agency cooperation and collaboration. If the need is for payroll support, for example, many federal agencies have "solved" that problem and could potentially provide services through an interagency agreement. Alternatively, it could be that to provide seamless services to the public, two or more agencies need to team together to acquire a solution. (This is the model that may well evolve with e-government solutions, given the president's proposal of a special fund for such initiatives.)

Second, agencies with similar needs may be able to provide lessons learned and best practices. For example, the Department of Commerce COMMITS office has frequently briefed other agencies on the process of establishing a Governmentwide Agency Contract (GWAC). Another agency that we are aware of is now conducting public-sector market research about seat management implementation in the federal government. So it is important for the integrated solutions team to talk to their counterparts in other agencies. Taking the time to do so may help avert problems that could otherwise arise in the acquisition.

Talk to private-sector companies before structuring the acquisition.

With regard to the more traditional private-sector market research, it is important to be knowledgeable about commercial offerings, capabilities, and practices before structuring the acquisition in any detail. This is one of the more significant changes brought about by acquisition reform.

Some of the traditional ways to do this include issuing "sources sought" type notices at **FedBizOps.gov**, conducting "industry days," issuing requests for information, and holding pre-solicitation conferences. But it is also okay to simply pick up the phone and call private-sector company representatives.

Contact with vendors and suppliers for purposes of market research is now encouraged. In fact, FAR 15.201(a) specifically promotes the exchange of information "among all interested parties, from the earliest identification of a requirement through receipt of proposals." The limitations that apply (once a procurement is underway) are that prospective contractors be treated fairly and impartially and that standards of procurement integrity (FAR 3.104) be maintained. But the real key is to begin market research before a procurement is underway.

Consider one-on-one meetings with industry.

While many may not realize it, one-on-one meetings with industry leaders are not only permissible—see Federal Acquisition Regulation 15.201(c)(4)—they are more effective than pre-solicitation or pre-proposal conferences. Note that when market research is conducted before a solicitation or performance work statement is drafted, the rules are different. FAR 15.201(f) provides, for example: "General information about agency mission needs and future requirements may be disclosed at any time." Since the requirements have not (or should not have) been defined, disclosure of procurement-sensitive information is not an issue.

It is effective to focus on commercial and industry best practices, performance metrics and measurements, innovative delivery methods for the required services, and incentive programs that providers have found particularly effective.

This type of market research can expand the range of potential solutions, change the very nature of the acquisition, establish the performance-based approach, and represent the agency's first step on the way to an "incentivized" partnership with a contractor.

Look for existing contracts.

FAR Part 10 requires that as part of market research, the Integrated Solutions Team must go to **www.contractdirectory.gov** to see if there is an existing contract available to meet agency requirements.

Document market research.

FAR Part 10 requires that a written market research report be placed in the contract file. The amount of research, given the time and expense should be commensurate with the size of the acquisition.

Step 4:
Develop PWS or SOO

There are two ways to develop a specification for a performance-based acquisition: by using a performance work statement (PWS) or an emerging methodology built around a statement of objectives (SOO).

The PWS process is discussed in most existing guides on perfor-

Tasks, Features, and Best Practices
PWS
■ Conduct an analysis.
■ Apply the "so what?" test.
■ Capture the results of the analysis in a matrix.
■ Write the performance work statement.
■ Let the contractor solve the problem, including the labor mix.
SOO
■ Begin with the acquisition's "elevator message."
■ Describe the scope.
■ Write the performance objectives into the SOO.
■ Make sure the government and the contractor share objectives.
■ Identify the constraints.
■ Develop the background.
■ Make the final checks and maintain perspective.
See Web site for additional information: www.acqnet.gov.

mance-based service contracting and in the *Federal Acquisition Regulation*. Among its key processes are the conduct of a job analysis and development of a performance work statement and quality assurance and surveillance plan. When people talk about performance-based contracting, this is typically the model they have in mind.

The alternative process—use of a SOO—is an emerging methodology that turns the acquisition process around and requires competing contractors to develop the statement of work, performance metrics and measurement plan, and quality assurance plan-all of which should be evaluated before contract award. It is described briefly in the Department of Defense "Handbook for Preparation of Statement of Work (SOW)" for example:

> The SOO is a government-prepared document incorporated into the RFP that states the overall solicitation objectives. It can be used in those solicitations where the intent is to provide the maximum flexibility to each offeror to propose an innovative development approach.

The SOO is a very short document (under 10 pages) that provides the basic, high-level objectives of the acquisition. It is provided in the solicitation in lieu of a government-written statement of work or performance work statement.

In this approach, the contractors' proposals contain statements of work and performance metrics and measures (which are based on their proposed solutions and existing commercial practices). Clearly, use of a SOO opens the acquisition up to a wider range of potential solutions. The Veterans Benefits Administration loan servicing acquisition discussed under step two and in this step was conducted (very successfully) using a SOO.

The integrated solutions team should consider these two approaches and determine which is more suitable: the use of a PWS or a SOO.

PWS—Conduct an analysis.

Preparing a PWS begins with an analytical process, often referred to as a "job analysis." It involves a close examination of the agency's requirements and tends to be a "bottom up" assessment with "reengineering" potential. This analysis is the basis for establishing performance requirements, developing performance standards, writing the performance work statement, and producing the quality assurance plan. Those responsible for the mission or program are essential to the performance of the job analysis.

A different approach to the analytical process is described in the "Guidebook for Performance-Based Services Acquisition (PBSA) in the Department of Defense." It describes three "analysis-oriented steps" that are "top-down" in nature:

■ Define the desired outcomes: What must be accomplished to satisfy the requirement?

■ Conduct an outcome analysis: What tasks must be accomplished to arrive at the desired outcomes?

■ Conduct a performance analysis: When or how will I know that the outcome has been satisfactorily achieved, and how much deviation from the performance standard will I allow the contractor, if any?

The integrated solutions team should consider the various approaches. Neither the OFPP nor DOD guide is mandatory; both describe an approach to analysis. (There are other guides and other approaches in the "seven steps" library as well.) Regardless of the analytical process adopted, the team's task under step four is to develop certain information:

■ A description of the requirement in terms of results or outcomes,

■ Measurable performance standards, and

■ Acceptable quality levels (AQLs).

The AQL establishes the allowable error rate or variation from the standard. OFPP's best-practices guide cites this example: In a requirement for taxi services, the performance standard might be "pickup within five minutes of an agreed upon time." The AQL then might be five percent—i.e., the taxi could be more than five minutes late no more than five percent of the time. Failure to perform within the AQL could result in a contract price reduction or other action.

With regard to performance standards and AQLs, the integrated solutions team should remember that an option is to permit contractors to propose standards of service, along with appropriate price adjustment or other action. This approach fosters a reliance on standard commercial practices. (Remember that all these points—performance standards, quality levels, and price—are negotiable.)

Apply the "so what?" test.

"There is nothing so useless as doing efficiently that which should not be done at all."

—Peter Drucker

An analysis of requirements is often, by its nature, a close examination of the status quo; that is, it is often an analysis of process and "how" things are done-exactly the type of detail that is not supposed to be in a PWS. The integrated solutions team needs to identify the essential inputs, processes, and outputs during job analysis. Otherwise, the danger is that contractors will bid back the work breakdown structure, and the agency will have failed to solicit innovative and streamlined approaches from the competitors.

One approach is to use the "so what?" test during job analysis. For example, once job analysis identifies outputs, the integrated solutions team should verify the continued need for the output. The team should ask questions like: Who needs the output? Why is the output needed? What is done with it? What occurs as a result? Is it worth the effort and cost? Would a different output be preferable?

Capture the results of the analysis in a matrix.

As the information is developed, the integrated solutions team should begin capturing the information in a performance matrix. The U.S. Department of Treasury guide, "Performance-Based Service Contracting," illustrates a six-column approach with the following:

- Desired Outcomes: What do we want to accomplish as the end result of this contract?

- Required Service: What task must be accomplished to give us the desired result? (Note: Be careful this doesn't become a "how" statement.)

- Performance Standard: What should the standards for completeness, reliability, accuracy, timeliness, customer satisfaction, quality and/or cost be?

- Acceptable Quality Level (AQL): How much error will we accept?

- Monitoring Method: How will we determine that success has been achieved?

■ Incentives/Disincentives for Meeting or Not Meeting the Performance Standards: What carrot or stick will best reward good performance or address poor performance? (This reflects priced and unpriced adjustments based on an established methodology. Reductions can be made for reduced value of performance.)

The U.S. Treasury guide provides templates for help desk, seat management, systems integration, software development, and system design/business process re-engineering services.

The Department of Defense approach is very similar: take the desired outcomes, performance objectives, performance standards, and acceptable quality levels that have been developed during the analytical process and document them in a performance requirements summary (PRS). The PRS matrix has five columns: performance objective, performance standard, acceptable quality level, monitoring method, and incentive. The PRS serves as the basis for the performance work statement.

Write the performance work statement.

There is not a standard template or outline for a PWS. The Federal Acquisition Regulation only requires that agencies

■ Describe requirements in terms of results rather than process,

■ Use measurable performance standards and quality assurance surveillance plans,

■ Provide for reductions of fees or price, and

■ Include performance incentives where appropriate.

In terms of organization of information, a SOW-like approach is suitable for a performance work statement: introduction, background information, scope, applicable documents, performance requirements, special requirements (such as security), and deliverables. However, the team can adapt this outline as appropriate. Before finishing, there should be final checks:

■ Examine every requirement carefully and delete any that are not essential.

■ Search for process descriptions or "how" statements and eliminate them.

Many agencies have posted examples of performance-based solicitations that can provide some guidance or helpful ideas. (See LINKS section.) However, since the nature of performance-based acquisition is (or should be) tied to mission-unique or program-unique needs, keep in mind that another agency's solution may not be a good model.

Let the contractor solve the problem, including the labor mix.

First, keep this important "lesson learned" in mind: *Don't spec the requirement so tightly that you get the same solution from each offeror.*

Second, performance-based service acquisition requires that the integrated solutions team usually must jettison some traditional approaches to buying services, like specifying labor categories, educational requirements, or number of hours of support required. Those are "how" approaches. Instead, let contractors propose the best people with the best skill sets to meet the need and fit the solution. The government can then evaluate the proposal based both on the quality of the solution and the experience of the proposed personnel. In making the shift to performance-based acquisition, remember this:

"The significant problems we face cannot be solved at the same level of thinking we were at when we created them."

—Albert Einstein

The Department of Defense addresses this in the "Guidebook for Performance-Based Services Acquisition (PBSA) in the Department of Defense." The guide provides as follows:

> Prescribing manpower requirements limits the ability of offerors to propose their best solutions, and it could preclude the use of qualified contractor personnel who may be well suited for performing the requirement but may be lacking— for example—a complete college degree or the exact years of specified experience.

For some services, in fact, such practices are prohibited. Congress passed a provision (Section 813) in the 2001 Defense Authorization Act, now implemented in the FAR (with governmentwide applicability, of course). It prescribes that, when acquiring information technology services, solicitations may not describe any minimum experience or educational requirements for proposed contractor personnel unless the contracting officer determines that needs of the agency either

(1) cannot be met without that requirement, or (2) require the use of other than a performance-based contract.

Remember that how the performance work statement is written will either empower the private sector to craft innovative solutions or limit or cripple that ability.

Using a SOO

As discussed previously, an alternative approach to development of the PWS is to develop a statement of objectives. There is no set format for a SOO, but one approach follows:

- Purpose,

- Scope,

- Period of performance,

- Place of performance (if known, if required),

- Background,

- Program objectives, and

- Constraints (may include security, privacy, safety, and accessibility).

The government-prepared SOO is usually incorporated into the RFP either as an attachment or as part of Section L. At contract award, the contractor-proposed statement of work (solution) can be incorporated by reference or integrated into Section C.

Begin with the acquisition's "elevator message."

How many solicitations have you seen that begin with a statement like, "This is a solicitation for a time-and-materials contract." Or what about this one: "The purpose of this solicitation is to acquire information technology hardware, software, and services." Or this one (true story): "This is a performance-based specification to acquire services on a time-and-materials basis." In the context of performance-based acquisition, all are bad starts.

The first statement made in a statement of objectives should be an explanation of how the acquisition relates to the agency's program or mission need and what problem needs solving (as identified under step two).

For example, in a recent task order solicitation by the Veterans Benefits Administration, this statement was made: *The purpose of this task order is to obtain loan servicing in support of VA's portfolio that will significantly improve loan guaranty operations and service to its customers.*

This simple statement was a signal that the acquisition had made a huge break from the predecessor contract, which had started with something like, "This is a requirement for information technology resources." The turnaround was the realization that the need was for loan servicing support services; technology was the enabler.

Describe the scope.

A short description of scope in the SOO helps the competitors get a grasp on the size and range of the services needed. The Veteran's Benefits Administration's scope statement follows:

> The purpose of this [task order] is to provide the full range of loan servicing support. This includes such activities as customer management, paying taxes and insurance, default management, accounting, foreclosure, bankruptcy, etc., as well as future actions associated with loan servicing. This Statement of Objectives reflects current VA policies and practices, allowing offerors to propose and price a solution to known requirements. It is anticipated that specific loan servicing requirements and resulting objectives will change over the life of this order. This will result in VA modifying this order to incorporate in-scope changes.

Another consideration for the integrated solutions team to consider is the budget authority (in dollars) available to fund the acquisition. In an acquisition approach as "wide open" as a statement of objectives, the competing contractors will need insight into funding authority so that they can size their solution to be both realistic and competitive. This may be listed as a constraint.

Write the performance objectives into the SOO.

In step two, the task of the integrated solutions team was to "decide what problem needs solving." The basis for that analysis was information in the agency's strategic and annual performance plans, program authorization documents, budget documents, and discussions with project owners and stakeholders. That information constitutes the core of the statement of objectives.

In the case of the Veterans Administration, for example, the acquisition's performance objectives were set forth in this opening statement:

> VA expects to improve its current loan servicing operations through this task order in several ways. Primary among these is to increase the number and value of saleable loans. In addition, VA wants to be assured that all payments for such items as taxes and insurance are always paid on time. As part of these activities, the VA also has an objective to improve information technology exchange and VA's access to automated information on an as required basis to have the information to meet customer needs and auditors' requirements.

What is immediately obvious is that these are mission-related, measurable objectives.

Make sure the government and the contractor share objectives.

When the acquisition's objectives are "grounded in" the plans and objectives found in agency strategic performance plans, program authorization documents, and budget and investment documents, then the government and the contractor are clearly working in a partnership toward shared goals. This is a far cry from the old-school acquisition approach, characterized by driving cost down and then berating the supplier to demand delivery. When the agency and the contractor share the same goals, the likelihood of successful performance rises dramatically.

Identify the constraints.

The purpose of a SOO is to provide contractors with maximum flexibility to conceive and propose innovative approaches and solutions. However, in some cases, there may be constraints that the government must place on those solutions. For example, core financial systems used by federal agencies must comply with requirements of OMB Circular A-127 and the guidance of the Joint Financial Management Improvement Program. Acquisitions related to technology will need to conform to the agency's information technology architecture and accessibility standards. In addition, there may be considerations of security, privacy, and safety that should be addressed. There also may be existing policies, directives, and standards that are constraining factors. The integrated solutions team should work with program managers, staff, customers, and stakeholders to identify these and to confirm their essentiality.

Develop the background.

The background and current environment set forth in a statement of objectives comprise important information for contractors. The Veterans Benefits Administration's statement of work included sections on

- VA loan servicing history,

- Current VA portfolio origination/acquisition process, and

- Overview of the current servicing process.

A best practice when using a SOO is to provide a brief overview of the program, listing links to Web-delivered information on the current contract, government-controlled, government-furnished equipment, and a hardware configuration or enterprise architecture, as appropriate. The development of this information is essential so that contractors can perform meaningful due diligence.

Make the final checks and maintain perspective.

Before finalizing the document, the integrated solutions team should examine the entire SOO carefully and delete anything that is not essential.

Even more so than performance work statements, it is extremely unlikely that another agency's SOO would prove very useful, but several examples are provided in the library. Since this is an emerging technique, the integrated solutions team should examine them critically. New processes take time to perfect and require ongoing experimentation and innovation.

Step 5:
Decide How to Measure & Manage Performance

Developing an approach to measuring and managing performance is a complex process that requires consideration of many factors: performance standards and measurement techniques, performance management approach, incentives, and more. This component of performance-based contracting is as important as developing the state-

---

Tasks, Features, and Best Practices

- Review the success determinants.
- Rely on commercial quality standards.
- Have the contractor propose the metrics and the quality assurance plan.
- Select only a few meaningful measures on which to judge success. Include contractual language for negoriated changes to the metrics and measures.
- Apply the contract-type order of precedence carefully.
- Use incentive-type contracts.
- Consider "award term."
- Consider other incentive tools.
- Recognize the power of profit as motivator.
- Most importantly, consider the relationship.

See Web site for additional information: www.acqnet.gov.

ment of work (SOW) or the statement of objectives (SOO) because this step establishes the strategy of managing the contract to achieve planned performance objectives.

Review the success determinants.

In step two, the integrated solutions team established a vision of what will constitute success for the project by answering two distinct questions: Where do I want to go, and how will I know when I get there?

The task now is to build the overall performance measurement and management approach on those success determinants.

Rely on commercial quality standards.

Rather than inventing metrics or quality or performance standards, the integrated solutions team should use existing commercial quality standards (identified during market research), such as International Standards Organization (ISO) 9000 or the Software Engineering Institute's Capability Maturity Models®.

ISO has established quality standards (the ISO 9000 series) that are increasingly being used by U.S. firms to identify suppliers who meet the quality standards. The term "ISO 9001 2000" refers to a set of new quality management standards which apply to all kinds of organizations in all kinds of areas. Some of these areas include manufacturing, processing, servicing, printing, electronics, computing, legal services, financial services, accounting, banking, aerospace, construction, textiles, publishing, energy, telecommunications, research, health care, utilities, aviation, food processing, government, education, software development, transportation, design, instrumentation, communications, biotechnology, chemicals, engineering, farming, entertainment, horticulture, consulting, insurance, and so on.

The Carnegie Mellon Software Engineering Institute, a federally funded research and development center, has developed Capability Maturity Models® (CMM) to "assist organizations in maturing their people, process, and technology assets to improve long-term business performance." (See Carnegie Mellon Software Engineering Institute, **www.sei.cmu.edu/managing/**.) SEI has developed CMMs for software, people, and software acquisition, and assisted in the development of CMMs for Systems Engineering and Integrated Product Development:

- SW-CMM® Capability Maturity Model for Software,

- P-CMM People Capability Maturity Model,

■ SA-CMM Software Acquisition Capability Maturity Model,

■ SE-CMM Systems Engineering Capability Maturity Model, and

■ IPD-CMM Integrated Product Development Capability Maturity Model.

The Capability Maturity Models express levels of maturation: the higher the number, the greater the level of maturity. There are five levels. Solicitations that require CMMs typically specify only level two or three.

The integrated solutions team can incorporate such commercial quality standards in the evaluation and selection criteria.

Have the contractor propose the metrics and the quality assurance plan.

One approach is to require the contractor to propose performance metrics and the quality assurance plan (QAP), rather than have the government develop it. This is especially suitable when using a SOO because the solution is not known until proposed. With a SOO, offerors are free to develop their own solutions, so it makes sense for them to develop and propose a QAP that is tailored to their solution and commercial practices. If the agency were to develop the QAP, it could very well limit what contractors can propose.

As the integrated solutions team considers what is required in a QAP, it may be useful to consider how the necessity for quality control and assurance has changed over time, especially as driven by acquisition reform. In short, QAPs were quite necessary when federal acquisition was dominated by low-cost selections. Think about the incentives at work: To win award but still protect some degree of profit margin, the contractor had to shave his costs, an action that could result in use of substandard materials or processes. With best-value selection and an emphasis on past-performance evaluation and reporting, entirely different incentives are at work.

The regulations have changed to some degree to reflect this reality. FAR 46.102 provides that contracts for commercial items "shall rely on a contractor's existing quality assurance system as a substitute for compliance with Government inspection and testing before tender for acceptance unless customary market practices for the commercial item being acquired permit in-process inspection."

Air Force Instruction 63-124 (April 1, 1999) goes farther. Among others, the AFI suggests these considerations in implementing a quality management system:

- Tailor the system to management risks and costs associated with the requirement.

- Use source selection criteria that promise the most potential to reduce government oversight and ensure the government is only receiving and paying for the services required.

- Rely on customer feedback where contract nonconformance can be validated.

- Allow variation in the extent of oversight to match changes in the quality of the contractor's performance.

- Allow the contractor to perform and report on surveillance of services as part of their quality assurance system. Some form of oversight (government QA, third-party audit) is needed to confirm surveillance results.

Remember the following key aspects. Performance metrics are negotiable and, wherever possible, address quality concerns by exception not inspection. Also, when contractors propose the metrics and the QAP, these become true discriminators among the proposals in best-value evaluation and source selection.

Select only a few meaningful measures on which to judge success.

Whether the measures are developed by the proposing contractor or by the integrated solutions team, it is important to limit the measures to those that are truly important and directly tied to the program objectives. The measures should be selected with some consideration of cost. For example, the team will want to determine that the cost of measurement does not exceed the value of the information—and that more expensive means of measurement are used for only the most risky and mission-critical requirements.

The American Productivity and Quality Center Web site (see **www. apqc.org/portal/apqc/site/generic;jsessionid=WBCE3AKIUEVARQF IAJICFEQ?path=/site/performance/overview.jhtml**) states that performance measures come in many types, including economic and financial measures such as return on investment, and other quantitative and qualitative measures. "Organizations are investing energy in developing measures that cover everything from capital adequacy and inventory turns to public image, innovation, customer value, learning, competency, error rate, cost of quality, customer contact, perfect orders, training hours, and re-engineering results." Each measure should relate directly to the objectives of the acquisition.

Include contractual language for negotiated changes to the metrics and measures.

One important step the integrated solutions team can take is to reserve the right to change the metrics and measures. One effective way to do this is for the agency and the contractor to meet regularly to review performance. The first question at each meeting should be, "Are we measuring the right thing?"

This requires that the contractual documents include such provisions as value engineering change provisions, share-in-savings options, or other provisions preserving the government's right to review and revise.

Apply the contract-type order of precedence carefully.

Under law and regulation, there is an order of preference in contract types used for performance-based contracting, as follows:

(i) A firm-fixed price performance-based contract or task order.

(ii) A performance-based contract or task order that is not firm-fixed price.

(iii) A contract or task order that is not performance-based.

Agencies must take care implementing this order of precedence. Be aware that a firm-fixed-price contract is not the best solution for every requirement. "Force fitting" the contract type can actually result in much higher prices as contractors seek to cover their risks.

This view is upheld by FAR 16.103(b), which indicates, A firm-fixed-price contract, which best utilizes the basic profit motive of business enterprise, shall be used when the risk involved is minimal or can be predicted with an acceptable degree of certainty. However, when a reasonable basis for firm pricing does not exist, other contract types should be considered, and negotiations should be directed toward selecting a contract type (or combination of types) that will appropriately tie profit to contractor performance.

Clearly, the decision about the appropriate type of contract to use is closely tied to the agency's need and can go a long way to motivating superior performance-or contributing to poor performance and results. Market research, informed business decision, and negotiation will determine the best contract type.

One final point: The decision on contract type is not necessarily "either/or." Hybrid contracts—those with both fixed-price and cost-type tasks—are common.

Use incentive-type contracts.

Although determining the type of contract to use is often the first type of incentive considered, it is important to understand that contract type is only part of the overall incentive approach and structure of a performance-based acquisition. Other aspects have become increasingly important as agencies and contractors have moved closer to partnering relationships.

Contract types differ in their allocation and balance of cost, schedule, and technical risks between government and contractor. As established by FAR Part 16 (Types of Contracts), contract types vary in terms of

- The degree and timing of the risk and responsibility assumed by the contractor for the costs of performance, and

- The amount and nature of the profit incentive offered to the contractor for achieving or exceeding specified standards or goals.

The government's obligation is to assess its requirements and the uncertainties involved in contract performance and select from the contractual spectrum a contract type and structure that places an appropriate degree of risk, responsibility, and incentives on the contractor for performance.

At one end of the contractual spectrum is the firm-fixed-price contract, under which the contractor is fully responsible for performance costs and enjoys (or suffers) resulting profits (or losses). At the other end of the spectrum is the cost-plus-fixed-fee contract, in which allowable and allocable costs are reimbursed and the negotiated fee (profit) is fixed—consequently, the contractor has minimal responsibility for, or incentive to control, performance costs. In between these extremes are various incentive contracts, including:

- Fixed-price incentive contracts (in which final contract price and profit are calculated based on a formula that relates final negotiated cost to target cost): these may be either firm target or successive targets.

■ Fixed-price contracts with award fees (used to "motivate a contractor" when contractor performance cannot be measured objectively, making other incentives inappropriate).

■ Cost-reimbursement incentive contracts (used when fixed-price contracts are inappropriate, due to uncertainty about probable costs): these may be either cost-plus-incentive-fee or cost-plus-award-fee.

Use of certain types of incentives may be limited by availability of funds. Fortunately, there are other types of incentives that can be tailored to the acquisition and performance goals, requirements, and risks. For example, agencies can also incorporate delivery incentives and performance incentives—the latter related to contractor performance and/or specific products' technical performance characteristics, such as speed or responsiveness. Incentives are based on meeting target performance standards, not minimum contractual requirements. These, too, are negotiable.

Consider "award term."

"Award term" is a contract performance incentive feature that ties the length of a contract's term to the performance of the contractor. The contract can be extended for "good" performance or reduced for "poor" performance.

Award term is a contracting tool used to promote efficient and quality contractor performance. In itself, it is not an acquisition strategy, nor is it a performance solution. As with any tool, its use requires careful planning, implementation, and management/measurement to ensure its success in incentivizing contractors and improving performance.

The award-term feature is similar to award-fee (FAR 16.405-2) contracting where contract performance goals, plans, assessments, and awards are made regularly during the life of a contract. Award-term solicitations and contracts should include a base period (e.g., three years) and a maximum term (e.g., 10 years), similar to quantity estimates used in indefinite quantity/indefinite delivery contracts for supplies (FAR 16.504).

When applying the award-term feature, agencies need to identify and understand the project or task:

■ Conditions, constraints, assumptions, and complexities;

- Schedule, performance, and cost-critical success factors; and

- Schedule, performance, and cost risks.

They also need to understand marketplace conditions and pricing realities. Only then can agencies establish meaningful and appropriate schedule, performance, and cost measures/parameters for a specific contract. These measures must be meaningful, accurate, and quantifiable to provide the right incentives and contract performance results. Specifics need to be incorporated and integrated in an award-term plan.

Award term is best applied when utilizing performance or solution-based requirements where a SOW or SOO describes the agency's required outcomes or results (the "what" and "when" of the agency's requirement) and where the contractor has the freedom to apply its own management and best performance practices (the "how" of the requirement) towards performing the contract. The award-term plan must specify success measurement criteria, regarding how performance will be measured (i.e., defines what is "good" or "poor" performance) and the award-term decision made.

There should also be a clear indication of the consequences of various levels of performance in terms of the contract's minimum, estimated, and maximum terms—and the agency needs to be prepared to follow up with those consequences. If contractor performance is below the standard set, the contract ends at the completion of the base period. The agency must be prepared to re-procure in a timely fashion.

The effort applied in managing an award term contract after award is critical. Too often, agencies and contractors don't invest the right people (numbers and skills) and management attention during the contract performance phase. Managing contracts with features like award term is not a "last minute," incidental, or a fill-out-a-survey job. As in the case of its "sister" award-fee approach, communication needs to be constant and clear with contractors, and not include so many evaluation elements that it dilutes the critical success factors.

Consider other incentive tools.

Incentives can be monetary or non-monetary. They should be positive, but include remedies as appropriate, when performance targets or objectives are missed.

Creating an incentive strategy is much the same as crafting an acquisition strategy. There is no single, perfect, "one-size-fits-all" approach; instead, the incentive structure should be geared to the acquisition, the characteristics of the marketplace, and the objectives the government seeks to achieve. While cost incentives are tied to a degree to contract-type decisions, there are other cost and non-cost incentives for the integrated solutions team to consider, such as

■ Contract length considerations (options and award term),

■ Strategic supplier alliances,

■ Performance-based payments,

■ Performance incentive bonus,

■ Schedule incentives,

■ Past performance evaluation,

■ Agency "supplier of the year" award programs,

■ Competitive considerations,

■ Non-performance remedies,

■ Value engineering change provisions,

■ Share-in-savings strategies, and

■ Letters of commendation.

Remember that performance incentives are negotiable. Developing an incentive strategy is a "study unto itself," and there are some excellent guides on the subject. (See step five's Additional Information).

Recognize the power of profit as motivator.

One of the keys to effective incentives involves recognizing and then acting on the private sector's chief motivator: profit. It is a simple fact that companies are motivated by generation return for their investors. One contractor was heard to say, "You give us the incentive, we will earn every available dollar."

The real opportunity is to make that work to the government's advantage. For example, link the incentive program to the mutually agreed-to contract performance measures and metrics. Then, incorporate value engineering change provisions (VECP) or share-in-savings strategies that reward the contractor for suggesting innovations that improve performance and reduce total overall cost. Put more simply: Set up the acquisition so that a contractor and the government can benefit from economies, efficiencies, and innovations delivered in contract performance.

If the incentives are right, and if the contractor and the agency share the same goals, risk is largely controlled and effective performance is almost the inevitable outcome. This approach will help ensure that the contractor is just as concerned—generated by self-interest in winning all available award fees and award terms—about every element of contract performance, whether maximizing operational efficiency overall, reducing subcontract costs, or ensuring the adequacy of post-award subcontractor competition and reasonableness of prices, as is the agency.

Most importantly, consider the relationship.

With regard to overall approach to contract performance management, the integrated solutions team should plan to rely less on management by contract and more on management by relationship. At its most fundamental level, a contract is much like a marriage. It takes work by both parties throughout the life of the relationship to make it successful. Consider, for example, the public-private partnership that was the Apollo Program.

Other more recent examples exist, but they all share the same common characteristics:

- Trust and open communication,

- Strong leadership on both sides,

- Ongoing and honest self-assessment,

- Ongoing interaction, and

- Mutual benefit or value created and maintained throughout the relationship.

There are several means to shift the focus from management by contract to management by relationship. For example, plan on meeting with the contractor to identify ways to improve efficiency and reduce the effect of the "cost drivers." Sometimes agencies require management reporting based on policy *without considering what the cost of the requirement is*. For example, in one contract, an agency required that certain reports be delivered regularly on Friday. When asked to recommend changes, the contractor suggested that report due date be shifted to Monday because weekend processing time costs less. An example is requiring earned-value reporting on every contractual process. For tasks of lesser risk, complexity, and expense, a less costly approach to measuring cost, schedule, and performance can be used. This type of collaborative action will set the stage for the contractor and government to work together to identify more effective and efficient ways to measure and manage the program.

Another effective means is to establish a Customer Process Improvement Working Group that includes contractor, program, and contracting representatives. This works especially well when the integrated solutions team's tasks migrate into contract performance and they take part in the working group. These meetings should always start with the question, are we measuring the right thing?

For major acquisitions, the team can consider the formation of a higher-level Board of Directors, comprised of top officials from the government and its winning partner, with a formal charter that requires continual open communication, self-assessment, and ongoing interaction.

The intent to "manage by relationship" should be documented in a contract administration plan that lays out the philosophies and approach to managing this effort, placing special emphasis on techniques that enhance the ability to adapt and incorporate changes.

Step 6:
Select the Right Contractor

Developing an acquisition strategy that will lead to selection of the "right contractor" is especially important in performance-based acquisition. The contractor must understand the performance-based approach, know or develop an understanding of the agency's requirement, have a history of performing exceptionally in the field, and have the processes and resources in place to support the mission. This goes a long way to successful mission accomplishment. In fact, selecting the right contractor and developing a partnership automatically solves many potential performance issues.

Keep in mind that large businesses have not "cornered the market" on good ideas.

Small firms can be nimble, quick thinking, and very dedicated to customer service. While there is a cost in proposing solutions, a small business with a good solution can win performance-based awards.

Tasks, Features, and Best Practices

- Compete the solution—use down-selection and "due diligence."
- Use oral presentations and other opportunities to communicate.
- Emphasize past performance in evaluation.
- Use best-value evaluation and source selection.
- Assess solutions for issues of conflict of interest.

See Web site for additional information: www.acqnet.gov.

Also, do not think you are limited to companies that specialize in the federal market. Information obtained from market research sessions has shown that often commercial companies—or commercial divisions of companies that do federal and commercial business—have significantly more experience with performance-based service delivery methods and techniques.

While there are many aspects to crafting an acquisition strategy, among the most important for performance-based acquisition are to "compete the solution," use down-selection and "due diligence," evaluate heavily on past performance information, and make a best-value source selection decision.

Compete the solution.

Too many government-issued statements of work try to "solve the problem." In such cases, the agency issues a detailed SOW, often with the assumption that "the tighter the spec the better," without realizing that this approach increases the government's risk. (This is because if the government specifications are not accurate or feasible, any increase in cost or time is at government expense.) The agency SOW establishes what to do, how to do it, what labor categories to provide, what minimum qualifications to meet, and how many hours to work. The agency then asks vendors to respond with a "mirror image" of the specifications in the proposal. The result is that the "competing" vendors bid to the same government-directed plan, and the agency awards the contract to the company with the best proposal writers...not the best ideas.

So, the first key to selecting the right contractor is to structure the acquisition so that the government describes the problem that needs to be solved and vendors compete by proposing solutions. The quality of the solution and the contractor-proposed performance measures and methodology then become true discriminators in best-value evaluation.

Use down-selection and "due diligence."

Responding to a performance-based solicitation, especially a SOO that seeks contractor-developed solutions, is substantial work for contractors. Likewise, evaluation of what may be significantly different approaches or solutions is much more substantial work for the integrated solutions team. The team will have to understand the contractor-proposed solutions, assess the associated risks and likelihood of success, identify the discriminators, and do the best-value tradeoff analysis.

Because of this, the acquisition strategy should consider some means of "down-selection," so that only those contractors with a significant likelihood of winning award will go through the expense of developing proposals. As to the integrated solutions team, evaluating dozens of solution-type proposals would be overly burdensome.

"Down-selection" is a means of limiting the competitive pool to those contractors most likely to offer a successful solution. There are four primary means of down-selection in current acquisition methodology: using the Federal Supply Service (FSS) Multiple-Award Schedule (MAS) competitive process, using the "fair opportunity" competitive process under an existing Governmentwide Agency Contract (GWAC) or multiple-award contract (MAC), using the multi-step advisory process in a negotiated procurement, or using a competitive range determination in a negotiated procurement. All of these methods provide a means to establish a small pool of the most qualified contractors, competing to provide the solution.

Once the competing pool of contractors is established, those contractors enter a period called due diligence. "Due diligence" is used in acquisitions to describe the period and process during which competitors take the time and make the effort to become knowledgeable about an agency's needs in order to propose a competitive solution. It usually includes site visits, meetings with key agency people, and research and analysis necessary to develop a competitive solution tailored to agency requirements. During this time, the competing contractors must have access to the integrated solutions team and program staff so that the contractors can learn as much as possible about the requirement. It is a far more open period of communication than is typical in more traditional acquisitions.

Use oral presentations and other opportunities to communicate.

One streamlining tool that eases the job of evaluation is the use of oral presentations (characterized by "real-time interactive dialogue"). These presentations provide information about the contractor's management and/or technical approach that the integrated solutions team will use in evaluation, selection, and award.

Oral presentations provide "face time," permitting the integrated solutions team to assess prospective contractors. Agencies have said that oral presentations remove the "screen" that professional proposal writers can erect in front of the contractor's key personnel. The integrated solutions team should take full advantage of "face time" by requiring that the project manager and key personnel (those who will do the work) make the presentations. This gives agency evaluators an opportunity to see part of the vendor-proposed solution team, to ask specific questions, and to gauge how well the team works together and would be likely to work with the agency.

Oral presentations can lay out the proposed solution and the contractor's capability and understanding of the requirement. Oral presentations *may substitute for, or augment, written information*. However, it's important to remember that statements made in oral presentations are not binding unless written into the contract. Note that oral presentations should be recorded in some way.

Communication with offerors is an important element of selecting the right contractor. Despite this fact, it is "trendy" in negotiated procurements to announce the intent to award without discussions. Given the complexities associated with performance-based proposals (i.e., different approaches and different performance metrics), it is nearly impossible to award without conducting discussions. While it may reduce time, it is important to use discussions to fully understand the quality of the solution, the pricing approach, incentive structure, and even the selection itself.

Emphasize past performance in evaluation.

A contractor's past performance record is arguably the key indicator for predicting future performance. As such, it is to the agency's advantage to use past performance in evaluating and selecting contractors for award. Evaluation of past performance is particularly important for service contracts. Properly conducted, the collection and use of such information provides significant benefits. It enhances the government's ability to predict both the performance quality and customer satisfaction. It also provides a powerful incentive for current contractors to maximize performance and customer satisfaction.

Past performance information can come from multiple sources. The two most familiar methods are asking the offerors to provide references and seeking information from past performance information databases. The Past Performance Information Retrieval System, or PPIRS, is the governmentwide repository for past performance information. It ties together a number of databases formerly independent of one another (see **www.ppirs.gov**).

There are other means of obtaining past performance information for evaluation. One very important means is through market research. Call counterparts in other agencies with similar work and ask them for the names of the best contractors they've worked with. Are there industry awards in the field of work? Who has won them? In fact, ask offerors to identify their awards and events of special recognition. Look for industry quality standards and certifications, such as ISO

9000 and SEI CMM® (discussed in step five). Ask offerors what they do to track customer satisfaction and to resolve performance issues. Is there an established and institutionalized approach? In short, the integrated solutions team must take past performance more seriously than just calling a few references. Make the answers to these questions part of the request for proposals. Rather than have a separate past performance team, integrate this evaluation into the technical and management proposal evaluation effort.

When used in the source selection evaluation process, past performance evaluation criteria must provide information that allows the source selection official to compare the "quality" of offerors against the agency requirement and assess the risk and likelihood of success of the proposed solution and success of contractor performance. This requires the information to be relevant, current and accurate. For example, the information requested of the contractor and evaluated by the integrated solutions team should be designed to determine how well, in contracts of similar size, scope, and complexity, the contractor

■ Conformed to the contract requirements and standards of good workmanship,

■ Adhered to contract schedules,

■ Forecasted and controlled costs,

■ Managed risk,

■ Provided reasonable and cooperative behavior and commitment to customer satisfaction, and

■ Demonstrated business-like concern for the interest of the customer.

The answers to the above list provide the source selection authority with information to make a comparative assessment for the award decision.

Use best-value evaluation and source selection.

"Best value" is a process used to select the most advantageous offer by evaluating and comparing factors in addition to cost or price. It allows flexibility in selection through tradeoffs, which the agency makes between the cost and non-cost evaluation factors with the intent of awarding to the contractor that will give the government the greatest or best value for its money.

Note that "the rules" for the best-value and tradeoff process (and the degree of documentation required) depend on two factors: the rules for the specific acquisition process being used and the rules the agency sets in the solicitation. For example, when conducting a negotiated procurement, the complex processes of FAR Subpart 15.1, "Source Selection Processes and Techniques," and FAR Subpart 15.3, "Source Selection," apply. When using Federal Supply Schedule contracts, the simpler provisions at FAR 8.404 apply. However, if the agency writes FAR 15-type rules into a Request for Quote under Federal Supply Schedule contracts, the rules in the RFQ control.

The integrated solutions team should consider including factors such as the following in the evaluation model:

- Quality and benefits of the solution,

- Quality of the performance metrics and measurement approach,

- Risks associated with the solution,

- Management approach and controls,

- Management team (limited number of key personnel),

- Past performance (how well the contractor has performed), and

- Past experience (what the contractor has done).

The General Accounting Office acknowledges broad agency discretion in selection; therefore, the integrated solution team evaluators and the source selection authority should expect to exercise good judgment. Quite simply, best-value source selection involves subjective analysis. It cannot, and should not, be reduced to a mechanical, mathematical exercise. The following, derived from GAO protest decision B-284270, reflects just how broad agency discretion is.

- Source selection officials have broad discretion to determine the manner and extent to which they will make use of the technical and price evaluation results in negotiated procurements.

- In deciding between competing proposals, price/technical tradeoffs may be made; the propriety of such tradeoffs turns not on the difference in technical scores or ratings per se, but on whether the source selection official's judgment concerning the significance of that difference was reasonable and adequately justified in light of the RFP evaluation scheme.

■ The discretion to determine whether the technical advantages associated with a higher-priced proposal are worth the price premium exists notwithstanding the fact that price is equal to or more important than other factors in the evaluation scheme.

■ In a best-value procurement, an agency's selection of a higher-priced, higher-rated offer should be supported by a determination that the technical superiority of the higher-priced offer warrants the additional cost involved.

Assess solutions for issues of conflict of interest.

An "organizational conflict of interest" exists when a contractor is or may be unable or unwilling to provide the government with impartial or objective assistance or advice. An organizational conflict of interest may result when factors create an actual or potential conflict of interest on a current contract or a potential future procurement.

While concerns about organizational conflict of interest are important, they should be tempered by good business sense. For example, sometimes software development is done in stages. Organizational conflict of interest would suggest that the contractor that does the initial systems design work be precluded from the follow-on code development due to unfair competitive advantage. However, this would also mean that the agency is excluding from consideration the contractor with the best understanding of the requirement. In this case, perhaps the acquisition approach should be reconsidered to allow the definer of the requirements to continue with the development.

Step 7:
Manage Performance

The final step of the seven steps of performance-based acquisition is the most important. Unlike legacy processes where the contract is awarded and the team disperses, there is a growing realization that "the real work" of acquisition is in contract management. This requires that agencies allocate sufficient resources, in both the contracting or program offices, to do the job well.

This is largely a problem of resource allocation and education. Again, legacy processes are much to blame. Many contracting staff learned their job when the culture was to maintain an arm's length distance (or more) from contractors—and by all means, limit the amount of contact the contractor has with program people. That approach won't work in today's environment and especially not in performance-based acquisition. The contractor must be part of the acquisition team itself—a reality recognized by the guiding principles

---

Tasks, Features, and Best Practices

- Keep the team together.
- Adjust roles and responsibilities.
- Assign accountability for managing contract performance.
- Add the contractor to the team at a formal "kick-off" meeting.
- Regularly review performance in a Contract Performance Improvement Working Group.
- Ask the right questions.
- Report on the contractor's "past performance."

See Web site for additional information: www.acqnet.gov.

of the federal acquisition system. FAR 1.102(c) provides:

> The acquisition team consists of all participants in government acquisition including not only representatives of the technical, supply, and procurement communities but also the customers they serve, and the contractors who provide the products and services.

Effective contract management is a mission-critical agency function. This goes to the heart of the need to maintain sufficient core capability in the federal government to manage its programs. If the contractor is flying blind in performance, then the agency will soon fly blind and without landing gear when the contract is over.

This step, contract performance, is guided far less by law, regulation, and policy than those described in the preceding steps. To a large degree, the management of contract performance is guided by the contract's terms and conditions and is achieved with the support of the business relationships and communications established between the contractor and the integrated solutions team. It is in the best interest of all parties concerned that the contract be successful.

Keep the team together.

To be successful in performance-based acquisition, the agency must retain at least a core of the integrated solutions team on the project for contract management. Those on the team have the most knowledge, experience, and insight into what needs to happen next and what is expected during contract performance. Contract award is not the final measure of success. Effective and efficient contract performance that delivers a solution is the goal. The team should stay together to see that end reached.

Acquisition team members are expected to collaborate with all requisite external organizations in order to provide the best possible service to the citizens. The most notable example, 20 years on the making, is the USDA's food stamp program. The federal government collaborated with state and local governments, banks, and supermarkets to move away from the paper food stamps to debit cards. This not only has helped ease the "stigma" of the food stamps but also has significantly reduced fraud.

Adjust roles and responsibilities.

Often the members of the acquisition team take on new roles during the contract performance phase. Typically, these responsibilities are shared between the program office and contracting office.

Given that the purpose of any acquisition (in part) is "to deliver on a timely basis the best value product or service to the customer" (as provided in FAR 1.102), meeting this objective requires the continued involvement of the program office in duties classified as contract administration as well as those more accurately described as program (or project) management.

Program management is concerned with maintaining the project's strategic focus and monitoring and measuring the contractor's performance. The integrated solutions team is ultimately responsible for ensuring that the contractor performs on time and within budget. On smaller acquisitions, the contracting officer's technical representative (COTR) may fill this role.

Contract administration involves the execution of the administrative processes and tasks necessary to see that the contractual requirements are met, by both contractor and agency. FAR Subpart 42.3 identifies the numerous but specific contract administration functions that may be delegated by the contracting office to a contract administration office, and in turn to a specific individual.

Assign accountability for managing contract performance.

Just as important as keeping the team together is assigning roles and responsibilities to the parties. Contracting officers have certain responsibilities that can't be delegated or assumed by the other members of the team. These include, for example, making any commitment relating to an award of a task, modification, or contract; negotiating technical or pricing issues with the contractor; or modifying the stated terms and conditions of the contract. Some roles and responsibilities are decreed-for example, agencies are required to establish capability and training requirements for contracting officers technical representatives (COTRs).

Make sure the people assigned the most direct roles for monitoring contract performance have read and understand the contract and have the knowledge, experience, skills, and ability to perform their roles. In performance-based organizations, they are held accountable for the success or failure of the program they lead. They should know the program needs in depth, understand the contractor's marketplace, have familiarity with the tools the contractor is using to perform, and have good interpersonal skills (with the capability to disagree constructively).

Enhanced professionalism in contract performance management is on the horizon. In November 2003, the Services Acquisition Reform

Act (SARA) was passed with a number of noteworthy provisions. Share-in-savings contracting is authorized for all types of acquisitions. (See **www.gsa.gov/shareinsavings.**) A fund is to be established in FY2005 to ensure government program managers are properly trained and certified to manage large projects. Certified project managers' names will appear on OMB Form 300 submissions. (See **www. pubklaw.com/legis/SARA2003ssa.pdf.**) Information on certification programs can be found at **www.pmi.org.** These requirements are part of a larger effort to link budget to performance, and to improve project management in order to reduce or eliminate wasteful spending.

Add the contractor to the team at a formal "kick-off" meeting.

It is often advisable—and sometimes required by the contract—to conduct a "kick-off meeting" or, more formally, a "post-award conference," attended by those who will be involved in contract performance. Even though a post-award conference may not be required by the contract, it is an especially good idea for performance-based contracts. This meeting can help both agency and contractor personnel achieve a clear and mutual understanding of contract requirements and further establish the foundation for good communications and a win-win relationship.

It is very important that the contractor be part of the integrated solutions team, and that agency and contractor personnel work closely together to fulfill the mission and program needs.

Regularly review performance in a Contract Performance Improvement Working Group.

Performance reviews should take place regularly, and that means much more than the annual "past performance" reviews required by regulation. These are contract management performance reviews, not for formal reporting and rebutting, but for keeping the project on course, measuring performance levels, and making adjustments as necessary. For most contracts, monthly or bi-monthly performance reviews would be appropriate. For contracts of extreme importance or contracts in performance trouble, more frequent meetings may be required.

Measuring and managing a project to the attainment of performance goals and objectives requires the continued involvement of the acquisition team, especially the program manager. It also requires considerable involvement by the acquisition team's new members-contractor personnel.

Ask the right questions.

It is important to keep the focus of the meetings on improving performance, not evaluating people. Each meeting should start with the questions, "Are we measuring the right thing?" and "How are we doing?" It is important to continually revisit the success measures the team identified during step two.

Other important questions are

- Is the acquisition achieving its cost, schedule, and performance goals?

- Is the contractor meeting or exceeding the contract's performance-based requirements?

- How effective is the contractor's performance in meeting or contributing to the agency's program performance goals?

- Are there problems or issues that we can address to mitigate risk?

There should be time in each meeting where the agency asks, "Is there anything we are requiring that is affecting the job you can do in terms of quality, cost, schedule, or delivering the solution?" Actions discussed should be recorded for the convenience of all parties, with responsibilities and due dates assigned.

Report on the contractor's "past performance."

There are many types of performance reporting that may be required of the integrated solutions team. For example, agency procedures may establish special requirements for acquisition teams to report to the agency's investment review board regarding the status of meeting a major acquisition's cost, schedule, and performance goals (as required by the Federal Acquisition Streamlining Act). The team may also be responsible for performance reporting under the Government Performance and Results Act, if the contractor's performance directly supports a GPRA performance goal. Refer to internal agency guidance on these processes.

However, one type of performance reporting requirement—evaluation of the contractor's performance—is dictated by the contract terms and conditions and by FAR 42.15. This requirement is generally referred to as past-performance evaluation.

The FAR now requires that agencies evaluate contractor performance for each contract in excess of $100,000. The performance evaluation and report is shared with the contractor, who has an opportunity to respond before the contracting officer finalizes the performance report. In well-managed contracts, there has been continual feedback and adjustment, so there should be no surprises on either side.

Conclusion

The intent of this guide is to make the subject of performance-based acquisition accessible and logical for all and shift the paradigm from traditional "acquisition think" into one of collaborative, performance-oriented teamwork with a focus on program performance, improvement, and innovation, not simply contract compliance. Performance-based acquisition offers the potential to dramatically transform the nature of service delivery, and permit the federal government to tap the enormous creative energy and innovative nature of private industry.

Let the acquisitions begin!

Appendix B
Acquisition Bid/No-Bid
Assessment Tool

Executive Summary

The Acquisition Bid/No-Bid Assessment Tool (ABAT) is designed to support the supplier's assessment of a potential opportunity viability before committing the resources required to develop a project plan and a customer bid or proposal. It is to be completed by the sales team closest to the customer project under evaluation, with support from the project management organization (PMO). The tool provides a high-level evaluation of the risks associated with a project. It will support the sales team and senior management in determining which opportunities to concentrate on and which risks must be managed to ensure project success. It is meant to provide assistance in making a bid/no-bid decision.

How to Use ABAT

The process for performing the project opportunity and risk assessment using the ABAT involves three basic steps:

- **Assessing the opportunity**—Answer a series of 10 questions on opportunity analysis , and calculate a score for each. The questions have been weighted on a scale of 1 (low weight) to 5 (high weight) in terms of their relative importance to each other. Calculate this score by multiplying the raw score (opportunity factor, or O) by a pre-established weight value (W). After each question has been scored, document it on the ABAT scoring sheet.

■ **Assessing the risk**—Answer a series of 11 questions on risk analysis, and calculate a score for each. Calculate the score by multiplying the raw score (Risk Factor, or R) by the pre-established weight value (W). After each question has been scored, document it on the ABAT scoring sheet.

■ **Plotting the opportunity and risk scores on the matrix**—Use the total scores for opportunity and risk, which were calculated on the ABAT scoring sheet, to create a plot on the matrix (See **Figure B.1** on p. 290) provided within the model. The location of this score on the matrix helps determine the quality of an opportunity and serves as an indicator of the level of risk that will need to be managed in order to ensure project success.

When to Use ABAT

The questions provided in this tool can be applied to a project at any time during the sales cycle before issuing a proposal to the customer. However, the complete process is intended to be used primarily when the project requirements are defined with such detail that the customer could issue or has issued a request for proposal (RFP), request for quotation (RFQ), or similar solicitation document. The model has been designed so that a core team should be able to complete it in an hour or less.

How to Assess the ABAT Results

Once the scores have been plotted on the model's matrix, the sales team including the bid/capture manager and the project manager can determine the next appropriate step. Normally, a meeting with management is held to review the opportunity. This meeting should include representation from each of the organizations that would be responsible for performing detailed assessment, developing a project plan, and providing input to the customer proposal. These same organizations will ultimately be responsible for project execution if the bid is won.

If the project assessment is unfavorable, the sales team—in conjunction with the project manager—may search for ways to improve the opportunity, to reduce the risk, or both before presenting the opportunity to management. Alternatively, the sales team—with concurrence from the capture manager—project manager and senior management, as appropriate—may conclude the opportunity should not be pursued.

OPPORTUNITY ANALYSIS
The Supplier's Perspective

A. Promotion of Supplier's Strategic Direction	Weight Factor (W)	x	Oppt. Factor (O)	=	Total Score (W x O)

Any project, if properly executed, will promote the reputation and image of the supplier. However, the more valuable opportunities are those that are consistent with the supplier's core business and strategic direction.

The projects do the following:
- Support our strategic market direction.
- Support our focus on key accounts.
- Use our knowledge of specific industries.
- Represent an excellent example of the type of business that the supplier seeks and that will serve as a reference for future sales efforts with other accounts.

The more of these attributes that a project has, the better the opportunity. If properly executed, a project that has all of the above attributes will promote the supplier as an industry leader.

Opportunity Factor (O)
How many of the supplier's major strategies are matched by this project?

1 2 3 4

_____ 5 x [| | |] = _____

1. One
2. Two
3. Three
4. Four

Notes

OPPORTUNITY ANALYSIS
The Supplier's Perspective

B. Revenue Plan

	Weight Factor (W)	x	Oppt. Factor (O)	=	Total Score (W x O)

At this point in the project assessment, exact pricing has not yet been performed. However, an estimate of the amount of revenue expected as a result of the project should be developed. The estimate should include only revenue that will be generated within the scope of the project as defined by the contract. The revenues should include all hardware, software, and service revenues. (Do not include future revenue potential that is beyond the scope of this project.)

Opportunity Factor (O)

What is the estimated value of the project in U.S. dollars, including all hardware, software, and services?

$$\underline{\quad 4 \quad} \quad x \quad \boxed{\begin{array}{|c|c|c|c|} 1 & 2 & 3 & 4 \end{array}} = \underline{\qquad}$$

1. $500,000 or less
2. Greater than $500,000, but less than $2,500,000
3. At least $2,500,000, but less than $5,000,000
4. $5,000,000 or greater

Notes
(Local currency could be substituted if necessary.)

OPPORTUNITY ANALYSIS
The Supplier's Perspective

C. Margin Plan

Weight Factor (W)	x	Oppt. Factor (O)	=	Total Score (W x O)

Estimate the percentage of the gross margin (GM) that is likely to be realized on the revenue generated by this project. This GM should be the aggregate for the project and should combine hardware, software, and service margins. Ideally, the margin should be consistent with the margin plan for the organization bidding on the project. However, competitive pressures and the need to win may cause the supplier to consider a break-even or a loss on the project. Such might be the case when the project will lead to a high volume of profitable business in the future. (When generating the profit estimate, do not include the margins generated by future revenues beyond the scope of this project.)

Opportunity Factor (O)

How does the GM in this project compare to the percentage of margin goals stated in the annual plan for the organization bidding on the project?

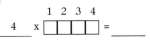

1. Negative margins or break-even
2. Margins up to 50 percent of annual plan
3. Margins greater than 50 percent, but less than 100 percent of annual plan
4. Margins equal to or in excess of annual plan

Example: An organization's annual plan states a 50-percent GM goal for a given year. For a project that is projected to generate up to 30 percent margin, you should select the second answer.

Notes

OPPORTUNITY ANALYSIS
The Supplier's Perspective

	Weight		Oppt.		Total
	Factor	x	Factor	=	Score
	(W)		(O)		(W x O)

D. Future Sales

A project may represent a good opportunity because of the future business potential. The project may provide the means to enter a new account, or may be required to protect an existing account. Participation in the project (either in whole or in part) may be required for the supplier to be considered for future business. Consider the need to do this project relative to its effect on the relationship between supplier and this customer, and the potential for future supplier hardware, software, and services opportunities with this customer.

Opportunity Factor (O)

What effect will successful conclusion of the project have on future supplier opportunities with this customer?

$$\underline{\quad 3 \quad} \times \begin{array}{|c|c|c|c|} \hline 1 & 2 & 3 & 4 \\ \hline \end{array} = \underline{\quad\quad}$$

1. The project has little or no bearing on future business
2. Future business is possible as a result of this project.
3. Future business is likely as a result of this project.
4. Future business is assured as a result of this project, or project participation is mandatory to remain a viable supplier.

Notes

OPPORTUNITY ANALYSIS
The Supplier's Perspective

E. Provision of Value-Added Experience or New Skills	Weight Factor (W)	x	Oppt. Factor (O)	=	Total Score (W x O)

Occasionally, a project is desirable for the education or experience to be gained by the supplier. While learning and experience occur on any project, those that will significantly improve the skills of the supplier project team or will develop previously nonexistent critical skills are the more favored projects. Skills such as managing the project, delivering new products and technologies, and supporting the customer are just a few examples.

Opportunity Factor (O)

What is the value of the experience and skills to be gained from the project?

1 2 3 4

3 x ☐☐☐☐ = _____

1. Little improvement in existing skills is expected because the project team is very experienced.
2. The project team members will gain significant improvement in existing skills.
3. Little improvement in existing skills is expected, but some new skills and expertise will be developed.
4. Significant improvement in existing skills is expected, and the project team members will develop new skills and expertise.

Notes

OPPORTUNITY ANALYSIS
The Supplier's Perspective

F. Resource Utilization

	Weight Factor (W)	x	Oppt. Factor (O)	=	Total Score (W x O)

A project may be highly desirable if it makes good use of the supplier's resources and assets that are either currently or projected to be underused. Even a project that might otherwise be declined may be desirable for its positive effect on the supplier's resource and asset use. The effect on the sales, project management, and support personnel and the use of technical facilities and equipment should be considered. Evaluate current resource use and the number and type of projects currently under way. Consider how senior management would react to requests for additional resources.

Opportunity Factor (O)

What effect will this project have on the supplier's resource and asset use?

$$\underline{2} \quad x \quad \boxed{\begin{array}{cccc} 1 & 2 & 3 & 4 \\ & & & \end{array}} = \underline{}$$

1. The project will drain significant resources allocated to other projects.
2. The project will drain some resources allocated to other projects.
3. The project will have a normal effect on resources.
4. The project will make use of currently underused resources.

Notes

OPPORTUNITY ANALYSIS
The Supplier's Perspective

G. Customer Who Favors the Supplier	Weight Factor (W)	x	Oppt. Factor (O)	=	Total Score (W x O)

A project involving a customer who favors the supplier (for reasons other than price) before the project has been proposed is highly desirable. Customers may prefer the supplier for any number of reasons, including technology, reputation, past experience, industry commitment, and so on. Of course, they may favor the competition for the same reasons. Consider the number of competitors vying for the project, as well as the customer's past experience with the supplier, the competition, or both.

Opportunity Factor (O)

How does the customer consider the supplier in comparison to the competition for this project?

$$\underline{\ \ 3\ \ } \ \text{x} \ \boxed{1\ 2\ 3\ 4} = \underline{\hspace{2cm}}$$

1. The customer favors the competition and is negative toward the supplier for this project.
2. The customer favors the competition and is neutral toward the supplier for this project.
3. The customer is neutral toward all potential suppliers for this project.
4. The customer prefers the supplier for this project.

Notes

OPPORTUNITY ANALYSIS
The Supplier's Perspective

H. Supplier's Revenue and Direct Control of Products and Services	Weight Factor (W)	x	Oppt. Factor (O)	=	Total Score (W x O)

Most projects will require some outsourcing of products, services, or both by other vendors or supply-chain partners. The more products and services are outsourced by various vendors, then generally the greater the risk and the lower the direct revenues.

Opportunity Factor (O)
What percentage of the revenue will be generated by the supplier's products and services?

$$\underline{2} \quad \text{x} \quad \boxed{} \quad = \quad \underline{}$$
1 2 3 4

1. Less than 50 percent of the project revenue will come from the supplier's products and services.
2. Between 50 percent and 70 percent of the project revenue will come from the supplier's products and services.
3. Between 70 percent and 90 percent of the project revenue will come from the supplier's products and services.
4. At least 90 percent or more of the project revenue will come from the supplier's products and services.

Notes

OPPORTUNITY ANALYSIS
The Supplier's Perspective

I. Proposal or Bid Expense

Weight Factor (W)	x	Oppt. Factor (O)	=	Total Score (W x O)

Every project has presale expense
associated with it. The amount of presale
expense varies greatly from bid to bid.
Some projects are largely a replication of an
existing project with this account or another
account. In other projects, a significant
amount of planning and even a demonstration
of the system (including a benchmark) may
be required before the bid is considered
by the account. Projects with little presale
expense are more desirable. Examples of
items that increase the level of presale
expense include the following:

- Additional local resources beyond those
  normally assigned to this account
- A benchmark system to be constructed
- Non-seller's product(s) to be acquired for
  evaluation before the proposal
  is generated
- Resources from other organizations,
  such as country or group home office
- Professional services from outside the
  supplier's sources

Opportunity Factor (O)
What is the estimated level of presale expense
for this project? (Use the items listed above
as a guide.

$$1 \quad x \quad \boxed{\begin{array}{cccc} 1 & 2 & 3 & 4 \\ \end{array}} \quad = \quad \underline{\hspace{2cm}}$$

1. High (all of the above apply)
2. Moderate (three or four of the above apply)
3. Low (one or two of the above apply)
4. Minimal presale expense is expected
   (none of the above)

Notes

OPPORTUNITY ANALYSIS
The Supplier's Perspective

	Weight Factor (W)	x	Oppt. Factor (O)	=	Total Score (W x O)

J. Sales Executive Assessment of Opportunity

The sales executive, with the support from the project leader, should provide an overall assessment of the need to win the opportunity. This is the point at which the sales executive and project leader can express an opinion that is about the need to win and is based on the more tangible aspects of the opportunity. Perhaps they are aware of other opportunity factors not yet considered.

Opportunity Factor (O)

On a scale of 1 (low need) to 10 (high need), which is the sales executive's overall assessment of the need to win this project business? (Briefly describe those reasons in the space provided below.)

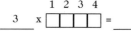

$$\underline{3} \quad x \quad \boxed{} \quad = \quad \underline{}$$

1. 5 or less
2. 6 or 7
3. 8 or 9
4. 10

Reasons for overall assessment:

RISK ANALYSIS
The Supplier's Perspective

A. Customer's Commitment

Weight Factor (W)	x	Oppt. Factor (R)	=	Total Score (W x R)

Customer commitment is a vital factor in the success of a project. A committed customer will place a high degree of importance on the project and will make it part of its business plan. A committed customer will apply resources, such as a project manager, as well as a budget to implement the project. A committed customer is less likely to change or cancel the project and, therefore, represents a lower risk.

Risk Factor (R)
How committed is the customer to the project?

$5 \quad x \quad \boxed{1\ 2\ 3\ 4} \quad = \quad \underline{\hspace{2cm}}$

1. The customer has assigned personnel and a budget.
2. The customer has assigned a budget, but no personnel.
3. The customer has assigned personnel, but no budget.
4. The customer has not assigned personnel or a budget.

Notes

RISK ANALYSIS
The Supplier's Perspective Score

	Weight Factor (W)	x	Oppt. Factor (R)	=	Total Score (W x R)

B. Project Delivery Schedule

All projects have a set start and completion date. The customer will normally require that the project be completed within a specific time. Typically, this is driven by the customer's business cycle and by end-customer demands. The ability to meet the project schedule requirements is highly dependent on the magnitude of the project and the availability and coordination of the right talent at the right time. A project schedule that is reasonable and can be established by the supplier, with no penalty clauses, represents the least risk.

Risk Factor (R)

How has the project delivery schedule been established?

$$4 \quad \text{x} \quad \boxed{\begin{array}{c|c|c|c} 1 & 2 & 3 & 4 \end{array}} = \underline{\hspace{1cm}}$$

1. Project start and end dates are flexible and will be established by the supplier.
2. Project start and end dates will be mutually established by the customer and the supplier.
3. Project start and end dates have been set by the customer. There is no penalty clause, but changing the schedule and milestones is difficult and must be negotiated with the customer.
4. Project start and end dates have been set by the customer and are not changeable. Penalty clauses may exist for not meeting milestones.

Notes

RISK ANALYSIS
The Supplier's Perspective

C. Project Performance Period

Weight Factor (W)	x	Oppt. Factor (R)	=	Total Score (W x R)

The performance period of the project has a bearing on the level of risk associated with the project. The longer the project, the greater the chance of significant changes. Personnel, customer environment, and business climate are a few examples of areas subject to significant change as time passes. Those changes can pose substantial risk to the project.

Risk Factor (R)

What is the estimated performance period of the project from the time a contract is awarded to the time it is expected to be completed?

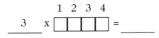

$$\underline{\hphantom{3}}3\underline{\hphantom{3}} \; x \; \boxed{\begin{array}{c|c|c|c} 1 & 2 & 3 & 4 \end{array}} \; = \; \underline{\hspace{1cm}}$$

1. From 3 months to 6 months
2. Between 6 months and 12 months
3. Exactly 1 year
4. More than 1 year

Notes

RISK ANALYSIS
The Supplier's Perspective

	Weight Factor (W)	x	Oppt. Factor (R)	=	Total Score (W x R)

D. Supplier's Experience

Experience with a previous project that was similar to this one can reduce risk. Determine how many of the project requirements can be met using products, technologies, or skills that have been used by the supplier on other projects.

Consider the following:
- What skills are available at the local level to manage and carry out this project
- How much of the system solution needs to be developed as opposed to having been done before somewhere within the supplier
- What the supplier's experience has been with the non-supplier's products needed for the solution
- That the supplier's experience is with the supply-chain partners and other customer-selected third parties.

Risk Factor (R)

What is the Supplier's experience with similar solutions?

$$\underline{\quad 4 \quad} \quad x \quad \boxed{\begin{array}{cccc} 1 & 2 & 3 & 4 \\ & & & \end{array}} = \underline{\qquad}$$

1. The project is a replication of a previous project managed locally.
2. A majority (50% or greater) of the project requirements replicate a previous project done by the supplier.
3. A minority (less than 50%) of the project requirements replicate a previous project done by the supplier.
4. None of the project requirements can be satisfied using previous experience, either local or worldwide.

Notes

RISK ANALYSIS
The Supplier's Perspective

E. The Supplier's Participation in Project Definition

| Weight Factor (W) | x | Oppt. Factor (R) | = | Total Score (W x R) |

Many customers develop project requirements without the participation of those who will bid on the projects. In this type of situation, those who bid will have had little or no input regarding schedules, technology, product selection, and so on. The less the supplier is involved in the development of the requirements, the higher the risk presented by the project.

Risk Factor (R)
Did the supplier have any involvement in the development of the requirements?

1. The supplier developed requirements for the customer.
2. The supplier guided the customer in developing requirements.
3. The supplier was asked for comments after requirements were developed.
4. The supplier had no involvement in developing the requirements.

1 2 3 4

3 x [| | | |] = _____

Notes

RISK ANALYSIS
The Supplier's Perspective

F. Level or Extent of Outsourcing	Weight Factor x (W)	Oppt. Factor (R)	Total = Score (W x R)

Most projects that provide a customized solution will outsource the resources of one or more vendors or subcontractors. External organizations can also include nonsupplier hardware and software manufacturers or distributors, application software developers, professional service providers, and consultants. The number of external organizations involved with a project directly relates to the amount of risk in the project; the more external resource coordination needed, the higher the risk.

Risk Factor (R)
Not including the customer, how many suppliers or subcontractors will need to be coordinated for this project?

$\underline{3}$ x [1 2 3 4] = $\underline{}$

1. None
2. 1 or 2
3. 3 to 5
4. 6 or more

Notes

RISK ANALYSIS
The Supplier's Perspective

G. Bid or Proposal Turnaround Time

Weight Factor (W)	x	Oppt. Factor (R)	=	Total Score (W x R)

Bid requests usually specify a date when a response must be returned to the requester. This time requirement presents an element of risk. A request requiring a quick response may not give the supplier the necessary time to do a thorough evaluation of the request. A complex project requiring a bid response (proposal) in 30 days or less could be considered aggressive. Conversely, a simple project allowing more than 30 days for a response could be considered conservative. The shorter the time allowed to develop a response, the higher the risk.

Risk Factor (R)
Which of the following best describes the time frame allotted for assessing customer requirements and generating a proposal?

3 x 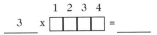 =

1. Not a significant factor
2. Moderate
3. Aggressive
4. Very aggressive

Notes

RISK ANALYSIS
The Supplier's Perspective

H. Technology and Product Maturity	Weight Factor (W)	x	Oppt. Factor (R)	=	Total Score (W x R)

Consider the maturity of the technologies and products to be used in this solution. Many products available today are so widely used that they have been accepted as industry standards. Products that have a substantial field population and have been in use for a year or more are considered mature. Those types of products are typically very reliable and pose little risk. However, prereleased and newly released products—or products using leading-edge technology—pose greater risks.

Risk Factor (R)
What percentage of the products needed to satisfy the requirements are mature?

$\underline{2}$ x $\begin{array}{|c|c|c|c|} \hline 1 & 2 & 3 & 4 \\ \hline \end{array}$ = $\underline{}$

1. All requirements can be satisfied with mature, released products.
2. Less than 30 percent of the products will be prereleased or new products, or will be products using leading-edge technology.
3. Between 30 percent to 70 percent of the products will be prereleased or new products, or will be products using leading-edge technology.
4. About 70 percent or more of the products will be prereleased or new products, or will be products using leading-edge technology.

Notes

RISK ANALYSIS
The Supplier's Perspective

I. Geographic Distribution

	Weight Factor (W)	x	Oppt. Factor (R)	=	Total Score (W x R)

The geographic distribution of the project adds complexity and risk. The greater the geographic distribution, the greater the risk caused by factors such as distance, time zone differential, and language barriers.

Risk Factor (R)

What is the geographic distribution of the project as it relates to the supplier's locations?

1. Confined to one location
2. Confined to one region, with multiple locations
3. Confined to one country
4. Distributed across multiple countries

1 2 3 4

1 x ☐☐☐☐ = ____

Notes

RISK ANALYSIS
The Supplier's Perspective

	Weight Factor (W)	x	Oppt. Factor (R)	=	Total Score (W x R)

J. Project Leader Assessment of Project

The project leader should provide an overall assessment of the doability of the project. At this point, the project leader can express an opinion on the likelihood that the organization could effectively manage the risk and could satisfy the customer's project requirements to deliver within the scope and terms of the contract. The project leader may be aware of other risk factors (such as economic or political instability) that were not yet considered.

Risk Factor (R)
On a scale of 1 (low risk) to 10 (high risk), what is the project leader's overall risk assessment of the supplier's ability to successfully manage this project?
(Briefly describe those reasons in the space provided below.)

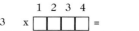

1. 5 or less—Manageable risk
2. 6 or 7—Risk mitigation likely
3. 8 or 9—Very high risk
4. 10—Extremely high risk

Reasons for overall assessment:

ABAT Scoring Sheet

Opportunity Analysis

Weight Factor x (W)	Oppt. Factor = (O)	Total Score (W x O)
A. __5__ x	=	
B. __4__ x	=	
C. __4__ x	=	
D. __3__ x	=	
E. __3__ x	=	
F. __2__ x	=	
G. __3__ x	=	
H. __2__ x	=	
I. __1__ x	=	
J. __3__ x	=	

Total Opportunity Score = _____

Risk Analysis

Weight Factor x (W)	Oppt. Factor = (R)	Total Score (W x R)
A. __5__ x	=	
B. __4__ x	=	
C. __3__ x	=	
D. __4__ x	=	
E. __3__ x	=	
F. __3__ x	=	
G. __3__ x	=	
H. __2__ x	=	
I. __2__ x	=	
J. __3__ x	=	

Total Risk Score = _____

Figure B.1 Acquisition Bid/No-Bid Matrix

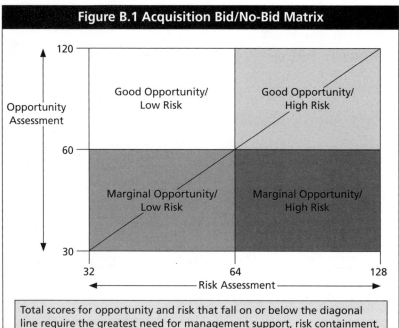

Total scores for opportunity and risk that fall on or below the diagonal line require the greatest need for management support, risk containment, contingency planning, and so on.

Appendix C
Glossary of Key Terms

acceptance
(1) The taking and receiving of anything in good part, and as if it were a tacit agreement to a preceding act, which might have been defeated or avoided if such acceptance had not been made. (2) Agreement to the terms offered in a contract. An acceptance must be communicated, and (in common law) it must be the mirror image of the offer.

acquisition cost
The money invested up front to bring in new customers.

acquisition plan
A plan for an acquisition that serves as the basis for initiating the individual contracting actions necessary to acquire a system or support a program.

acquisition strategy
The conceptual framework for conducting systems acquisition. It encompasses the broad concepts and objectives that direct and control the overall development, production, and deployment of a system.

act of God
An inevitable, accidental, or extraordinary event that cannot be

foreseen and guarded against, such as lightning, tornadoes, or earthquakes.

actual authority

The power that the principal intentionally confers on the agent or allows the agent to believe he or she possesses.

actual damages

See *compensatory damages*.

affidavit

A written and signed statement sworn to under oath.

agency

A relationship that exists when there is a delegation of authority to perform all acts connected within a particular trade, business, or company. It gives authority to the agent to act in all matters relating to the business of the principal.

agent

An employee (usually a contract manager) empowered to bind his or her organization legally in contract negotiations.

allowable cost

A cost that is reasonable, allocable, and within accepted standards, or otherwise conforms to generally accepted accounting principles, specific limitations or exclusions, or agreed-on terms between contractual parties.

alternative dispute resolution

Any procedure that is used, in lieu of litigation, to resolve issues in controversy, including but not limited to, settlement negotiations, conciliation, facilitation, mediation, fact finding, mini-trials and arbitration.

amortization

Process of spreading the cost of an intangible asset over the expected useful life of the asset.

apparent authority

The power that the principal permits the perceived agent to exercise, although not actually granted.

as is

A contract phrase referring to the condition of property to be sold or leased; generally pertains to a disclaimer of liability; property sold in as-is condition is generally not guaranteed.

assign

To convey or transfer to another, as to assign property, rights, or interests to another.

assignment

The transfer of property by an assignor to an assignee.

audits

The systematic examination of records and documents and/or the securing of other evidence by confirmation, physical inspection, or otherwise, for one or more of the following purposes: determining the propriety or legality of proposed or completed transactions; ascertaining whether all transactions have been recorded and are reflected accurately in accounts; determining the existence of recorded assets and inclusiveness of recorded liabilities; determining the accuracy of financial or statistical statements or reports and the fairness of the facts they represent; determining the degree of compliance with established policies and procedures in terms of financial transactions and business management; and appraising an account system and making recommendations concerning it.

base profit

The money a company is paid by a customer, which exceeds the company's cost.

best value

The best trade-off between competing factors for a particular purchase requirement. The key to successful best-value contracting is consideration of life-cycle costs, including the use of quantitative as well as qualitative techniques to measure price and technical performance trade-offs between various proposals. The best-value concept applies to acquisitions in which price or price-related factors are not the primary determinant of who receives the contract award.

bid

An offer in response to an invitation for bids (IFB).

bid development

All of the work activities required to design and price the product and service solution and accurately articulate this in a proposal for a customer.

bid phase

The period of time a seller of goods and/or services uses to develop a bid/proposal, conduct internal bid reviews, and obtain stakeholder approval to submit a bid/proposal.

bilateral contract

A contract formed if an offer states that acceptance requires only for the accepting party to promise to perform. In contrast, a *unilateral contract* is formed if an offer requires actual performance for acceptance.

bond

A written instrument executed by a seller and a second party (the surety or sureties) to ensure fulfillment of the principal's obligations to a third party (the obligee or buyer), identified in the bond. If the principal's obligations are not met, the bond ensures payment, to the extent stipulated, of any loss sustained by the obligee.

breach of contract

(1) The failure, without legal excuse, to perform any promise that forms the whole or part of a contract. (2) The ending of a contract that occurs when one or both of the parties fail to keep their promises; this could lead to arbitration or litigation.

buyer

The party contracting for goods and/or services with one or more sellers.

cancellation

The withdrawal of the requirement to purchase goods and/or services by the buyer.

capture management

The art and science of winning more business.

capture management life cycle

The art and science of winning more business throughout the entire business cycle.

capture project plan

A document or game plan of who needs to do what, when, where, how often and how much to win business.

change in scope

An amendment to approved program requirements or specifications after negotiation of a basic contract. It may result in an increase or decrease.

change order/purchase order amendment

A written order directing the seller to make changes according to the provisions of the contract documents.

claim

A demand by one party to contract for something from another party, usually but not necessarily for more money or more time. Claims are usually based on an argument that the party making the demand is entitled to an adjustment by virtue of the contract terms or some violation of those terms by the other party. The word does not imply any disagreement between the parties, although claims often lead to disagreements. This book uses the term *dispute* to refer to disagreements that have become intractable.

clause

A statement of one of the rights and/or obligations of the parties to a contract. A contract consists of a series of clauses.

collaboration software

Automated tools that allow for the real-time exchange of visual information using personal computers.

collateral benefit

The degree to which pursuit of an opportunity will improve the existing skill level or develop new skills which will positively affect other or future business opportunities.

compensable delay

A delay for which the buyer is contractually responsible that excuses the seller's failure to perform and is compensable.

compensatory damages

Damages that will compensate the injured party for the loss sustained and nothing more. They are awarded by the court as the measure of actual loss, and not as punishment for outrageous conduct or to deter future transgressions. Compensatory damages are often referred to as "actual damages." See also *incidental* and *punitive damages*.

competitive intelligence

Information on competitors or competitive teams which is specific to an opportunity.

competitive negotiation

A method of contracting involving a request for proposals that states the buyer's requirements and criteria for evaluation; submission of timely proposals by a maximum number of offerors; discussions with those offerors found to be within the competitive range; and award of a contract to the one offeror whose offer, price, and other consideration factors are most advantageous to the buyer.

condition precedent

A condition that activates a term in a contract.

condition subsequent

A condition that suspends a term in a contract.

conflict of interest

Term used in connection with public officials and fiduciaries and their relationships to matters of private interest or gain to them. Ethical problems connected therewith are covered by statutes in most jurisdictions and by federal statutes on the federal level. A conflict of interest arises when an employee's personal or financial interest conflicts or appears to conflict with his or her official responsibility.

consideration

(1) The thing of value (amount of money or acts to be done or not done) that must change hands between the parties to a contract. (2) The inducement to a contract—the cause, motive, price, or

impelling influence that induces a contracting party to enter into a contract.

contract negotiation

Is the process of unifying different positions into a unanimous joint decision, regarding the buying and selling of products and/ or services.

contract negotiation process

A three phased approach composed of planning, negotiating, and documenting a contractual agreement between two or more parties to buy or sell products and/or services.

constructive change

An oral or written act or omission by an authorized or unauthorized agent that is of such a nature that it is construed to have the same effect as a written change order.

contingency

The quality of being contingent or casual; an event that may but does not have to occur; a possibility.

contingent contract

A contract that provides for the possibility of its termination when a specified occurrence takes place or does not take place.

contra proferentem

A legal phrase used in connection with the construction of written documents to the effect that an ambiguous provision is construed most strongly against the person who selected the language.

contract

(1) A relationship between two parties, such as a buyer and seller, that is defined by an agreement about their respective rights and responsibilities. (2) A document that describes such an agreement.

contract administration

The process of ensuring compliance with contractual terms and conditions during contract performance up to contract closeout or termination.

contract closeout

The process of verifying that all administrative matters are concluded on a contract that is otherwise physically complete—in other words, the seller has delivered the required supplies or performed the required services, and the buyer has inspected and accepted the supplies or services.

contract fulfillment

The joint buyer/seller actions taken to successfully perform and administer a contractual agreement and met or exceed all contract obligations, including effective changes management and timely contract closeout.

contract interpretation

The entire process of determining what the parties agreed to in their bargain. The basic objective of contract interpretation is to determine the intent of the parties. Rules calling for interpretation of the documents against the drafter, and imposing a duty to seek clarification on the drafter, allocate risks of contractual ambiguities by resolving disputes in favor of the party least responsible for the ambiguity.

contract management

The art and science of managing a contractual agreement(s) throughout the contracting process.

contract type

A specific pricing arrangement used for the performance of work under the contract.

contractor

The seller or provider of goods and/or services.

controversy

A litigated question. A civil action or suit may not be instigated unless it is based on a "justifiable" dispute. This term is important in that judicial power of the courts extends only to cases and "controversies."

copyright

A royalty-free, nonexclusive, and irrevocable license to reproduce, translate, publish, use, and dispose of written or recorded material, and to authorize others to do so.

cost

The amount of money expended in acquiring a product or obtaining a service, or the total of acquisition costs plus all expenses related to operating and maintaining an item once acquired.

cost of good sold (COGS)

Direct costs of producing finished goods for sale.

cost accounting standards

Federal standards designed to provide consistency and coherency in defense and other government contract accounting.

cost-plus-award-fee (CPAF) contract

A type of cost-reimbursement contract with special incentive fee provisions used to motivate excellent contract performance in such areas as quality, timeliness, ingenuity, and cost-effectiveness.

cost-plus-fixed-fee (CPFF) contract

A type of cost-reimbursement contract that provides for the payment of a fixed fee to the contractor. It does not vary with actual costs, but may be adjusted if there are any changes in the work or services to be performed under the contract.

cost-plus-incentive-fee (CPIF) contract

A type of cost-reimbursement contract with provision for a fee that is adjusted by a formula in accordance with the relationship between total allowable costs and target costs.

cost-plus-a-percentage-of-cost (CPPC) contract

A type of cost-reimbursement contract that provides for a reimbursement of the allowable cost of services performed plus an agreed-on percentage of the estimated cost as profit.

cost-reimbursement (CR) contract

A type of contract that usually includes an estimate of project cost, a provision for reimbursing the seller's expenses, and a provision for paying a fee as profit. CR contracts are often used when there is high uncertainty about costs. They normally also include a limitation on the buyer's cost liability.

cost-sharing contract

A cost-reimbursement contract in which the seller receives no fee and is reimbursed only for an agreed-on portion of its allowable costs.

cost contract

The simplest type of cost-reimbursement contract. Governments commonly use this type when contracting with universities and nonprofit organizations for research projects. The contract provides for reimbursing contractually allowable costs, with no allowance given for profit.

cost proposal

The instrument required of an offeror for the submission or identification of cost or pricing data by which an offeror submits to the buyer a summary of estimated (or incurred) costs, suitable for detailed review and analysis.

counteroffer

An offer made in response to an original offer that changes the terms of the original.

customer revenue growth

The increased revenues achieved by keeping a customer for an extended period of time.

customer support costs

Costs expended by a company to provide information and advice concerning purchases.

default termination

The termination of a contract, under the standard default clause, because of a buyer's or seller's failure to perform any of the terms of the contract.

defect

The absence of something necessary for completeness or perfection. A deficiency in something essential to the proper use of a thing. Some structural weakness in a part or component that is responsible for damage.

defect, latent

A defect that existed at the time of acceptance but would not have been discovered by a reasonable inspection.

defect, patent

A defect that can be discovered without undue effort. If the defect was actually known to the buyer at the time of acceptance, it is patent, even though it otherwise might not have been discoverable by a reasonable inspection.

definite-quantity contract

A contractual instrument that provides for a definite quantity of supplies or services to be delivered at some later, unspecified date.

delay, excusable

A contractual provision designed to protect the seller from sanctions for late performance. To the extent that it has been excusably delayed, the seller is protected from default termination or liquidated damages. Examples of excusable delay are acts of God, acts of the government, fire, flood, quarantines, strikes, epidemics, unusually severe weather, and embargoes. See also *forbearance* and *force majeure clause.*

depreciation

Amount of expense charged against earnings by a company to write off the cost of a plant or machine over its useful live, giving consideration to wear and tear, obsolescence, and salvage value.

design specification

(1) A document (including drawings) setting forth the required characteristics of a particular component, part, subsystem, system, or construction item. (2) A purchase description that establishes precise measurements, tolerances, materials, in-process and finished product tests, quality control, inspection requirements, and other specific details of the deliverable.

direct cost

The costs specifically identifiable with a contract requirement, including but not restricted to costs of material and/or labor directly incorporated into an end item.

direct labor

All work that is obviously related and specifically and conveniently traceable to specific products.

direct material

Items, including raw material, purchased parts, and subcontracted items, directly incorporated into an end item, which are identifiable to a contract requirement.

discount rate

Interest rate used in calculating present value.

discounted cash flow (DCF)

Combined present value of cash flow and tangible assets minus present value of liabilities.

discounts, allowances and returns

Price discounts, returned merchandise.

dispute

A disagreement not settled by mutual consent that could be decided by litigation or arbitration. Also see *claim*.

e-business

Technology-enabled business that focuses on seamless integration between each business, the company, and its supply partners.

EBITDA

Earnings Before Interest, Taxes, Depreciation and Amortization, but after all product/service, sales and overhead (SG&A) costs are accounted for. Sometimes referred to as operating profit.

EBITDARM

Acronym for earnings before interest, taxes, depreciation, amortization, rent and management fees.

e-commerce

A subset of e-business, Internet-based electronic transactions.

electronic data interchange (EDI)

Private networks used for simple data transactions, which are typically batch- processed.

elements of a contract
The items that must be present in a contract if the contract is to be binding, including an offer, acceptance (agreement), consideration, execution by competent parties, and legality of purpose.

enterprise resource planning (ERP)
An electronic framework for integrating all organizational functions, evolved from manufacturing resource planning (MRP).

entire contract
A contract that is considered entire on both sides and cannot be made severable.

e-procurement
Technology-enabled buying and selling of goods and services.

estimate at completion (EAC)
The actual direct costs, plus indirect costs allocable to the contract, plus the estimate of costs (direct or indirect) for authorized work remaining.

estoppel
A rule of law that bars, prevents, and precludes a party from alleging or denying certain facts because of a previous allegation or denial or because of its previous conduct or admission.

ethics
Of or relating to moral action, conduct, motive, or character (such as ethical emotion). Also, treating of moral feelings, duties, or conduct; containing precepts of morality; moral. Professionally right or befitting; conforming to professional standards of conduct.

e-tool
An electronic device, program, system, or software application used to facilitate business.

exculpatory clause
The contract language designed to shift responsibility to the other party. A "no damages for delay" clause would be an example of one used by buyers.

excusable delay

See *delay, excusable*.

executed contract

A contract that is formed and performed at the same time. If performed in part, it is partially executed and partially executory.

executed contract (document)

A written document, signed by both parties and mailed or otherwise furnished to each party, that expresses the requirements, terms, and conditions to be met by both parties in the performance of the contract.

executory contract

A contract that has not yet been fully performed.

express

Something put in writing, for example, "express authority."

fair and reasonable

A subjective evaluation of what each party deems as equitable consideration in areas such as terms and conditions, cost or price, assured quality, timeliness of contract performance, and/or any other areas subject to negotiation.

Federal Acquisition Regulation (FAR)

The government-wide procurement regulation mandated by Congress and issued by the Department of Defense, the General Services Administration, and the National Aeronautics and Space Administration. Effective April 1, 1984, the *FAR* supersedes both the *Defense Acquisition Regulation (DAR)* and the *Federal Procurement Regulation (FPR)*. All federal agencies are authorized to issue regulations implementing the *FAR*.

fee

An agreed-to amount of reimbursement beyond the initial estimate of costs. The term "fee" is used when discussing cost-reimbursement contracts, whereas the term "profit" is used in relation to fixed-price contracts.

firm-fixed-price (FFP) contract

The simplest and most common business pricing arrangement.

The seller agrees to supply a quantity of goods or to provide a service for a specified price.

fixed cost

Operating expenses that are incurred to provide facilities and organization that are kept in readiness to do business without regard to actual volumes of production and sales. Examples of fixed costs consist of rent, property tax, and interest expense.

fixed price

A form of pricing that includes a ceiling beyond which the buyer bears no responsibility for payment.

fixed-price incentive (FPI) contract

A type of contract that provides for adjusting profit and establishing the final contract price using a formula based on the relationship of total final negotiated cost to total target cost. The final price is subject to a price ceiling, negotiated at the outset.

fixed-price redeterminable (FPR) contract

A type of fixed-price contract that contains provisions for subsequently negotiated adjustment, in whole or in part, of the initially negotiated base price.

fixed-price with economic price adjustment

A fixed-price contract that permits an element of cost to fluctuate to reflect current market prices.

forbearance

An intentional failure of a party to enforce a contract requirement, usually done for an act of immediate or future consideration from the other party. Sometimes forbearance is referred to as a nonwaiver or as a one-time waiver, but not as a relinquishment of rights.

force majeure clause

Major or irresistible force. Such a contract clause protects the parties in the event that a part of the contract cannot be performed due to causes outside the control of the parties and could not be avoided by exercise of due care. Excusable conditions for nonperformance, such as strikes and acts of God (e.g., typhoons) are contained in this clause.

fraud

An intentional perversion of truth to induce another in reliance upon it to part with something of value belonging to him or her or to surrender a legal right. A false representation of a matter of fact, whether by words or conduct, by false or misleading allegations, or by concealment of that which should have been disclosed, that deceives and is intended to deceive another so that he or she shall act upon it to his or her legal injury. Anything calculated to deceive.

free on board (FOB)

A term used in conjunction with a physical point to determine (a) the responsibility and basis for payment of freight charges and (b) unless otherwise agreed, the point at which title for goods passes to the buyer or consignee. *FOB origin*—The seller places the goods on the conveyance by which they are to be transported. Cost of shipping and risk of loss are borne by the buyer. *FOB destination*—The seller delivers the goods on the seller's conveyance at destination. Cost of shipping and risk of loss are borne by the seller.

functional specification

A purchase description that describes the deliverable in terms of performance characteristics and intended use, including those characteristics that at minimum are necessary to satisfy the intended use.

general and administrative (G&A)

(1) The indirect expenses related to the overall business. Expenses for a company's general and executive offices, executive compensation, staff services, and other miscellaneous support purposes. (2) Any indirect management, financial, or other expense that (a) is not assignable to a program's direct overhead charges for engineering, manufacturing, material, and so on, but (b) is routinely incurred by or allotted to a business unit, and (c) is for the general management and administration of the business as a whole.

general accepted accounting principles (GAAP)

A term encompassing conventions, rules, and procedures of accounting that are "generally accepted" and have "substantial authoritative support." The GAAP have been developed by agreement on the basis of experience, reason, custom, usage, and to a certain extent, practical necessity, rather than being derived from a formal set of theories.

General Agreement on Tariffs and Trade (GATT)
A multi-national trade agreement, signed in 1947 by 23 nations.

gross profit margin
Net sales minus cost of goods sold. Also called gross margin, gross profit, or gross loss

gross profit margin % or ratio
Gross profit margin $ divided by net sales.

gross sales
Total revenues at invoice value before any discounts or allowances.

horizontal exchange
A marketplace that deals with goods and services that are not specific to one industry.

imply
To indirectly convey meaning or intent; to leave the determination of meaning up to the receiver of the communication based on circumstances, general language used, or conduct of those involved.

incidental damages
Any commercially reasonable charges, expenses, or commissions incurred in stopping delivery; in the transportation, care and custody of goods after the buyer's breach; or in connection with the return or resale of the goods or otherwise resulting from the breach.

indefinite-delivery/indefinite-quantity (IDIQ) contract
A type of contract in which the exact date of delivery or the exact quantity, or a combination of both, is not specified at the time the contract is executed; provisions are placed in the contract to later stipulate these elements of the contract.

indemnification clause
A contract clause by which one party engages to secure another against an anticipated loss resulting from an act or forbearance

on the part of one of the parties or of some third person.

indemnify
To make good; to compensate; to reimburse a person in case of an anticipated loss.

indirect cost
Any cost not directly identifiable with a specific cost objective but subject to two or more cost objectives.

indirect labor
All work that is not specifically associated with or cannot be practically traced to specific units of output.

intellectual property
The kind of property that results from the fruits of mental labor.

Internet
The World Wide Web.

interactive chat
A feature provided by automated tools that allow for users to establish a voice connection between one or more parties and exchange text or graphics via a virtual bulletin board.

intranet
An organization-specific internal secure network.

joint contract
A contract in which the parties bind themselves both individually and as a unit.

liquidated damages
A contract provision providing for the assessment of damages on the seller for its failure to comply with certain performance or delivery requirements of the contract; used when the time of delivery or performance is of such importance that the buyer may reasonably expect to suffer damages if the delivery or performance is delinquent.

mailbox rule
The idea that the acceptance of an offer is effective when depos-

ited in the mail if the envelope is properly addressed.

marketing

Activities that direct the flow of goods and services from the producer to the consumers.

market intelligence

Information on your competitors or competitive teams operating in the marketplace or industry.

market research

The process used to collect and analyze information about an entire market to help determine the most suitable approach to acquiring, distributing, and supporting supplies and services.

memorandum of agreement (MOA)/memorandum of understanding (MOU)

The documentation of a mutually agreed-to statement of facts, intentions, procedures, and parameters for future actions and matters of coordination. A "memorandum of understanding" may express mutual understanding of an issue without implying commitments by parties to the understanding.

method of procurement

The process used for soliciting offers, evaluating offers, and awarding a contract.

modifications

Any written alterations in the specification, delivery point, rate of delivery, contract period, price, quantity, or other provision of an existing contract, accomplished in accordance with a contract clause; may be unilateral or bilateral.

monopoly

A market structure in which the entire market for a good or service is supplied by a single seller or firm.

monopsony

A market structure in which a single buyer purchases a good or service.

NCMA CMBOK
Definitive descriptions of the elements making up the body of professional knowledge that applies to contract management.

negotiation
A process between buyers and sellers seeking to reach mutual agreement on a matter of common concern through fact-finding, bargaining, and persuasion.

net marketplace
Two-sided exchange where buyers and sellers negotiate prices, usually with a bid-and-ask system, and where prices move both up and down.

net present value (NPV)
The lifetime customer revenue stream discounted by the investment costs and operations costs.

net sales
Gross sales minus discounts, allowances and returns.

North America Free Trade Agreement (NAFTA)
A trilateral trade and investment agreement, between Canada, Mexico, and the United States ratified on January 1, 1994.

novation agreement
A legal instrument executed by (a) the contractor (transferor), (b) the successor in interest (transferee), and (c) the buyer by which, among other things, the transferor guarantees performance of the contract, the transferee assumes all obligations under the contract, and the buyer recognizes the transfer of the contract and related assets.

offer
(1) The manifestation of willingness to enter into a bargain, so made as to justify another person in understanding that his or her assent to that bargain is invited and will conclude it. (2) An unequivocal and intentionally communicated statement of proposed terms made to another party. An offer is presumed revocable unless it specifically states that it is irrevocable. An offer once made will be open for a reasonable period of time and is binding on the offeror unless revoked by the offeror before the

other party's acceptance.

oligopoly

A market dominated by a few sellers.

operating expenses

SG&A plus depreciation and amortization.

opportunity

A potential or actual favorable event.

opportunity engagement

The degree to which your company or your competitors were involved in establishing the customer's requirements.

opportunity profile

A stage of the capture management life cycle, during which a seller evaluates and describes the opportunity in terms of what it means to your customer, what it means to your company, and what will be required to succeed.

option

A unilateral right in a contract by which, for a specified time, the buyer may elect to purchase additional quantities of the supplies or services called for in the contract, or may elect to extend the period of performance of the contract.

order of precedence

A solicitation provision that establishes priorities so that contradictions within the solicitation can be resolved.

Organizational Breakdown Structure (OBS)

A organized structure which represents how individual team members are grouped to complete assigned work tasks.

outsourcing

A contractual process of obtaining another party to provide goods and/or services that were previously done internal to an organization.

overhead

An accounting cost category that typically includes general indirect expenses that are necessary to operate a business but are not directly assignable to a specific good or service produced. Examples include building rent, utilities, salaries of corporate officers, janitorial services, office supplies, and furniture.

overtime

The time worked by a seller's employee in excess of the employee's normal workweek.

parol evidence

Oral or verbal evidence; in contract law, the evidence drawn from sources exterior to the written instrument.

parol evidence rule

A rule that seeks to preserve the integrity of written agreements by refusing to permit contracting parties to attempt to alter a written contract with evidence of any contradictory prior or contemporaneous oral agreement (parol to the contract).

payments

The amount payable under the contract supporting data required to be submitted with invoices, and other payment terms such as time for payment and retention.

payment bond

A bond that secures the appropriate payment of subcontracts for their completed and acceptable goods and/or services.

performance-based contract (PBC)

A documented business arrangement, in which the buyer and seller agree to use: a Performance work statement, performance-based metrics, and a quality assurance plan to ensure contract requirements are met or exceeded.

performance bond

A bond that secures the performance and fulfillment of all the undertakings, covenants, terms, conditions, and agreements contained in the contract.

performance specification

A purchase description that describes the deliverable in terms of desired operational characteristics. Performance specifications tend to be more restrictive than functional specifications, in that they limit alternatives that the buyer will consider and define separate performance standards for each such alternative.

performance work statement (PWS)

A statement of work expressed in terms of desired performance results, often including specific measurable objectives.

post-bid phase

The period of time after a seller submits a bid/proposal to a buyer through source selection, negotiations, contract formation, contract fulfillment, contract closeout, and follow-on opportunity management.

pre-bid phase

The period of time a seller of goods and/or services uses to identify business opportunities prior to the release of a customer solicitation.

pricing arrangement

An agreed-to basis between contractual parties for the payment of amounts for specified performance; usually expressed in terms of a specific cost-reimbursement or fixed-price arrangement.

prime/prime contractor

The principal seller performing under the contract.

private exchange

A marketplace hosted by a single company inside a company's firewall and used for procurement from among a group of preauthorized sellers.

privity of contract

The legal relationship that exists between the parties to a contract that allows either party to (a) enforce contractual rights against the other party and (b) seek remedy directly from the other party.

procurement

The complete action or process of acquiring or obtaining goods or services using any of several authorized means.

procurement planning

The process of identifying which business needs can be best met by procuring products or services outside the organization.

profit

The net proceeds from selling a product or service when costs are subtracted from revenues. May be positive (profit) or negative (loss).

program management

Planning and execution of multiple projects that are related to one another.

progress payments

An interim payment for delivered work in accordance with contract terms; generally tied to meeting specified performance milestones.

project management

Planning and ensuring the quality, on-time delivery, and cost of a specific set of related activities with a definite beginning and end.

promotion

Publicizing the attributes of the product/service through media and personal contacts and presentations, e.g., technical articles/presentations, new releases, advertising, and sales calls.

proposal

Normally, a written offer by a seller describing its offering terms. Proposals may be issued in response to a specific request or may be made unilaterally when a seller feels there may be an interest in its offer (which is also known as an unsolicited proposal).

proposal evaluation

An assessment of both the proposal and the offeror's ability (as conveyed by the proposal) to successfully accomplish the prospective contract. An agency shall evaluate competitive proposals solely on the factors specified in the solicitation.

protest

A written objection by an interested party to (a) a solicitation or other request by an agency for offers for a contract for the procurement of property or services, (b) the cancellation of the solicitation or other request, (c) an award or proposed award of the contract, or (d) a termination or cancellation of an award of the contract, if the written objection contains an allegation that the termination or cancellation is based in whole or in part on improprieties concerning the award of the contract.

punitive damages

Those damages awarded to the plaintiff over and above what will barely compensate for his or her loss. Unlike compensatory damages, punitive damages are based on actively different public policy consideration, that of punishing the defendant or of setting an example for similar wrongdoers.

purchasing

The outright acquisition of items, mostly off-the-shelf or catalog, manufactured outside the buyer's premises.

quality assurance

The planned and systematic actions necessary to provide adequate confidence that the performed service or supplied goods will serve satisfactorily for the intended and specified purpose.

quotation

A statement of price, either written or oral, which may include, among other things, a description of the product or service; the terms of sale, delivery, or period of performance; and payment. Such statements are usually issued by sellers at the request of potential buyers.

reasonable cost

A cost is reasonable if, in its nature and amount, it does not exceed that which would be incurred by a prudent person in the conduct of competitive business.

request for information (RFI)

A formal invitation to submit general and/or specific information concerning the potential future purchase of goods and/or services.

request for proposals (RFP)

A formal invitation that contains a scope of work and seeks a formal response (proposal), describing both methodology and compensation, to form the basis of a contract.

request for quotations (RFQ)
A formal invitation to submit a price for goods and/or services as specified.

request for technical proposals (RFTP)
Solicitation document used in two-step sealed bidding. Normally in letter form, it asks only for technical information; price and cost breakdowns are forbidden.

revenue value
The monetary value of an opportunity.

risk
Exposure or potential of an injury or loss.

sealed-bid procedure
A method of procurement involving the unrestricted solicitation of bids, an opening, and award of a contract to the lowest responsible bidder.

selling, general & administrative (SG&A) expenses
Administrative costs of running business.

severable contract
A contract divisible into separate parts. A default of one section does not invalidate the whole contract.

several
A circumstance when more than two parties are involved with the contract.

single source
One source among others in a competitive marketplace that, for justifiable reason, is found to be most worthy to receive a contract award.

small business concerns
A small business is one that is independently owned and operated, and is not dominant in its field; a business concern that meets government size standards for its particular industry type.

socioeconomic programs

Programs designed to benefit particular groups. They represent a multitude of program interests and objectives unrelated to procurement objectives. Some examples of these are preferences for small business and for American products, required sources for specific items, and minimum labor pay levels mandated for contractors.

solicitation

A process through which a buyer requests, bids, quotes, tenders, or proposes orally, in writing, or electronically. Solicitations can take the following forms: request for proposals (RFP), request for quotations (RFQ), request for tenders, invitation to bid (ITB), invitation for bids, and invitation for negotiation.

solicitation planning

The preparation of the documents needed to support a solicitation.

source selection

The process by which the buyer evaluates offers, selects a seller, negotiates terms and conditions, and awards the contract.

Source Selection Advisory Council

A group of people who are appointed by the Source Selection Authority (SSA). The council is responsible for reviewing and approving the source selection plan (SSP) and the solicitation of competitive awards for major and certain less-than-major procurements. The council also determines what proposals are in the competitive range and provides recommendations to the SSA for final selection.

source selection plan (SSP)

The document that describes the selection criteria, the process, and the organization to be used in evaluating proposals for competitively awarded contracts.

specification

A description of the technical requirements for a material, product, or service that includes the criteria for determining that the requirements have been met. There are generally three types of specifications used in contracting: performance, functional, and design.

stakeholders

Individuals who control the resources in a company needed to pursue opportunities or deliver solutions to customers.

standard

A document that establishes engineering and technical limitations and applications of items, materials, processes, methods, designs, and engineering practices. It includes any related criteria deemed essential to achieve the highest practical degree of uniformity in materials or products, or interchangeability of parts used in those products.

standards of conduct

The ethical conduct of personnel involved in the acquisition of goods and services. Within the federal government, business shall be conducted in a manner above reproach and, except as authorized by law or regulation, with complete impartiality and without preferential treatment.

statement of work (SOW)

That portion of a contract describing the actual work to be done by means of specifications or other minimum requirements, quantities, performance date, and a statement of the requisite quality.

statute of limitations

The legislative enactment prescribing the periods within which legal actions may be brought upon certain claims or within which certain rights may be enforced.

stop-work order

A request for interim stoppage of work due to nonconformance, funding, or technical considerations.

subcontract

A contract between a buyer and a seller in which a significant part of the supplies or services being obtained is for eventual use in a prime contract.

subcontractor

A seller who enters into a contract with a prime contractor or a subcontractor of the prime contractor.

supplementary agreement

A contract modification that is accomplished by the mutual action of parties.

technical factor

A factor other than price used in evaluating offers for award. Examples include technical excellence, management capability, personnel qualifications, prior experience, past performance, and schedule compliance.

technical leveling

The process of helping a seller bring its proposal up to the level of other proposals through successive rounds of discussion, such as by pointing out weaknesses resulting from the seller's lack of diligence, competence, or inventiveness in preparing the proposal.

technical/management proposal

That part of the offer that describes the seller's approach to meeting the buyer's requirement.

technical transfusion

The disclosure of technical information pertaining to a proposal that re-suits in improvement of a competing proposal. This practice is not allowed in federal government contracting.

term

A part of a contract that addresses a specific subject.

termination

An action taken pursuant to a contract clause in which the buyer unilaterally ends all or part of the work.

terms and conditions (Ts and Cs)

All clauses in a contract, including time of delivery, packing and shipping, applicable standard clauses, and special provisions.

unallowable cost

Any cost that, under the provisions of any pertinent law, regulation, or contract, cannot be included in prices, cost-reimbursements, or settlements under a government contract to which it is allocable.

uncompensated overtime

The work that exempt employees perform above and beyond 40 hours per week. Also known as competitive time, deflated hourly rates, direct allocation of salary costs, discounted hourly rates, extended work week, full-time accounting, and green time.

Uniform Commercial Code (UCC)

A U.S. model law developed to standardize commercial contracting law among the states. It has been adopted by 49 states (and in significant portions by Louisiana). The UCC comprises articles that deal with specific commercial subject matters, including sales and letters of credit.

unilateral

See *bilateral contract*.

unsolicited proposal

A research or development proposal that is made by a prospective contractor without prior formal or informal solicitation from a purchasing activity.

variable costs

Costs associated with production that change directly with the amount of production, e.g., the direct material or labor required to complete the build or manufacturing of a product.

variance

The difference between projected and actual performance, especially relating to costs.

vertical exchange

A marketplace that is specific to a single industry.

waiver

The voluntary and unilateral relinquishment a person of a right that he or she has. See also *forbearance*.

warranty

A promise or affirmation given by a seller to a buyer regarding the nature, usefulness, or condition of the goods or services furnished under a contract. Generally, a warranty's purpose is to delineate the rights and obligations for defective goods and services and to foster quality performance.

warranty, express

A written statement arising out of a sale to the consumer of a consumer good, pursuant to which the manufacturer, distributor, or retailer undertakes to preserve or maintain the utility or performance of the consumer good or provide compensation if there is a failure in utility or performance. It is not necessary to the creation of an express warranty that formal words such as "warrant" or "guarantee" be used, or that a specific intention to make a warranty be present.

warranty, implied

A promise arising by operation of law that something that is sold shall be fit for the purpose for which the seller has reason to know that it is required. Types of implied warranties include implied warranty of merchantability, of title, and of wholesomeness.

warranty of fitness

A warranty by the seller that goods sold are suitable for the special purpose of the buyer.

warranty of merchantability

A warranty that goods are fit for the ordinary purposes for which such goods are used and conform to the promises or affirmations of fact made on the container or label.

warranty of title

An express or implied (arising by operation of law) promise that the seller owns the item offered for sale and, therefore, is able to transfer a good title and that the goods, as delivered, are free from any security interest of which the buyer at the time of contracting has no knowledge.

Web portals

A public exchange in which a company or group of companies list products or services for sale or provide other transmission of business information.

win strategy

A collection of messages or points designed to guide the customer's perception of you, your solution, and your competitors.

work breakdown structure (WBS)
A logical, organized, decomposition of the work tasks within a given project, typically uses a hierarchical numeric coding scheme.

World Trade Organization (WTO)
A multi-national legal entity which serves as the champion of fair trade globally, established April 15, 1995.

References

Atkinson, William. "Beyond the Basics." *PM Network Magazine*. Newtown Square, PA: PMI, May 2003. pp. 78-80.

Badgerow, Dana B., Gregory A. Garrett, Dominic F. DiClementi, and Barbara M. Weaver. *Managing Contracts for Peak Performance*. Vienna, VA: National Contract Management Association, 1990.

Bain & Co. *Benchmarking Study: Use of Balanced Scorecards*. London: Bain & Co., 2003.

Barkley, Bruce T., and James H. Saylor. *Customer-Driven Project Management: A New Paradigm in Total Quality Implementation*. New York: McGraw-Hill, 1991.

Bergeron, Bryan. *Essentials of CRM: A Guide to Customer Relationship Management*. New York: John Wiley & Sons, 2002.

Bonaldo, Guy. "Interview with Business 2.0 Magazine." *Business Intelligence*. February 2003, pp. 21-24.

Booz Allen Hamilton Study. "Enterprise Architecture." *Government Executive Magazine*. National Journal Group Inc., Washington, DC, December 2004, pp. 44-47.

Bossidy, Larry, and Ram Charan. *Confronting Realty: Doing What Matters to Get Things Right*. New York: Crown Business, 2004.

Bruce, David L., Marlys Norby, and Victor Ramos. *Guide to the Contract Management Body of Knowledge (CMBOK)*. McLean, VA: National Contract Management Association, 2002.

Burk, Karen B., and Douglas W. Webster. *Activity-Based Casting and Performance (ABC&P)*. Fairfax, VA: American Management Systems, 1994.

Burt, David, Donald Dolber, and Stephen Starling. *World-Class Supply Management*. New York: McGraw-Hill, 2003.

Cleland, David I. *Project Management: Strategic Design and Implementation*. New York: McGraw-Hill, 1994.

Cleland, David I., and William R. King. *Project Management Handbook*. 2nd ed. New York: Van Nostrand Reinhold, 1988.

Collins, Jim. *Good to Great: Why Some Companies Make the Leap ... and Others Don't*. New York: HarperCollins, 2001.

Coulson-Thomas, Colin. *Creating the Global Company*. New York: McGraw-Hill, 1992.

Covey, Stephen R. *The Seven Habits of Highly Effective People*. New York: Simon and Schuster, 1989.

Deming, W. Edwards. *Total Quality Management Seminar*. Columbus, OH: Ohio State University, 1987.

Dickey, Beth. "Bright Ideas." *Government Executive Magazine*. National Journal Group Inc., Washington, DC, December 2004, pp. 58-60.

Fisher, Roger, Elizabeth Kopelman, and Andrea K. Schneider. *Beyond Machiavelli: Tools for Coping with Conflict*. Cambridge: Harvard University Press, 1994.

Forsberg, Kevin, Hal Mooz, and Howard Cotterman. *Visualizing Project Management*. New York: John Wiley & Sons, 2001.

———. *Communicating Project Management*. New York: John Wiley & Sons, 2003.

Foti, Ross. "Louder Than Words." *PM Network Magazine*. Newtown Square, PA: PMI, December 2002: 34-36.

———. "CH2M HILL Interview." *PM Network Magazine*. Newtown Square, PA: PMI, January 2003: 47-48.

———. "Saudi Aramaco's Hawiyah Gas Plant." *PM Network Magazine*. Newtown Square, PA: PMI, January 2003: 61-64.

Freed, Richard C., Joe Romano, and Shervin Freed. *Writing Winning Business Proposals*. New York: McGraw-Hill, 2003.

Garrett, Gregory A. "Achieving Customer Loyalty." *Contract Management Magazine*. National Contract Management Association, Vienna, VA, August 2002.

———. *World-Class Contracting: How Winning Companies Build Successful Partnerships in the e-Business Age*. 3rd ed. Chicago: CCH Incorporated, 2003.

———. *Managing Complex Outsourced Projects*. Chicago: CCH Incorporated, 2004.

Garrett, Gregory A., and Ed. Bunnik. "Creating a World-Class PM Organization." *PM Network Magazine*. Newtown Square, PA: PMI, September 2000: 61-64.

Garrett, Gregory A., and Reginald J. Kipke. *The Capture Management Life Cycle: Winning More Business*. Chicago: CCH Incorporated, 2003.

Garrett, Gregory A., and Rene G. Rendon. *Contract Management Organizational Assessment Tool*. McLean, VA: National Contract Management Association, 2005.

Gates, Bill. *Business @ The Speed of Thought: Using a Digital Nervous System*. New York: Warner Books USA, 1999.

General Accounting Office (GAO). "Best Practices: Using Spend Analysis to Help Agencies Take a More Strategic Approach to Procurement." GAO Report 04-870, Washington, DC, September 2004.

Harris, Phillip R., and Robert T. Moran. *Managing Cultural Differences*. Houston, TX: Gulf Publishing Company, 1996.

Hassan, Harnold, and Robert Blackwell. *Global Marketing*. New York: Harcourt Brace, 1994.

Hernandaz, Richard J. and Delane F. Moeller. "Negotiating a Quality Contract." National Contract Management Association, 1992.

Horton, Sharon. "Creating and Using Supplier Scorecards." *Contract Management Magazine*. National Contract Management Association, McLean, VA, September 2004a, pp. 22–25.

———. "Successful Supplier Performance Programs." *Contract Management Magazine*. National Contract Management Association, McLean, VA, September 2004, p. 167.

Jones, Gerard, Michael Mickaliger, and Joseph Witzgtall. "Performance Sunrise: Blending Contract Management with Project Management." *NCMA Contract Management Magazine*. National Contract Management Association, McLean, VA, April 2004, pp. 20-25.

Jones, Kathryn. "The Dell Way." *Business 2.0 Magazine*. NY: Fortune Publishing, February 2003, pp. 27-32.

Kalakota, Ravi, and Marcia Robinson. *e-Business 2.0*. Boston: Addison-Wesley, 2004.

Kantin, Bob. *Sales Proposals Kit for Dummies*. New York: Hungry Minds, 2001.

Kaplan, Robert, and David Norton. *Balanced Scorecard*. Boston: HBS Press, 2001.

Kearney, A. T. 1997 CEO Global Business Study. New York, 1997.

Kerzner, Harold. *In Search of Excellence in Project Management*. New York: Van Nostrand Reinhold, 1998.

Kirk, Dorothy. "Managing Expectations." *PM Network Magazine*. Newtown Square, PA: PMI, August 2000.

Lewis, James P. *Mastering Project Management: Applying Advanced Concepts of Systems Thinking, Control and Evaluation, Resource Allocation*. New York: McGraw-Hill, 1998.

Liker, Jeffrey K., and Thomas Y. Choi. "Building Deep Supplier Relationships." *Harvard Business Review*. Boston, MA: Harvard Business School Press, December 2004. pp. 104–13.

Lisagor, Megan. "e-Mentoring: A Tool for Federal Workers." *Federal Computer Week*. January 24, 2005, p. 50.

Lubeck, Jeffrey A. "Beyond an Adequate Accounting System." *Contract Management* May 2004. McLean, VA: NCMA, 2004. pp. 27-30.

McRae, Hamish. *The World in 2020: Power, Culture, and Prosperity*, Boston: HBS Press, 1994.

Monroe, Kent B. *Pricing: Making Profitable Decisions*. 2nd ed. New York: McGraw-Hill, 1990.

Moran, Robert T., and John R. Riesenberger. *The Global Challenge*. New York: McGraw-Hill, 1994.

Nair, Mohan. *Essentials of Balanced Scorecard*. New York: John Wiley & Sons, 2004.

National Contract Management Association. *The Desktop Guide to Basic Contracting Terms*. 4th ed. Vienna, VA: National Contract Management Association, 1994.

O'Connell, Brian. B2B.com: *Cashing-in on the Business-to-Business e-Commerce Bonanz*. Holbrook, MA: Adams Media Corporation, 2000.

Ohmae, Kenichi. *The Borderless World: Power and Strategy in the Interlinked Economy*. New York: HarperCollins, 1991).

———. *The Evolving Global Economy*. Boston, MA: Harvard Business School Press, 1995.

Patel, Jemin. "Establishing Mutual Equity for Buyers and Sellers with e-Sourcing." *Contract Management Magazine*. National Contract Management Association, McLean, VA, March 2005.

Patterson, Shirley. "Supply Base Optimization and Integrated Supply-Chain Management." *Contract Management Magazine*. National Contract Management Association, McLean, VA, January 2005, pp. 24–35.

Pennypacker, James S, and Kevin P. Grant. "Project Management Maturity: An Industry Benchmark." *Project Management Journal*. Newtown Square, PA: PMI, March 2003. pp. 44-51.

Peterson, Marissa. "Sun Microsystems: Leveraging Project Management Expertise" *PM Network Magazine*. Newtown Square, PA: PMI, January 2003.

Project Management Institute (PMI) Newsletter, Newtown Square, PA, April 2005.

Project Management Institute Standards Committee. *A Guide to the Project Management Body of Knowledge*. Upper Darby, PA.: Project Management Institute, 2001.

Reichheld, Frederick F. *The Loyalty Effect*. Boston: Harvard Business School Press, 1996.

Richards, Kent M. "Not a Johnny-Come-Latte." *USA Today*. September 9, 2003, p. 3B.

Salameri, Phil, Best Value Source Selection Seminar Manual, 2004.

Tichy, Noel. *The Leadership Engine*. New York: Harper Business, 1997.

Tracy, Michael, and Fred Wiersema. *Discipline of Market Leaders*. Boston: Harvard Business School Press, 2003.

Walker, Darryl L. "Is Your Estimating System Asking for Trouble." *Contract Management Magazine*. National Contract Management Association, McLean, VA, May 2004, pp. 31-34.

Webster's Dictionary: *The New Lexicon of the English Language.* New York: Lexicon Publications, 1989.

Welborn, Ralph. "Interview with Business 2.0 Magazine." *Business Intelligence*, New York, February 2003.

Wilson, Greg. "Proposal Automation Tools." *Journal of the Association of Proposal Management*. Reston, VA: Association of Proposal Management Professionals, Spring/Summer 2002.

Wilson, Mark. *Executive Presentation: Visualizing Project Management.* Chantilly, VA: Center for Systems Management, 2002.

About the Author

GREGORY A. GARRETT is a respected international educator, bestselling author, dynamic speaker, and practicing industry leader. He has successfully led more than $30 billion of high-technology contracts and projects during the past 25 years. He has taught, consulted, and led contract and project teams in more than 40 countries. He has served as a lecturer for the Law School and the School of Business and Public Management at The George Washington University. He is the president and CEO of Garrett Consulting Services.

With Lucent Technologies, since 1997, Garrett currently serves as the chief compliance officer for all U.S. federal government programs. He has served as vice president, Program Management, North America Wireless, as chairman, Lucent Technologies Project Management Leadership Council, representing more than 2,000 Lucent project managers globally; and as director, Global Program Management Platform, at the company headquarters.

At ESI International, Garrett served as executive director of Global Business, where he led the sales, marketing, negotiation, and implementation of bid and proposal management, project management, commercial contracting, and government contract management training and consulting programs for numerous Fortune 100 multinational corporations, government agencies, and small businesses worldwide, including the following: ABB, AT&T, BellSouth, Boeing, IBM, Inter-American Development Bank, Israel Aircraft Industries, Lucent Technologies, Motorola, NCR, NTT, Panama Canal Commission, SBC, U.S. Trade Development Agency, United Nations, the U.S. Department of Energy, and U.S. Department of Defense.

Formerly, Garrett served as a highly decorated military officer for the U.S. Air Force (USAF), having been awarded more than 17 medals, badges, and citations. He completed his active duty career as the youngest acquisition action officer in the Colonel's Group Headquarters, USAF, at the Pentagon. He was the youngest division chief and professor of contracting management at the Air Force Institute of Technology, where he taught advanced courses in contract administration and program management to more than 5,000 people from the Department of Defense and NASA.

Previously, he was the youngest procurement contracting officer for the USAF Aeronautical Systems Center, where he led more than 50 multimillion dollar negotiations and managed the contract administration of more than $15 billion in contracts for major weapon systems. He served as a program manager at the Space Systems Center, where he managed a $300 million space communications project.

Garrett is a Certified Purchasing Manager of the Institute for Supply Management. He is a Certified Project Management Professional of the Project Management Institute (PMI) and has received the prestigious PMI Eric Jenett Project Management Excellence Award and the PMI David I. Cleland Project Management Literature Award. He is a Certified Professional Contracts Manager, a Fellow, and a member of the Board of Advisors of the National Contract Management Association (NCMA). He has received the NCMA National Achievement Award, the NCMA National Educational Award, and the Blanche Witte Memorial Award for outstanding service to the contract management profession.

A prolific writer, Garrett coauthored the book *Managing Contracts for Peak Performance* (NCMA, 1990); authored the best-selling books *World-Class Contracting* (third edition, CCH, 2003), *Managing Complex Outsourced Projects*, (CCH, 2004), and *Contract Negotiations* (CCH, 2005); and co-authored the books *The Capture Management Life-Cycle* (CCH, 2003) and *Contract Management Organizational Assessment Tools* (NCMA, 2005). In addition, he has written more than 50 published articles on bid and proposal management, supply chain management, contracting, project management, and leadership.

He resides in Oakton, Virginia, with his wife, Carolyn, and three children: Christopher, Scott, and Jennifer.

Index